Rechtsvergleichung und Rechtsvereinheitlichung

Herausgegeben von der
Gesellschaft für Rechtsvergleichung e.V.

41

AF684146

The Significance of Religion for Today's Labour and Social Legislation

Edited by

Ulrich Becker, Sebastian Krebber and Achim Seifert

Mohr Siebeck

Ulrich Becker is Director of the Max Planck Institute for Social Law and Social Policy, Munich.

Sebastian Krebber is Professor of Law at the University of Freiburg/Br.

Achim Seifert is Professor of Law at the University of Jena.

ISBN 978-3-16-155019-5
ISSN 1861-5449 (Rechtsvergleichung und Rechtsvereinheitlichung)

Die Deutsche Nationalbibliothek lists this publication in the Deutsche Nationalbibliographie; detailed bibliographic data are available on the Internet at *http://dnb.dnb.de*.

© 2017 by Mohr Siebeck Tübingen, Germany. www.mohr.de

This book may not be reproduced, in whole or in part, in any form (beyond that permitted by copyright law) without the publisher's written permission. This applies particularly to reproductions, translations, microfilms and storage and processing in electronic systems.

The book was typeset by Martin Fischer in Tübingen and printed and bound by Gulde Druck in Tübingen.

Printed in Germany.

Preface

The search for the fundamental principles coining society and holding it together has once more become acute in these times of crisis. Connected to this is the question of the values or fundamental views underlying legal systems. They find expression in the constitutional framework and yet are not identical with it. An essential part of the answer to that question consists in the investigation of whether and to what extent law may be influenced by ideologies and, especially in Europe, by the belief system.

At its 35th Conference in 2015, the section for labour law and social law of the Society for Comparative Law [*Gesellschaft für Rechtsvergleichung*] did not seek to delve into the mentioned issues on either a general or an abstract level. Rather, its intention was to pursue the question of whether and in what respect the predominantly still nationally shaped labour and social legislations are influenced by religious convictions. Such an elaboration requires a relatively broad approach which must attempt to work out, by way of specific evidence, the bases of our current legal systems – as well as to take into account the significance of work and the legal structure of the interrelationship between the individual, social institutions and the political community.

Fortunately, we have been able to convince six esteemed colleagues to take part in our endeavour, to participate in the conference that was held in Bayreuth in September 2015, and to send us their final papers for publication in this volume of the *Schriftenreihe der Gesellschaft für Rechtsvergleichung*. The selection of countries to be included was mainly based on the provisions set by the respective social policies and the rules on the relation between religion and government. In this regard, the publication attempts to inform about various models. Apart from Germany, which represents the corporatist welfare state that grants the various religious groups special roles (the so-called cooperation model), it includes France with its laicist system; Sweden, whose farewell to a state Church was only effected at the turn of the millennium; and the USA, where the Churches are not deployed for state objectives but where religious freedom is protected and the Churches, in turn, seek room for development based on the prohibition of discrimination, if nothing else (cf. for the respective models *Pollack*, Rückkehr des Religiösen?, 2009, p. 161 ff.). Furthermore, by also including Turkey and Israel we have examined two countries whose jurisdictions reflect a non-Christian religious orientation.

The first chapter has been written from the perspective of the social sciences (cf. for a closer examination of the different countries from other scientific perspectives *Gabriel / Reuter / Kurschat / Leibold* [eds.], Religion und Wohlfahrtsstaatlichkeit in Europa. Konstellationen – Kulturen – Konflikte, 2013), and it serves as a general basis in the form of an overview of the significance of ideological and religious values for the legal and economic system. It reflects social policy research on the various welfare state models which also, to some extent, focuses on the influence of religion (*Esping-Andersen,* The Three Worlds of Welfare Capitalism, 1990; *Manow,* Religion und Sozialstaat, 2008). The following chapters further look into the significance of religion for the various national labour and social legislations. We have asked the respective authors to take into consideration four points: First, fundamental principles which might be explained with regard to the guiding social policy principles, and with regard to the constitutional position of religions within the state or, in other words, to the relationship between the political community and religion. Second, specific problems pertaining to labour and social law are addressed and their legal solutions in the different jurisdictions are examined. Within this rough framework, the authors were free to choose their priorities and to put those topics to the fore that they considered to be the most significant.

We are deeply grateful to the authors for their contributions as well as for their commitment, and also for their patience. We would also like to thank *Christina McAllister* for the proofreading and *Julian Zinn* for his help with the formalities (both working with the Max Planck Institute for Social Law and Social Policy in Munich), as well as the editors of the *Schriftenreihe* for the publication.

September 2016

Ulrich Becker, München
Sebastian Krebber, Freiburg
Achim Seifert, Jena

Table of Contents

What Determines Social Spending?

The Impact of Economics, Politics, and Religion on the Welfare State

Jörg Althammer

The origin and the development of modern welfare states is a standing research question of applied social policy analysis. Why do some countries spend a greater part than others of their GDP on social issues? Why has the welfare state in some countries evolved at an early stage of economic development, and much later in others? And finally, why don't all countries adopt the same welfare institutions after some time but crystallize into rather distinct regime-clusters? These questions are not only relevant from an economic point of view. They are also of utmost importance for social theory and the normative evaluation of societies. The structural principles of the welfare state reflect the normative value society puts on the person, his or her entitlements to society and the relationship between the state, the individual and civil society. Thus, the size and the structure of the welfare state are the most visible signs of commonly shared beliefs and social values in a society.

Theoretical reasoning on these issues can be traced back to the 19th century, when German economist *Adolph Wagner* published his idea that industrialization leads to rising state activities, the nowadays well-known "Wagner's law". Theoretically akin to Karl Marx, *Wagner* interpreted the rise of the welfare state as a functional reaction to the demands of industrialization and capital accumulation. These ideas were later on taken up by *Golphorpe*[1], *Wilensky*[2] and *Stinchcombe*[3], who formulated models to explain welfare spending in a socio-functionalist manner. In the following decades, various accounts from the different branches of social science were made to get an understanding of the causes of welfare state expansion.

In the last years, empirical research on the determinants of the social state showed a significant turn. Besides looking at the economic structure and the political institutions of a society, researchers began to put more emphasis on explaining people's willingness to maintain social programs that put them in the position of a net payer. This new line of research had its starting point in *Alesina's*[4] seminal paper on the impact of racial heterogeneity on welfare programs. Currently it is discussed in the context of *Manow's*[5] hypothesis on the impact of a society's religious basis on welfare spending.

This paper gives an overview of the empirical literature concerning the determinants of the emergence and the development of modern welfare states. The paper is organized as follows. The next section gives a brief classification of and an overview on the main empirical approaches on the determinants of social state development. Section II. summarizes the economic and religious factors that determine welfare state expansion. Section III. reviews the empirical evidence on welfare state development with an emphasis on the impact of religion on social policy design. Section IV. concludes.

I. Classification

The empirical literature on the determinants of the welfare state falls into two categories: descriptive and explanatory. Descriptive models provide an empiri-

[1] *J.H. Golthorpe*, Social Stratification in Industrial Society, in: C.S. Heller (ed.): Structured Social Inequality, A Reader in Comparative Social Stratification, London 1969, pp. 452–465.

[2] *H.L. Wilensky*, The Welfare State and Equality, Structural and Ideological Roots of Public Expenditure, Berkeley 1975.

[3] *A. Stinchcombe*, Constructing Social Theories, New York 1968.

[4] *A. Alesina et al.*, Why doesn't the United States Have a European-Style Welfare State?, Brookings Papers on Economic Activity, 2001, Vol. 2, pp. 187–254.

[5] *Ph. Manow*, The Good, the Bad and the Ugly, Esping-Andersen's Regime Typology and the Religious Roots of the Western Welfare State, MPIfG Working Paper 3, Cologne 2007; *Ph. Manow*, Religion und Sozialstaat, Die konfessionellen Grundlagen europäischer Wohlfahrtsstaatsregime, Frankfurt/New York 2008.

cal assessment of the structural dimensions of welfare states and the differences therein without any explanatory content. The empirical models used in this branch of literature are descriptive as well, predominantly cluster analyses. This, however, does not mean that descriptive models lack theoretical content. Quite the contrary. As the clusters generated by the analytical model are supposed to be meaningful and to represent some kind of prototypes of welfare regimes, cluster analysis is a natural starting point for any further investigation of welfare state regimes. And the selection of the variables that indicate a specific regime has to be done on theoretical grounds as well. Thus, a theoretical notion of the welfare state lies at the beginning and at the end of any descriptive approach to welfare state analysis. Descriptive models can mainly be found in the literature on the *Varieties of Capitalism*, i.e. the theories of *Hall/Soskice/Gingerich and Gosta Esping-Andersen*.

Explanatory models start with a specific hypothesis concerning the determinants of social state installment and expansion. The role of the empirical model is to quantify the impact of a specific socio-economic or political variable (or a combination of variables) on welfare state development. The numerous approaches that fall under this line of research will be briefly sketched in paragraph 1.2.

1. Descriptive models

a) Varieties of Capitalism I: Hall – Soskice – Gingerich

A first descriptive approach to classify welfare state regimes is the distinction between Liberal Market Economies (LMEs) on the one side and Coordinated Market Economies (CMEs) on the other by *Hall, Soskice and Gingerich*. The authors argue that the main actors in any market economy are firms, not the people[6]. Thus, the size and the institutional design of the welfare state can mainly be addressed as issues of coordination between firms and their relevant stakeholders. They differentiate between two modes of coordination: markets and strategic management. Their main hypothesis is that in order to ensure dynamic efficiency, political, social and economic structures have to be complementary to the main mode of coordinating at firm level.

In case of market coordination, wage setting and industrial relations mainly take place at firm level. Employment protection is weak and social spending is well below average. Firms are mainly controlled by shareholders with widespread share holdings and thus a high dispersion of control. Typical liberal market economies are the United States, the UK, Australia, Canada and New Zealand. Coordinated market economies, on the other hand, are characterized by

[6] *P.A. Hall, D.W. Gingerich,* Varieties of Capitalism and Institutional Complementarities in the Political Economy, British Journal of Political Science, 2009, 39 (3), pp. 449–482 (452).

a high union density and centralized wage bargaining, a rigid labor market and a high degree of social protection. Corporate governance is based on a limited number of controlling shareholders and is mainly manager-oriented. Typical CMEs are Germany, Austria, Japan and – to a somewhat lower extent – the "Nordic" countries. So-called "mixed economies" are France, Italy, Greece, Spain and Portugal.

The main finding is that macroeconomic development relies predominantly on the institutional complementarities of economic activities. Both, purely liberal and purely coordinated economies show a positive macroeconomic performance in terms of GDP growth and unemployment, whereas mixed economies lag behind. To put it differently, we would expect all developed countries sooner or later to crystallize into one of the two ideal types in order to ensure satisfactory macroeconomic outcomes.

b) Varieties of Capitalism II: Esping-Andersen

The most prominent classification of welfare state regimes is undoubtedly Danish sociologist *Gosta Esping-Andersen's* "Varieties of Capitalism" approach. *Esping-Andersen* distinguishes welfare states according to two criteria: social stratification and decommodification. Stratification refers to the degree to which divergent social groups are being integrated into a homogeneous welfare system. Thus, universal social systems do not discern eligibility rules or social entitlements according to class, occupation or social status, whereas particularized systems differentiate in these respects. Universalism is thus equivalent to a social system that is egalitarian in structure, but not necessarily in outcomes. Decommodification denotes the adjournment of labor treated as a marketable commodity. It refers to the extent to which workers are free to pursue their life plans without being forced to supply their labor on the market at any cost. Thus decommodification is "the degree to which individuals, or families, can uphold a socially acceptable standard of living independent of market participation"[7]. This commodification-stratification dimension led to a classification of the welfare state that arranges social policy regimes according to the underlying political ideas generating specific welfare programs: the Liberal model, the Social-Democratic model and the Conservative model. The liberal Anglo-Saxon welfare system is characterized by a low degree of decommodification and a strong emphasis on self-reliance and individual responsibility. The Scandinavian model, on the other hand, shows a high degree of universalism and decommodification. Finally, *Esping-Andersen* identifies a third cluster that combines moderate decommodification with intermediate stratification of the social system. This specific combination can be traced back to a history of corporatism and etatism prevalent

[7] *G. Esping-Andersen*, The three worlds of welfare capitalism, Princeton New Jersey 1990, p. 30.

mainly in continental European countries, Germany being the prototype. This ultimately leads to his well-known "three regimes" typology of the liberal, social-democratic and conservative-corporatist (or Bismarckian) welfare regimes.

c) Criticism

The identification of different "welfare regimes" and the underlying typologies has had an enormous impact both on science and politics. Furthermore, it has spurred on a number of similar follow-up studies. This remarkable success should not obscure the fact that the ideal-typical distinction by *Esping-Andersen* suffers from serious drawbacks. One is the specific choice of countries under consideration. It has often been criticized that *Esping-Andersen* disregarded South European countries, i.e. Greece, Portugal and Spain. Whereas some authors consider these countries as specific sub-cases of the Continental-Bismarckian variety[8], others pool them into a separate category which they name "Southern Rim"[9]. The same holds true for the Eastern European welfare regimes[10]. Up to now it is not clear if these countries can be subsumed under one of the traditional clusters (and – if so – which one), whether they form a homogenous type distinct of the others or if they fall into different categories.[11]

A second difficulty arises from the micronumerosity problem associated with the classification of political regimes. Descriptive approaches use data mining methods which were designed to analyze huge data sets and to condense this information to a manageable size. In the analysis of welfare systems, there is, however, only a limited number of policy regimes that can be evaluated. Most studies use less than 20 observations. This makes the qualitative results highly sensitive to the underlying specification. A different classification of only one or two observations may influence the qualitative results significantly. Germany can be taken as a prominent example. In their seminal work, *Hall et al.* classify Germany as a typical Coordinated Market Economy (CME). Thus, they put Ger-

[8] *G. S. Katrougalos,* The South European Welfare Model: The Greek Welfare State in Search of an Identity, Journal of European Social Policy, 1996, 6 (1), pp. 39–60.

[9] *S. Leibfried,* Towards a European Welfare State? On Integrating Poverty Regimes into the European Community, in: Z. Ferge, J.E. Kohlberg (eds.): Social Policy in a Changing Europe, Frankfurt 1992; *M. Ferrera,* The Southern Model of Welfare in Social Europe, Journal of European Social Policy, 1996, 6 (1), pp. 17–37; *G. Bonoli,* Classifying Welfare States, A Two-Dimension Approach, Journal of Social Policy, 1997, (26) 3, pp. 351–372; *R. Trifiletti,* Mediterranean Welfare Regimes and the Worsening position of Women, Journal of European Social Policy, 1999, 4, pp. 63–78.

[10] *H.J.M. Fenger,* Welfare Regimes in Central and Eastern Europe: Incorporating Post-Communist Countries in a Welfare Regime Typology, CIIS Working Paper, Netherlands 2007.

[11] For example, *Fenger* (Fn. 10) distinguishes three distinct post-communist welfare regimes: the former USSR type (Belarus, Estonia, Latvia, Lithuania, Russia, Ukraine), the post-communist European type (Bulgaria, Croatia, Czech Republic, Hungary, Poland, Slovakia) and developing welfare states type (Georgia, Moldova, Romania).

many in one cluster together with Nordic countries such as Sweden or Norway. But on the other hand, in an earlier study, *Calmfors/Driffill*[12] took Germany to be the prototype of an economy with an "intermediate" degree of centralization of wage bargaining, which would identify Germany as a typical Mixed Market Economy (MME). Re-classifying a country like Germany from one cluster into another has severe implications for the qualitative results of these studies.

Finally, the different clustering approaches are only partly overlapping. If one interrelates the Coordination and the Decommodification/Stratification approach, there is a number of countries that fall into the same cluster. Unambiguous results can be found e.g. with the US, UK, Australia and New Zealand (Liberal type) and the Nordic Countries Sweden, Finland, Norway and Denmark, which fall into the Social-Democratic/Coordinated type (see table 1). Besides the Netherlands and Switzerland, two countries that already caused severe problems in *Esping-Andersen's* typology, Germany, Australia and Japan lack a clear categorization. The different ideal types of welfare regimes should thus be interpreted cautiously and with care.

Table 1: Typologies of Welfare Regimes.

		Coordination Regimes (Hall/Soskice/Gingerich)		
		Liberal Market Economies (LME)	Mixed Market Economies (MME)	Coordinated Market Economies (CME)
Decommodification and Stratification (Esping-Andersen et al.)	Liberal	United States, United Kingdom, Australia, Canada, New Zealand, Ireland		Netherlands, Belgium, Switzerland
	Conservative-corporatist/ Southern Rim		France, Italy, Portugal, Spain, Greece	Germany, Austria,
	Social-Democratic			Finland, Sweden, Denmark, Norway

[12] *L. Calmfors, J. Driffill*, Bargaining Structure, Corporatism and Macroeconomic Performance, Economic Policy, 1988, 3 (6), pp. 13–61.

2. Causal models

In contrast to the descriptive approach mentioned above, causal models try to discover the influences of exogenous variables on the size and/or the structure of welfare states using regression models. As (quasi-)natural experiments are impossible due to data limitations, causality has to be theoretically detected and tested by correlation analysis. As reversed causality and spurious regression is a severe problem in this context, all results have to be interpreted with extreme care. There is an exhaustive literature that uses correlation analysis to examine the influence of factors such as economic growth, the political system, the strength of left-wing parties or social fractionalization and globalization on social expenditure. The main results will be described in Section III. in the context of a comprehensive economic and political model.

II. Economic and Confessional Determinants of the Welfare State

1. Economic models of the Welfare State

In their seminal paper, *Alesina et al.*[13] present a model that comprises different approaches of economic and political theory to explain the level of redistribution. They assume utility maximizing agents with altruistic preferences in a median voter economy. According to *Alesina's* model, redistribution is mainly caused by five factors:

- by the number of people with an income below average and the severity (or "depth") of poverty. The depth of poverty is measured as the difference between actual income and mean income in society. As an efficient system of redistribution requires incomes to be reallocated from the rich to the poor, redistribution increases with the number of poor persons and with inequality in society. Put differently, one would expect redistribution to increase with rising inequality of gross income, i.e. with income before government intervention.
- by the welfare loss associated with redistribution. As any market intervention is supposed to affect economic efficiency, the welfare gain of redistribution has to be weighed against the loss incurred by taxation. It can be shown that there is a demand for state activity only whenever the social cost of redistribution does not exceed the ratio of median and mean income[14].
- by income insecurity. The impact of income fluctuation on the demand of government intervention is ambiguous. In a stationary environment, income

[13] *A. Alesina et al.*, Brookings Papers on Economic Activity (Fn. 4).
[14] *A. Alesina et al.*, Brookings Papers on Economic Activity (Fn. 4), p. 206.

volatility causes moderated state intervention via e. g. progressive taxation, as individuals tend to be risk-averse and thus prefer stable to volatile incomes over time[15]. However, this may change in a dynamic environment. With increasing incomes, the demand for redistribution might go down, as the median voter will be subject to redistributive taxation in the future. According to the "Prospect of Upward Mobility" (POUM) hypothesis, redistribution is supposed to decline. Thus, if this argument holds true, we would expect income growth and redistribution to be *negatively* correlated.

- by the degree of representation of the poor in the political process. The more the disadvantaged are capable of articulating themselves politically and of influencing the public agenda according to their preferences, the higher the degree of redistribution. Political theory suggests that this is more likely the case in a parliamentary democracy with proportional representation.
- by the degree of altruism in society. This determinant, which is crucial for any kind of redistribution in a welfare-based approach, is introduced into the model in a rather *ad hoc* fashion and not explained any further. A rising degree of altruism would lead – ceteris paribus – to an increase in redistribution.

German economist and social theorist *Heinz Lampert* offers a somewhat different view on the determinants of welfare spending[16]. In his integrative approach, he tries to subsume the main factors of welfare state expansion under three aspects. *Lampert* summarizes the main determinants of welfare expansion by the *urgency* of social problems, society's *ability* to solve these issues as well as the *willingness* of a society to engage in distributive activities. *Urgency* refers to objective differences in people's personal circumstances and their living conditions. Indicators for the urgency of social issues are, for instance, the poverty rate, the unemployment rate or the old-age dependancy ratio. *Ability* is mainly determined by the level of economic development. Thus, we find a significant difference to the prediction of *Alesina's* model. Whilst *Alesina* expects redistribution to decline with economic growth, this model predicts an increase in social expenditure with economic development. *Willingness* is a socio-political concept. It comprises political institutions (e. g. the degree of democratization or the political decision-making process) as well as societal predispositions towards liberty, equality and the social status of the individual. Thus, besides institutional factors, the concept of *willingness* also comprises the predominant ethics in a society.

[15] *A. Alesina et al.*, Brookings Papers on Economic Activity (Fn. 4), p. 203.

[16] *J. Althammer, H. Lampert,* Lehrbuch der Sozialpolitik, 9th ed., Berlin 2014, p. 145.

2. *Confessional determinants of the Welfare State*

a) General remarks

Normative predispositions and commonly shared ethical beliefs are rather complex and intangible analytical concepts that cause severe problems with respect to operationalization and measurement. The substantial progress made in the last decades notwithstanding, there is no overall consensus on how to measure normative attitudes and ethical beliefs in society. Partly due to the lack of a more convincing analytical concept, ethical values are usually approximated by the predominant religious beliefs in a country.

The impact of religious confessions on the size and the institutional structure of social policy arrangements have been analyzed in detail by *Philip Manow*[17] and the successive literature. To *Manow*, the formation as well as the development of western welfare states can only be understood by taking the predominant religious motives of a society into account. For western welfare states, he identifies three influential religious sources: Catholic Social Teaching (CST), the Lutheran established church and Protestant congregational chapels (e. g. Calvinism and the so called "dissenters"). Before analyzing the differences in the attitude to welfare state intervention between the different Christian confessions in more detail, I will briefly sketch the common grounds that characterize Christian social ethics irrespective of the specific denomination.

Constitutive for a Christian approach to social ethics is the conception of man being an image of God (*imago dei*). The belief that man was created in God's image is the foundation of the Christian notion of human dignity and constitutes specific rights that are assumed to pre-exist social conventions and positive law. In sharp contrast to classical liberalism, these rights are conceptualized not merely as negative rights, but as positive, social entitlements. Human dignity implies a right to those basic goods that are essential to lead a self-determined and meaningful life. The basic principle of Christian ethics is the personality principle that serves as a point of reference to the principles of solidarity, subsidiarity or the common good. The personality principle has a twofold implication. On the one hand, it postulates the duty to self-provision and the responsibility for oneself. On the other, the personality principle constitutes a duty for solidarity and outside help to those who lack the necessary means to take care of themselves. The command to charity – which, according to Christian thought, ranks equal to the command to love God – constitutes a responsibility to aid for the needy and to mutual assistance whenever necessary.

[17] *Ph. Manow*, Religion und Sozialstaat, Die konfessionellen Grundlagen europäischer Wohlfahrtsstaatsregime (Fn. 5).

b) The Catholic tradition

This congruency in Christian social thought notwithstanding, the various Christian denominations put their emphasis on different aspects of the means of individual responsibility and social interaction[18]. This has ultimately led to different conceptions of the welfare state and diverging demands for state intervention. For Southern European countries and – in a somewhat modified fashion – for France and Germany, Catholic Social Teaching plays a dominant role in the evolution and the shaping of the welfare state. According to the well-established definition by German sociologist *Franz-Xaver Kaufmann*[19], Catholic Social Teaching can be viewed as being anti-socialist, anti-statist and anti-liberal. It is anti-socialist, as it refutes the materialistic conception of man as well as class struggle as an instrument to achieve social goals. The working class concept of solidarity is refuted as well, as this specific notion of solidarity is directed towards specific groups in society and is thus excluding in nature. According to Christian ethics, solidarity is rather a concept that "encompasses the whole of mankind"[20]. Thus, solidarity in a Christian understanding is directed towards social inclusion and embedding. Secondly, Social Catholicism is conceptualized as anti-liberal, as the unregulated coordination of private activities via free markets is assumed to be insufficient to solve the social question. The responsibility for poverty, unemployment or social exclusion is not mainly assigned to the individual person, but is conceptualized as a social phenomenon which is mainly caused by structural circumstances. To address this phenomenon, the theology of liberation coined the phrase "structures of sin". This phrase was taken up by Pope *John Paul II.* in his encyclical "Sollitudo Rei Socialis" ("On Social Concern"). As poverty and exclusion are assumed to be determined by economic structures and institutions, Catholic Social Teaching demands collective action to overcome social stratification. This task, however, is not primarily the business of the welfare state, but of civil society. Therefore, charitable and not-for-profit organizations as well as parafiscal institutions play a predominant role in the social agenda of the Catholic Church. That is why the Catholic social model is rightly characterized as being "anti-statist".

The description of the Catholic social model would be highly fragmentary if one did not address the traditional gender roles and the specific division of labor that are associated with that arrangement. The Catholic conception of the welfare state relies heavily on the family as the producer of social services and on the male breadwinner model. Social services such as child-rearing and the care of the elderly are supposed to be supplied by family members, i. e. women who resign

[18] *Ph. Manow*, Religion und Sozialstaat, Die konfessionellen Grundlagen europäischer Wohlfahrtsstaatsregime (Fn. 5).

[19] *F. X. Kaufmann,* Christentum und Wohlfahrtsstaat, Zeitschrift für Sozialreform, 1988, 34 (2), pp. 65–89.

[20] *K. Bayertz,* Begriff und Problem der Solidarität, in: K. Bayertz (ed.): Solidarität, Frankfurt 1998, pp. 1–23.

from gainful employment. Social insurance for non-working family members is safeguarded by claims derived from the primary earner. Thus, the Catholic social model is based on specific social institutions such as (life-long) marriage, a continuous work biography for the breadwinner and labor income that guarantees a sufficient living standard for the family as a whole. Thus, changing gender roles and the increasing fragility of marriage have put this model under pressure and demand major adjustments.

c) The Lutheran established Church

A second branch of confessional influence on the social state stems from the Lutheran established church. Lutheranism exhibited its impact on the design of the welfare state mainly in the Nordic countries. According to Lutheran understanding, the solution to the social question lies predominantly in the hand of the secular government. It is the government that has the moral obligation to protect the people from poverty and to raise the living conditions of its population.

According to the confessional thesis, this specific "alliance of throne and altar" is the main reason for the comprehensiveness and the universalism of Scandinavian social systems. With the moral duties of the state outlined above, non-governmental organizations play only a minor role in designing social policy measures and deciding on welfare programs. If NGOs have an impact on the basic principles of the welfare state, their influence is mainly indirect and linked to the political system. This functional assignment in welfare policy was especially productive for the theoretical underpinning of social policy and the formulation of a theory of the welfare state. It is not by chance that the so called "Kathedersozialisten" such as *Adoph Wagner*, *Werner Sombart* or *Gustav Schmoller* were Protestants, as were leading proponents of the German Ordo-Liberal school of economics. Thus, the German concept of a Social Market Economy refers not only to Catholic Social Teaching, but is strongly rooted in Protestant political thought as well.

d) The Free Protestant tradition

Finally, a substantial, even though retarding, influence on the welfare state is ascribed to the free Protestant churches, such as Non-Conformist, Dissenters and the Reform Protestant movements. Although similar in theory, free Protestant churches emphasize a stern distinction between the Church and the state. This is mainly due to their experience of religious discrimination, social exclusion and repression, which ultimately culminated in lasting skepticism concerning the authority of the state. Additionally, one's own responsibility and a strong labor ethics are emphasized. The main reason for social exclusion and poverty are not traced back to the economic structures of capitalism, but attributed to the individual himself. Safeguarding the means of living for oneself and one's dependants is mainly the duty of the individual person, not that of the state or of collective institutions such as a social insurance program. Poverty relief is mainly due to private charity, which is pivotal to this concept. Finally, all public services are means-tested and due to a case-by-case review. This retarding effect of Reform Protestantism on the development of the welfare state can be seen in the US and Great Britain, but also in Switzerland and the Netherlands.

A common element to all Protestant social ethics is the high degree of emancipation and autonomy of women in the workplace. Protestant welfare policy is less family-centred than are concepts based on Catholic Social Thought. As a consequence, public social services are more developed in countries with a strong Protestant culture.

III. Empirical Evidence

1. Economic and socio-demographic characteristics

The determinants of welfare state expansion have been analyzed extensively in the literature. In his exhaustive literature survey, *Eschbach*[21] identifies 36 studies analyzing more than 80 variables in over 160 regressions. Although the specification of the model and the operationalization of the dependent variable differ considerably between these studies, there are some common features that can be derived from the empirical evidence. Some of them are so predominant in the literature that they can be taken as stylized facts of welfare state development. One of these is the positive influence of gross domestic product (GDP) on the level of social spending. Irrespective of the formal specification of the model and the operationalization of the GDP variable – be it real GDP, GDP per capita or GDP growth – a higher value of income is generally associated with higher levels of social spending and a higher share of social expenditures to national income. The same holds true for the old age dependency ratio. An increase of the share of elderly people in the population increases absolute social expenditure as well as the share of social expenditure to GDP. Thus, demographic change is one of the main driving forces of welfare state expansion.

The impact of distribution, or of "problem solving urgency", is less evident and quite often contrary to expectations. *Alesina* reports rather mixed and ambiguous results concerning the influence of income inequality on the size of the welfare state. The Gini coefficient of income before taxes and transfers (pre-tax Gini) turns out to be insignificant in various specifications. Different measures of income inequality such as the quintile distance or the relation of median to mean income even show the wrong – i. e. negative – sign. One can only hypothesize on the cause. One probable reason is the distributive inefficiency of welfare state

[21] *A. Eschbach*, Pfade in den Leviathanstaat? Determinanten der öffentlichen Sozialausgaben in 21 OECD-Ländern 1980–2005, Berlin 2011.

programs. Due to tax-avoiding reactions of the private actors, the welfare state might be unable to influence the income distribution profoundly in the long run. Another explanation is that extensive welfare states not only redistribute in terms of monetary measures, but also via labour market regulations, unionization etc. Thus, the pre-tax income distribution is flatter in developed welfare states, which might explain the lack of significance of this indicator.

2. *The impact of religious denomination*

The impact of religious denomination on welfare state development – or what will be called the "Manow Hypothesis" below – has up to now attracted only minor attention in the empirical literature. *Manow*[22] himself reports a negative impact of the free Protestant churches on welfare expenditure, but he does not distinguish between Lutheran and Catholic countries. In an explorative study, *Poole* rejects the hypothesis that Catholic states show higher welfare expenditures or a higher share of social expenditure to GDP than Protestant ones. *Eschbach*[23] reports insignificant results as well.

In order to investigate the impact of the three Christian denominations on the level and the structure of the welfare state in more detail, we regress the ratio of social expenditure on GDP and the share of transfers in kind to total social expenditure on the different denominations and a set of control variables such as GDP (in logs), the dependency ratio and the unemployment rate. We use a panel of 33 countries covering the period from 1990 to 2010 in 5-years intervals. The equation we estimate is given by (1) $Y_{it} = \alpha_i + \gamma R + \tau X_{it} + \varepsilon_{it}$ with Y being the variable under consideration (share of social expenditure or in-kind transfers), R denotes the religious denomination with non-Christian denominations as the reference category and X is a set of control variables. The results are represented in table 2 (absolute t-values in parentheses).

Table 2: The impact of religious denominations on size and structure of the welfare state.

	Share of social expenditure	*Share of transfers in kind*
log (GDP)	2.15 (2.02)	9.98 (3.18)
Old-age dependency ratio	0.36 (2.26)	−0.21 (0.44)
Unemployment ratio	0.45 (4.04)	−0.49 (1.5)
Catholic	4.96 (3.32)	−7.53 (1.69)
Lutheran	8.67 (4.94)	−5.27 (1.00)
Free Protestant	2.04 (1.26)	−2.45 (0.50)
N	165	165

[22] *Ph. Manow*, Religion und Sozialstaat, Die konfessionellen Grundlagen europäischer Wohlfahrtsstaatsregime (Fn. 5).

[23] *A. Eschbach*, Pfade in den Leviathanstaat? Determinanten der öffentlichen Sozialausgaben in 21 OECD-Ländern 1980–2005 (Fn. 21).

The table shows, that higher per capital GDP is positively correlated to social expenditure. The same holds true for the old-age dependency ratio and the unemployment rate. All these findings are in line with expectations and existing studies. It is interesting to note, that higher GDP positively associated with a higher fraction of in-kind transfers. This means that more developed countries put a larger emphasis on in-kind transfers such as public infrastructure compared to cash benefits. The relationship between in-kind transfers and unemployment or the old-age dependency ratio turns out to be statistically insignificant.

In contrast to the prevailing part of previous research, our results support *Manow's* hypothesis on the influence of Christian denomination on the size and – to a somewhat lesser extent – on the structure of the welfare state. Countries influenced by Free Protestantism have a considerably lower level of social expenditure, and they spend more on in-kind transfers than on cash payments. Catholic countries, on the other hand, show an intermediate level of welfare expenditure and the highest level of cash benefits. Finally, Lutheran countries have the highest level of social spending and an intermediate level of in-kind transfers. The results on social expenditure are statistically significant and robust to a number of re-specifications. With respect to the allocation of social spending in cash vs. in-kind, only the indicator for Catholicism turns out to be significant. We thus conclude that the dominant religious ideology in fact has a long-run influence mainly on the size of the welfare state.

IV. Conclusion

The literature on the varieties of capitalism convincingly shows that even in an economically and culturally rather homogenous community, there exist divergent norms and beliefs concerning the role of the individual in society. These commonly shared attitudes ultimately lead to different specifications and characteristics of the welfare state. Even the member states of the European Union show a wide range of diversity concerning the level and the structure of welfare policy. Thus, up to now, a "European Social Policy" is only visible in its contours. Although all these countries had to respond to industrialization and to the challenges of globalization, and although all western welfare states evolved within a culture that was dominated by Christian values and attitudes, social policy is still diverging with respect to scope and structure. Religion obviously deploys long-lasting normative impacts that are still effective even though the crucial precondition – strong religious commitment and denominational bonding – has considerably eroded.

The Significance of Religion for French Labour and Social Legislation

Gwenola Bargain

"Without faith, how open and beautiful and terrifying the world must have seemed to him"[1]

Modern societies are confronted with the resurgence of religion in the public sphere. The growth of "religious individualism"[2] gives rise to new specific conflicts and the extent to which the freedom of religion should be enjoyed in the workplace is a contentious debate in many western countries[3]. Religion is less regarded as private matter and, as a consequence, individuals are more likely to express religious beliefs in the workplace. Some conflicts could lead to very strong oppositions since some believers consider religion as being at the core of their identity. Religious claims raise new challenges facing labour law. However,

---

[1] *I. Mc Ewan*, The Children Act, London, Vintage, 2014, p. 212.

[2] *F. Gaudu*, "La religion dans l'entreprise", Droit social, 2010, p. 65.

[3] See *L. Vickers*, "Religion and belief discrimination in employment under the Employment Equality Directive: a comparative analysis", European equality law review, 2015, n°1, p. 25.

the statement, as in other countries[4], is that religious beliefs create few problems in the workplace[5].

Two distinctive topics relate to the relationship between labour law and religion: the impact of religion on labour law; and the expression of religion in the workplace. These are two different but interconnected matters. Religion obviously constitutes a normative framework. Several authors analysed the way the Church's social doctrine has influenced and partly informed French labour law[6]. According to Professor F. Gaudu, "the religious inspiration of French Labor Law cannot be ignored; however, this is barely recognized, at least since World War II"[7]. In the context of the secular (*laïc*) Republic, the influence of religion on labour law has decreased. In addition, the normative framework informing the evolution of the labour law rules has shifted towards a kind of "market framework". The influence of "models" of the market, shaped by economic analysis, is tangible[8] and it should be taken into account for analysing the current change of contemporary labour law[9]. To some extent, "every country [...] is affected by the dogma of the Total Market and by the growing number of claims concerning personal status"[10].

The growth of claims concerning "personal status" and related to religious beliefs has brought French labour law jurists to revise theirs concepts. A kind of "automatic" response was to refer to the "*laïcité* framework" to consider the interaction of religion and work. To some extent, this "reflex"[11] was based on a political rather than a legal view. It was related to a positive conception of "*laïcité*", a "positive secularism that respects religious beliefs but keeps them limited to the personal life of the employee" [12].

---

[4] See the report by *M. Mitchell, K. Beninger, A. Donald* et *E. Howard*, Religion or belief in the workplace and service delivery, Equality and Human Rights Commission, 2015.

[5] See Association française de Droit du travail, "Le fait religieux en entreprise", Synthèse des travaux du groupe AFDT, 22 January 2016, http://www.afdt-asso.fr/wp-content/uploads/2016/01/AFDT-Le-fait-religieux-au-travail-groupe-AFDT.pdf.

[6] *A. Supiot*, "A propos d'un centenaire: la dimension juridique de la doctrine sociale de l'Église", Droit social, 1991, p. 916.

[7] *F. Gaudu*, "Labor law and religion", Comparative Labor Law and Policy Journal, 2009, vol. 30, p. 507.

[8] See *S. Deakin*, "Conceptions of the Market in Labour Law", in *A. Numhauser-Henning* et *M. Rönnmar* (dir.), Normative patterns and legal developments in the social dimension of the EU, Oxford; Portland, Hart Publishing, 2013, p. 142.

[9] *A. Supiot*, L'esprit de Philadelphie: la justice sociale face au marché total, Paris, Seuil, 2010.

[10] *A. Supiot*, "Orare/Laborare", Comparative Labor Law and Policy Journal, 2009, vol. 30, p. 641.

[11] See *Ph. Auvergnon*, "L'expression des convictions religieuses sur le lieu de travail", in Droit et religion en Europe, Etudes en l'honneur de Francis Messner, Strasbourg, Presses universitaires de Strasbourg, 2014, p. 31.

[12] See *Ph. Waquet*, "La vie personnelle du salarié", Mélanges J.-M. Verdier, Dalloz, 2000, p. 520; *F. Gaudu*, "Labor law and religion", Comparative Labor Law and Policy Journal, 2009, vol. 30, p. 512.

The conception of a secularized enterprise guarantying religious freedom on a neutral ground therefore prevailed until a recent case, the *Baby Loup* case[13] (I). This case sheds light on the weakness of the usual reasoning regarding religion in the workplace. In addition, the prevailing line of reasoning, namely the reference to a secular workplace, was under question as the legal framework has deeply evolved. On the one hand, the Employment Equality Framework Directive 2000/78 of the EU has been implemented by the Law of 27 May 2008 providing diverse adaptations of Community law in the field of the fight against discriminations. On the other hand, the European Court of Human Rights has strengthened its approach of religious freedom by recognizing that religious beliefs have to be protected in the context of the workplace[14]. Through the lens of an "anti-discrimination" law framework, new legal answers will have to be shaped (II).

I. Laïcité and labour law: from the veil of ignorance to the ban on the wearing of the veil in nurseries

Laïcité lies at the core of the French Republic and yet, for a long time, as a legal principle, labour law jurists ignored it. Perceived as an overarching requirement, it was not considered useful for solving issues dealing with religion in the workplace[15]. However, over the past few years, *laïcité* has generated legal debates with regard to the *Baby Loup* case; six years of litigation have been devoted to this affair and "the *laïcité* principle has haunted labour jurists"[16].

Before analysing the case (2.), the complex meaning of *laïcité* should be presented (1.).

1. The complex meaning of laïcité

To what extent is *laïcité* a central concept for understanding the relationship between French labour law and religion? The place of religion in France is intrinsically connected to the secularist nature of the State. Nonetheless, secularism is not the key concept to answer to religious claims in the workplace. It may be considered that secularism is always used as a feeble argument when the freedom of religion is at stake.

---

[13] Cass., Ass. plén., 25 June 2014, Recueil Dalloz, p. 1386.

[14] ECHR, Case n°48420/10, Eweida and Others v. the United Kingdom, 15 January 2013.

[15] *P. Adam*, "Les laïcités et l'entreprise privée; représentation(s) dans un théâtre d'ombres", Droit social, 2015, p. 708.

[16] *P. Adam*, "Les laïcités et l'entreprise privée; représentation(s) dans un théâtre d'ombres", Droit social, 2015, p. 708.

a) Roots

There is no legal definition of *laïcité*. From a political view, there is not one but several models of *laïcité*. As a consequence, different definitions, depending on cultures, histories and political opinions, would be appropriate. To such an extent, according to one author, "there is no such thing as a French model of *laïcité* but different representations"[17].

Religious freedom is protected under the Declaration of the Rights of Man and of the Citizen of 1789. Article 10 provides that "No one shall be disquieted on account of his opinions, including his religious views, provided their manifestation does not disturb the public order established by law." As a fundamental value of the French Republic since 1946, *laïcité* is enshrined in Article 1 of the French Constitution of 1958:

> "France shall be an indivisible, secular, democratic and social Republic. It shall ensure the equality of all citizens before the law, without distinction of origin, race or religion. It shall respect all beliefs".

The absence of definition in the Constitution is intended to leave room for interpretation.

Nevertheless, French law has ignored the strict idea of *laïcité* for a long time. It appears late in the legislation, at the end of the twentieth century[18]. Even the Law on the Separation of Church and State (1905), "the real keystone of French secularism" according to the European Court of Human Rights[19], does not contain the word "secularism". The Law on the Separation of Church and State puts an end to the Concordat (except in two departments, Alsace and Moselle) and affirms in Article 1:

> "The Republic ensures freedom of conscience. It guarantees the free exercise of all forms of worship, subject only to the restrictions enacted hereafter in the interest of public order".

Freedom of worship, freedom of religion and separation of Church and State are thus organized by this legislation.

The *Conseil constitutionnel*, in a priority preliminary ruling on the issue of constitutionality, held that

> "the principle of secularism is one of the rights and freedoms guaranteed by the Constitution; that it follows that the State must be neutral; that it also follows that the Republic does not recognise any religion; that the principle of secularism requires in particular that all beliefs be respected, the equality of all citizens before the law without distinction based

---

[17] *J. Bauberot*, *Les 7* laïcités françaises, le modèle français de laïcité n'existe pas, Paris, Éditions de la Maison des sciences de l'homme, 2015, p. 16.

[18] *J. Bauberot*, Histoire de la laïcité en France, 6ème éd., Que-sais-je, PUF, 2013.

[19] ECHR, 4 December 2008, Dogru v. France, n°27005805, § 18.

on religion also be respected, and that the Republic guarantee the free exercise of religion; that it implies that it shall not subsidise any religion"[20].

Attempts to clarify the legal meaning of the concept did not prevent misunderstandings and misinterpretations of this political and legal principle[21].

However, different values lie at the core of this concept: freedom of conscience, equality of all citizens, universality. *Laïcité* is not – obviously – a way to eradicate religious belief. It refers both to the neutrality of the State and to religious freedom. As the European Court stated, "it implies an acknowledgement of religious pluralism and State neutrality towards religions. In return for protection of his or her freedom of religion, the citizen must respect the public arena that is shared by all"[22].

b) Secularism through the lens of labour law

While *laïcité* informs the way French society deals with religious issues, it should be acknowledged that labour law academics for a long time did not pay much attention to secularism[23]. From a labour law perspective, the issue of religious freedom in the workplace is a recent one[24]. As in other western countries, context is changing and it forces lawyers to revisit the current legal framework[25]. According to one author, this evolution is connected with the growth of "personal status": "Demands shift here from having to being, from the realm of the socio-economic to that of identity, with not only groups but also individuals wanting to become their own law-givers"[26]. In contemporary society, individuals are more inclined to assert their religious identity, even in the "social sphere". Several cases have arisen recently in national courts[27].

The idea of a secular workplace has tainted the debates related to religion and belief at work. The meaning of *laïcité* has always been understood in various ways. *Laïcité* was sometimes viewed as enshrining a closed sphere of freedom in the workplace, as "a secular enterprise does not inquire about the religion of

---

[20] Decision No. 2012–297, QPC of 21 February 2013, Association for the Promotion and Expansion of Secular Thought (Treatment of pastors from consistorial churches in the Departments of Bas-Rhin, Haut-Rhin and Moselle).

[21] See *J. Bauberot*, Les 7 laïcités françaises, le modèle français de laïcité n'existe pas, Paris, Éditions de la Maison des sciences de l'homme, 2015.

[22] CEDH, 4 December 2008, Dogru v. France, n°27005805, § 18.

[23] *P. Adam*, "Les laïcités et l'entreprise privée; représentation(s) dans un théâtre d'ombres", Droit social, 2015, p. 709.

[24] *F. Gaudu*, "Labor law and religion", Comparative Labor Law and Policy Journal, vol. 30, p. 507.

[25] See *Seifert A*, "Religious expression in the workplace: the case of the Federal Republic of Germany", Comparative Labor Law and Policy Journal, 2009, p. 529.

[26] *A. Supiot*, "Orare/Laborare", Comparative Labor Law and Policy Journal, 2009, vol. 30, p. 651.

[27] *F. Gaudu*, "La religion dans l'entreprise", Droit social, 2010, p. 65.

its employees"[28]. Solutions were, in accordance with the requirements of the *laïcité* principle, conceived with a view to protecting the freedom of conscience, equality of rights and the free exercise of worship. Nonetheless, labour law is currently "the main scene of disputes concerning the way of thinking *laïcité*"[29].

It may be surprising that regarding the Labour Code, no reference is made to this principle. Two kinds of boundaries have been elaborated to guaranty individual freedoms, including religious freedom, in an employment context. First, under Article L. 1121–1 of the Labour code, restrictions on personal rights as well as individual and collective freedoms should be "justified by the nature of the task to be accomplished" and "proportionate to the targeted objective". This very general article, dated from 1992[30], is aimed to protect individual freedoms in the workplace by limiting the employer's prerogatives. *A contrario*, the employer is entitled to adopt restrictions if it is justified and proportionate to a legitimate aim. Second, under Article L. 1132–1, discrimination based on religious beliefs is forbidden. Any discriminatory measure on religious beliefs is void. No employee may be punished, dismissed or discriminated, directly or indirectly, on that ground.

As Professor Gaudu analysed it, it is the non-intrusion of the employer that is the main question under the Labour Code. Nevertheless, debates dealing with freedom of religion in the workplace tend to refer to the idea of *laïcité*.

2. The erroneous reference to laïcité in the Baby Loup case

Concerning religion at work, the focus had for a long time been on cases dealing with the status of the clergy[31]. Decisions relating to the requirements set by an employer and the religious expression of an employee were unusual. With the *Baby Loup* case, for the first time, the Court of Cassation had to deal with a conflict between freedom of religion, claimed by an employee, and the requirements set by an employer. The judges had to decide on whether a private employer was entitled to require his employees to adopt religious neutrality. Answering to this question, some judges referred to *laïcité*, building on contradictory interpretations of the principle. The *Baby Loup* dispute lasted six years and raised several issues: political, philosophical, and ideological …[32]

---

[28] *F. Gaudu*, "Labor law and religion", Comparative Labor Law and Policy Journal, 2009, vol. 30, p. 507.

[29] *P. Adam*, "Les laïcités et l'entreprise privée; représentation(s) dans un théâtre d'ombres", Droit social, 2015, p. 708.

[30] Loi n° 92–1446 du 31 décembre 1992 relative à l'emploi, au développement du travail à temps partiel et à l'assurance chômage.

[31] *F. Gaudu*, "Labor law and religion", Comparative Labour Law and Policy Journal, 2009, vol. 30, p. 507.

[32] In English, see *M. Peyronnet* et *C. Radé*, "Employment law: The ban on the wearing of the Islamic veil in crèches", Montesquieu Law Review, n°1, January, 2015.

Baby Loup is a private non-profit organization, namely a crèche (nursery), and its purpose is "to develop activities directed at young children from disadvantaged backgrounds". One employee of the nursery, returning from parental leave, arrived at work wearing an Islamic veil (a non-face-covering Islamic scarf). She refused to remove her veil as required by the provisions of the internal regulations, and was dismissed. The nursery's internal regulation provided that

> "the principle of freedom of conscience and religion of all members of staff shall not prevent the observance of the principles of secularism and neutrality that apply in the performance of any and all activities developed by Baby Loup, both on the premises of the crèche or annexes and outside when accompanying children entrusted to the crèche".

The employee challenged the legality of her dismissal, claiming that it was contrary to the protection of religious freedom and the prohibition of religious discrimination. While the case seems easy, five hearings reached different decisions based on divergent legal reasoning. One employment law tribunal ruling, two Court of Appeal decisions, and two Court of Cassation decisions were involved.

The first instance tribunal, the *Conseil de prud'hommes* at *Mantes-la-Jolie*, in its judgment of 13 December 2010 held that the nursery could be characterized as a service of public interest and that its employees could be legally required to abide by the neutrality principle enshrined in the internal regulation[33]. Then the issue was brought before the Court of Appeal at Versailles. With no reference to the idea of *laïcité*, the Court of Appeal rejected the qualification and characterized the nursery as a private employer. Nevertheless, according to the judges, the dismissal was deemed legal on the ground that the nursery was entitled to guaranty the religious neutrality of its staff given its mission: to offer care to all children regardless of their religion and cultural background[34].

In 2013, the Social Chamber of the Court of Cassation quashed the decision of the Court of Appeal. Drawing a distinction between private employer and public employer, the Social Chamber ruled that *laïcité* does not apply to private sector employees who do not operate a public service. Offering care to young children was not a public service mission. On that ground, the general clause of the internal regulation was considered as imposing a general restriction to freedom of religion and was consequently deemed invalid. With this ruling, the Court of Cassation asserted that a private employer was outside the scope of *laïcité*[35]. *Laïcité* could not justify a restriction on religious freedom.

---

[33] Decision of Conseil de prud'hommes de Mantes la Jolie, 13 December 2010, n°10/00587, Dalloz, 2012, p. 901, obs. *P. Lokiec* et *J. Porta*; Revue de droit du travail, 2011, p. 182, obs. *P. Adam*.

[34] Court of Appeal at Versailles, CA Versailles, 27 October 2011, n°10/05642; Dalloz, 2012, p. 901, obs. *P. Lokiec* et *J. Porta*.

[35] "The principle of secularism established by Article 1 of the Constitution not being applicable to the salarie[d] employees of private-sector employers who do not run a public service … it may consequently not be relied upon in order to deprive them of the protection that is guar-

Pursuant to the French civil procedure, the Baby Loup case had to be heard again but this time by the Court of Appeal of Paris[36]. The Court of Appeal of Paris came to a different conclusion from the one reached by the Court of Cassation[37]. The Court of Appeal ruled that the nursery should be characterized in terms of an "*entreprise de tendance*" (or "confessionally-oriented enterprise"). According to the judges, Baby Loup was entitled to impose greater restrictions upon employees' individual religious freedoms than what would normally be allowed, given the aim to promote a special secular ("laic") ethos.

This characterization was rejected by the Court of Cassation in its plenary chamber. The Court held that the purpose of the nursery "was not to promote and defend religious, political or philosophical convictions" but "to develop activities directed at young children from disadvantaged backgrounds and to work for the social and professional reinsertion of women [...] whatever their political or religious affiliations"[38]. However, using a different legal argument from the Court of Appeal, it decided that the dismissal was lawful. To the Court of Cassation, it is legitimate for a private entity to place limits on its employees' freedom to express their religious beliefs in the workplace if these limits are justified and proportionate. In this second decision, the Court of Cassation considered that this was the case here. The nursery is a small business; it employs only 18 workers who come into continual contact with young children and their parents. Therefore the prohibition was not general and was precise enough and justified by the nature of the work. The reasoning of the Court is *in concreto*.

It should be noted that the principle of *laïcité* is not mentioned anymore in the ruling. Uncertainty remains with regard to the scope of this principle. As some authors have remarked,

> "this judgment does not shed any light on the powers of employers in matters concerning the management of religion within the company – and that is fortunate. It is not for the courts to decree such a demarcation where a fundamental freedom is at stake"[39].

Many questions are left unanswered by this case. Given the very contextual ruling of the Court of Cassation in the Baby Loup case, it is still difficult to

anteed to them under the provisions of the Code du travail"; Soc. 19 March 2013, n°11–28845; *E. Dockès,* Droit social, 2013, p. 388; *F. Laronze,* Droit social, 2014, p. 100; *P. Adam,* Revue de droit du travail, 2013, p. 385.

[36] The Court of Cassation has to decide whether the lower courts have correctly applied the rules of law. When the decision of the Court of Appeal is quashed, the case has consequently to be heard again by another Court of Appel.

[37] CA Paris, 27 November 2013, n°13/02981; *J. Mouly*, "L'affaire *Baby Loup* devant la Cour de renvoi: la revanche de la laïcité ?", Dalloz, 2014, p. 65.

[38] Cass. Ass. Plén., 25 June 2014, n°13–28.369; *J. Mouly*, "L'affaire Baby-Loup devant l'Assemblée plénière: quelques accommodements avec les principes", Droit social, 2014, p. 811; *P. Adam*, "Affaire Baby-Loup: vues du sommet", Revue de droit du travail, 2014, p. 607.

[39] See *M. Peyronnet* et *C. Radé*, "Employment law: The ban on the wearing of the Islamic veil in crèches", Montesquieu Law Review, n°1, January, 2015.

determine whether an employer can require his employees to remove their veil. In Baby Loup, the Court of Cassation ruled on the ground of Article L. 1121–1, which provides that restrictions on personal rights as well as individual and collective freedoms, should be "justified by the nature of the task to be accomplished" and be "proportionate to the targeted objective". The approach of the Court was only based on a proportionality test. A lot of comments have pointed out that the judgment ignored Article L. 1132–1, which forbids discrimination based on "religious beliefs". What about restriction being a form of discrimination? Could it be proportionated and justified? The legal framework does not give a clear answer and the "anti-discrimination" framework could be an even more disruptive element.

II. Religion in the workplace: a confused legal framework

For a long time, a kind of tacit compromise has regulated religious matters in the workplace. Indeed, in a secular Republic, labour relations were part of a "secularized undertaking"[40]. While still in place, this compromise has clearly evolved[41]. Individuals are more inclined to claim their religious beliefs in the workplace. The French labour law framework has to cope with new expectations. The extent to which religious beliefs can be expressed in the workplace depends on the legal characterization of the employer (A) and the behaviour of the employee (B).

1. The employer

Through the prism of religious freedom, a unitary analysis of the employer does not seem possible. A distinction has to be made between three, maybe four, kinds of organizations with different rules (rather uncertain rules) applicable to employees. This evolution reveals how problematic the growth of religious individualism could be for labour law.

a) Public service

Laïcité is enforced in the public sector. Public services employees have to abide by religious neutrality requirements, even in private institutions, as soon as a public service mission has been delegated to this institution. A public service mission requires an activity of general interest carried out under the control of

[40] *F. Gaudu*, "Labor law and religion", Comparative Labor Law and Policy Journal, 2009, vol. 30, p. 507.

[41] *Ph. Auvergnon*, "L'expression des convictions religieuses sur le lieu de travail", in Droit et religion en Europe, Etudes en l'honneur de Francis Messner, Strasbourg, Presses universitaires de Strasbourg, 2014, p. 31.

public authorities. In accordance with the administrative law jurisprudence, the Social Chamber of the Court of Cassation held, the same day as judgment was delivered in the *Baby Loup* case, that the principles of neutrality and secularism within public services were applicable to all public services. This includes

> "those instances where such services are provided by bodies governed by private law; and, while the provisions of the Code du travail are intended to apply to employees [of private institutions], the latter are nevertheless subject to specific constraints resulting from the fact that they perform public service functions, which forbid them in particular from displaying their religious beliefs through external symbols, and particularly their clothing"[42].

The case was dealing with a salaried employee who had no contact with the users of the public service in question (*a caisse primaire d'assurance maladie*, or local sickness insurance fund), and who had been dismissed for wearing a knotted headscarf in the workplace.

According to the European Court of Human Rights, this existing legal framework does not breach the Human Rights Convention[43]. The question was raised in a case involving a decision of a public hospital not to renew a French social worker's contract given her refusal to remove her veil. The European Court has considered that the freedom of consciousness of employees should be reconciled with the neutrality duty applicable in public services. Focusing on the legitimate aim of the religious neutrality requirement, the European judges held that this requirement was based on the necessity of protecting the rights and liberties of others, namely respecting everyone's religion. The French national courts had taken into consideration that the requirement was necessary to protect hospital patients from any risks of influence or partiality to their own freedom of conscience. The European Court follows this line of reasoning by underlining that the worker had contact with the patients. Then, in assessing the proportionality of the restriction, the European judges referred to the margin of appreciation of the State in its application of the Convention. The reasoning of the Court may be different from other rulings. The objective not to disrupt the French model of *laïcité* may explain the basis of the resolution.

In a different context, another kind of question has been raised with regard to secularism: does an "enterprise of secular belief" actually exist?

b) Entreprise de tendance (ethos-based enterprise)

Unknown to French labour law, the concept of "entreprise de tendance" is neither defined by the law nor subjected to any specific national regulation. Analysed by the doctrine, the concept of "entreprise de tendance" is defined by reference to the European Convention on Human Rights. This kind of enterprise, created to support the exercise of individual freedoms enshrined by the

[42] Soc. 19 March 2013, n°12–11.690, CPAM de Seine-Saint-Denis c/ M. X.

[43] ECHR, Ebrahimian v. France, 26 November 2015, n°64846/11, § 54.

Convention[44] in a collective way, could require its employees to be submitted to a reinforced loyalty duty[45]. It expressly promotes an ideology, morality, philosophy or policy and consequently could impose religious or ideological requirements on staff.

According to EU law and Employment Equality Directive 2000/78[46],

"in the case of occupational activities within churches and other public or private organisations the ethos of which is based on religion or belief, a difference of treatment based on a person's religion or belief shall not constitute discrimination where, by reason of the nature of these activities or of the context in which they are carried out, a person's religion or belief constitute a genuine, legitimate and justified occupational requirement, having regard to the organisation's ethos"[47].

Given their specific purpose, public or private organisations "the ethos of which is based on religion or belief", are entitled to act "in conformity with national constitutions and laws, to require individuals working for them to act in good faith and with loyalty to the organisation's ethos". In France, this Article has not yet been directly transposed.

Although French labour law does not distinguish the "entreprise de tendance" from others, the concept is not unknown to case law[48]. In one famous case, *Mme Roy*, of the plenary chamber of the Court of Cassation, on 19 May 1978, held that the dismissal of a teacher by a Catholic education institution on grounds of the former's remarriage after divorce was lawful. According to the judges,

"when the Association Saint-Marthe concluded a contract with Dame Roy, her religious beliefs had been taken into account and this element of the contract, which usually remains outside labour relations, was intentionally included into the contract, becoming an essential and determining part".

Another ruling of the Social Chamber on 20 November 1986 held that

"Article L. 122–45 of the Labour Code, stipulating that no employee can be punished or fired because of his religious beliefs, is not applicable when the worker, who was hired to achieve a task implying that he shares the beliefs and faith of his employer, ignores the obligations resulting from this commitment"[49].

However, since the 1990s, no case has raised a similar question.

---

[44] Freedom of thought, freedom of conscience and religion (art. 9), freedom of expression, opinion and communication (art. 10), freedom of association (art. 11).

[45] See *M. Morand*, "Entreprises identitaires et religions", Semaine Sociale Lamy, 2013, n°1611 Supplément; G. *Calvès*, "Devoir de réserve imposé aux salariés de la crèche Baby-Loup", Revue de droit du travail, 2014, p. 94.

[46] Directive 2000/78/EC of 27 November 2000 establishing a general framework for equal treatment in employment and occupation.

[47] Art. 4.2 of Directive 2000/78/EC.

[48] *Ph. Waquet*, "Convient-il d'interdire le port des signes religieux dans l'entreprise?", Revue de droit du travail, 2009, p. 485.

[49] Cass. Soc., 20 November 1986, Droit social, 1987, p. 379, note *J. Savatier*.

The specific ethos of such an enterprise does not imply that the employer is entitled to discriminate employees. To an organization the ethos of which is based on religion, the element of religion forms part of the contract, and thus the employer may take it into account. It does not mean that enterprises of this sort can behave in a discriminatory way: "the '*entreprises de tendance*' remain enterprises and are therefore submitted to the labour regulations"[50]. A kind of professional discretion could be required, while complete compliance with the purposes of the enterprise cannot. One could ask, however, whether such an employer would be entitled to invoke Article L. 1133–1 of the Labour Code, which provides that the justification of discrimination is to be "an essential and direct occupational requirement". Because of the nature of the occupation, a person's religious belief could constitute an occupational requirement for having and keeping the job. Imposing that requirement would be proportionate and the resulting discrimination would be considered lawful.

What remains disputable is whether an "*entreprise de tendance*" may restrict individual freedoms, for instance by taking into consideration the personal life of employees. The question is a sensitive one and to date there has been no clear answer from the judges[51]. According to Professor Gaudu,

> "in committing himself to an enterprise whose activities have religious aims, the employee restricts his personal freedom to a certain extent. In principle, the employer is not allowed to sanction or discharge an employee for facts related to his personal life that are external to the working relations. However, in the [entreprise de tendance], the employer can rely in exceptional cases on such facts"[52].

This statement must be put into perspective. A ruling by the Social Chamber of the Court of Cassation held that the personal life of an employee should be protected and dismissal cannot be based on a fact related to his personal life, unless this fact creates a serious disturbance within the enterprise[53]. As a consequence, the dismissal of a homosexual on grounds of his mores cannot be justified unless his behaviour has created a disturbance within the respective Catholic association. Moreover, a disciplinary dismissal based on a fact related to the personal life of an employee can only be justified by a breach of his contractual commitment[54]. The issue is whether an "*entreprise de tendance*" can impose a personal contractual commitment that goes beyond the usual occupational requirements.

---

[50] *F. Gaudu*, "Labor law and religion", Comparative Labor Law and Policy Journal, 2009, vol. 30, p. 515.

[51] See, *J.-P Marguenaud* et *J. Mouly*, "Les droits de l'homme salarié de l'entreprise identitaire", Dalloz, 2011, p. 1637.

[52] *F. Gaudu*, "Labor law and religion", Comparative Labor Law and Policy Journal, 2009, vol. 30, p. 515.

[53] Cass. Soc., 17 April 1991, n°90–42636; Droit social, 1991, p. 485, note *J. Savatier.*

[54] Cass. Soc., 3 May 2011, n°09–67464.

The lawfulness of such restrictions would depend on the context and the nature of the position. According to the ECHR,

"an employer whose ethos is based on religion or on a philosophical belief may impose specific duties of loyalty on its employees, a decision to dismiss based on a breach of such duty cannot be subjected, on the basis of the employer's right of autonomy, only to a limited judicial scrutiny exercised by the relevant domestic employment tribunal without having regard to the nature of the post in question and without properly balancing the interests involved in accordance with the principle of proportionality"[55].

The religious freedom of the employer should be balanced against other competing interests such as the right to privacy and personal rights of employees. The European judges have considered that an employee, in signing his or her employment contract, has accepted a duty of loyalty towards the Church, which limited the employee's rights "to respect for its private life to a certain degree". However, such commitments do not imply a complete waiver of an employee's right to a private life: the Court considers that

"the applicant's signature on the contract cannot be interpreted as a personal unequivocal undertaking to live a life of abstinence in the event of separation or divorce. An interpretation of that kind would affect the very heart of the right to respect for the private life of the person concerned, particularly since, as the employment tribunals found, the applicant was not bound by heightened duties of loyalty"[56].

It should be acknowledged that, given the margin of appreciation of the State and the proportionality test, the outcome of the matter is difficult to predict.

The question has arisen whether *laïcité* could be conceived as a belief promoted by an organization. In the *Baby Loup* case, the Court of Appeal referred to the expression of "*entreprise de conviction*, within the meaning of the case law of the European Court of Human Rights", and conceptualized secularism as a kind of promoted conviction to which the nursery was devoted [57]. Professor F. Gaudu defended this argument. According to him, the association had chosen a specific orientation, i. e. political and religious neutrality. It was entitled to impose on its employees this ethos:

"the restriction on personal rights is less strong than for organizations that promote a strict belief. The restriction is nevertheless more pronounced than the one which could be admitted in an ordinary enterprise. Baby Loup is an entreprise de conviction laïque (an 'enterprise of secular belief')"[58].

It is an ideological choice to refer to secularism, a *laïc ethos*.

---

[55] ECHR, 23 September 2010, Schüth v. Allemagne, req. n° 1620/03, § 69. See, *J.-P Marguenaud* et *J. Mouly*, "Les droits de l'homme salarié de l'entreprise identitaire", Dalloz, 2011, p. 1637.

[56] ECHR, 23 September 2010, Schüth v. Allemagne, req. n° 1620/03, § 71.

[57] CA Paris, 27 November 2013, n°13/02981.

[58] *F. Gaudu*, L'entreprise de tendance laïque, Droit social, 2011, p. 1186.

The plenary chamber of the Court of Cassation rejected this characterization, on the ground that the purpose of the nursery was not to promote or defend religious, political or philosophical beliefs but to develop activities directed at young children from disadvantaged backgrounds. This argument is questionable since the concept of "*entreprise de tendance*" may be viewed as a "flexible concept" applicable to a great variety of situations[59]. EU law does not restrict the aim of these enterprises to the promotion of a religion or a specific belief. The European Court of Human Rights has admitted that

> "the supporters of secularism are able to lay claim to views attaining the 'level of cogency, seriousness, cohesion and importance' required for them to be considered 'convictions' within the meaning of Articles 9 of the Convention and 2 of Protocol No. 1. More precisely, their views must be regarded as 'philosophical convictions', within the meaning of the second sentence of Article 2 of Protocol No. 1"[60].

Following this line of reasoning, secularism could be protected in terms of a political conviction[61].

However, *laïcité* should not be limited to a conviction; it would impoverish its signification. Some authors argued that *laïcité* is not a conviction as this concept would imply the acceptance of the expression of all convictions: "a crèche claiming to be secular or neutral does not defend a belief: it accepts them all"[62]. It could not be limited to be a belief among others, a kind of faith that people can adopt or not; "whether we like it or not, we live in France in a system of *laïcité*"[63]. By scrutinizing the purpose of the nursery without paying attention to its commitment to religious neutrality, the Court of Cassation clearly reveals a reluctance to validate the concept of *entreprise de conviction laïque*[64]. As has been explained,

> "the recognition of an entreprise de tendance ou de conviction laïque would necessarily bring about a marked decline in religion within companies, as all denominational businesses could potentially arm themselves with a neutrality clause in their internal regulations (whether it be in order to remain neutral in the eyes of their clientele or to ease relations within the company, for example)"[65].

---

[59] *F. Gaudu*, L'entreprise de tendance laïque, Droit social, 2011, p. 1186.

[60] ECHR, Lautsi et autres v. Italie, 18 March 2011, n° 30814/06, § 53.

[61] See the "rapport du conseiller *J.-G Huglo*" in the Baby Loup case.

[62] See *E. Dockès*, interview by *N. Hervieu*, "Entretiens croisé des Professeurs Gwénaële Calvès et Emmanuel Dockès sur le retentissant arrêt Baby Loup", La revue des droits de l'Homme, 2014, § 37, p. 7.

[63] *A. Supiot*, "La religion au travail", Mélanges en l'honneur du Professeur J. Hauser, Dalloz, 2012, p. 1040.

[64] *G. Calvès*, interview by *N. Hervieu*, "Entretiens croisé des Professeurs Gwénaële Calvès et Emmanuel Dockès sur le retentissant arrêt Baby Loup", La revue des droits de l'Homme, 2014, § 35.

[65] *M. Peyronnet* et *C. Radé*, "Employment law: The ban on the wearing of the Islamic veil in crèches", Montesquieu Law Review, n°1, January, 2015, p. 5.

c) Private nursery

Given the questions left unanswered by the Court of Cassation in the *Baby Loup* case, a specific legal framework is under discussion in Parliament with regard to the legal situation of the private *crèches*. The project aims to extend the application of the religious neutrality principle to all nurseries and facilities caring for young children[66]. However, it only plans for the neutrality duty to be applicable in private facilities operating a public service mission; this kind of legal disposition is not relevant since under the existing legal framework the neutrality duty is already enforced in such organizations. The project also takes into consideration that a private crèche can restrict one's religious freedom if it is justified and proportionate to the pursued objective. However, such a consideration adds nothing to the current legal framework.

d) Private enterprise

Unlike public services, private enterprises that do not operate a public service mission are not entitled to require their employees to comply with a general religious neutrality duty. As religious freedom is protected, employers have to respect the religious beliefs of their employees. However, under the current French legal framework, religion in the workplace is tolerated rather than supported. To some extent, occupational requirements apply in accordance with the respective labour contract provisions.

With regard to religious claims of staff related to dress codes, it should be acknowledged that many questions have been left unanswered by the *Baby Loup* case. Issues have arisen involving the question as to whether a private employer may prohibit his staff from wearing religious symbols in the workplace. In a recent case, an employee was dismissed because of a client complaining about the veil she was wearing[67]. The problem is different from the one in the *Baby Loup* case in that the staff were in contact with a different clientele. The solution in the *Baby Loup* case was dictated by the fact that the employee was working in a nursery, in contact with children, fulfilling the sensitive duties of a care worker. In the new case, the employee was working as a computer engineer in a consulting and engineering company. Moreover, being a private company, no internal regulation contained any general rule addressing religious neutrality. The employee was sent by her employer to deal with clients. One of them, a company, complained that the veil she was wearing "embarrassed" the company's employees. Her employer asked her not to wear her veil when she was in contact with clients. As she refused, she was dismissed. Complaining about direct discrimination on grounds

---

[66] Proposition de loi visant à étendre l'obligation de neutralité aux structures privées en charge de la petite enfance et à assurer le respect du principe de laïcité, 25 October 2011.

[67] Soc. 9 April 2015, n°13–19855, Dalloz, 2015, p. 1132, note *J. Mouly.*

of religion, the plaintiff stresses that no occupational requirements could justify such discrimination based on religious beliefs. Regarding this argument, the question is whether the demands of a client can be characterized as determining occupational requirements related to a commercial context. The Court of Cassation decided to refer to the Court of Justice to have this question resolved[68].

Two different ways of reasoning may be considered. Under Article L. 1121–1, a restriction should be justified and proportionate. Under Article L. 1132–1, religious discrimination is forbidden. The question is whether freedom and discrimination could be overlapping issues? As has been pointed out, an infringement of freedom is not necessarily discrimination but discrimination is an infringement of freedom[69]. Considering Article L. 1121–1 and Article L. 1132–1, the justification of an infringement of freedom is different than that of discrimination. It seems difficult to assert that the dismissal of an employee based on the wearing of an Islamic veil is not connected to her religious beliefs. This quite obviously constitutes a discrimination under Article L. 1132–1. This was the reasoning of the Social Chamber in the *Baby Loup* case[70].

How can such a discrimination be justified? Pursuant to European law, Article L. 1133–1 provides that inequality of treatment may be justified by "an essential and direct occupational requirement provided that the objective is legitimate and the requirement is proportionate". This notion of "essential and direct occupational requirement" comes from a transposition of Article 4§ 1 of the Employment Equality Directive 2000/78[71]. The substance of this requirement is not clear and not familiar to French Labour law. The justification may be conceived as narrower than the restriction justified and proportionate to freedom under Article L. 1121–1. In the reference for a preliminary question, the Court of Cassation mentions the *Feryn* case, in which an employer asserted that "customers would be unfavourably disposed towards employees of a certain ethnic

[68] "Must Article 4(1) of Council Directive 78/2000/EC of 27 November 2000 establishing a general framework for equal treatment in employment and occupation be interpreted as meaning that the wish of a customer of an information technology consulting company no longer to have the information technology services of that company provided by an employee, a design engineer, wearing an Islamic headscarf, is a genuine and determining occupational requirement, by reason of the nature of the particular occupational activities concerned or of the context in which they are carried out?"; Case C-188/15, Asma Bougnaoui, Association de défense des droits de l'homme (ADDH) v Micropole Univers SA, lodged on 24 April 2015.

[69] See *J. Mouly*, "Le voile dans l'entreprise: nouveaux rebondissements sous l'angle de la discrimination", Recueil Dalloz, 2015, p. 1132.

[70] Soc. 19 March 2013, n°11–28845.

[71] "Member States may provide that a difference of treatment which is based on a characteristic related to any of the grounds referred to in Article 1 shall not constitute discrimination where, by reason of the nature of the particular occupational activities concerned or of the context in which they are carried out, such a characteristic constitutes a genuine and determining occupational requirement, provided that the objective is legitimate and the requirement is proportionate". Article 4§ 1 of Directive 2000/78/EC of 27 November 2000 establishing a general framework for equal treatment in employment and occupation.

origin", in order to justify the fact that he had declared publicly that his company would not recruit employees of a certain ethnic or racial origin. The French judges quoted the conclusion of Advocate-General Maduro. According to him,

> "that is wholly irrelevant to the question whether the Directive applies. Even if that contention were true, it would only illustrate that 'markets will not cure discrimination' and that regulatory intervention is essential. The question of proportionality will remain pivotal".

A different line of reasoning may be considered. As one author explained, this kind of dismissal could be justified by the serious disturbance within the enterprise that such behaviour created. French labour law, for instance, prohibits dismissals grounded on sickness but admits the dismissal of a sick worker as its extended absence creates serious problems for the company. The justification is based on the objective situation faced by the employer and not on an uncertain occupational requirement justifying discrimination. By referring to problems, it is less about justifying the discrimination *a posteriori* than excluding it *a priori*[72]. It should be acknowledged, however, that the definition of an "objective disturbance" is not clearly defined. Given the fluctuant nature of case law, this could lead to a widening of the restriction admitted without meeting a proportionality criterion.

2. Religious behaviour of the employee

A different issue is the question whether individuals may demand accommodations based on their religious beliefs. Some situations are recurrent and different kinds of behaviour have been identified[73]. More broadly, the concern is that the growth of individualism may lead to an "implosion of collective interests"[74] or to the implosion of the collective *status* granted by labour law.

a) Time off for religious observance

Some employees may have to work during a religious holiday. As the labour contract applies, the employer could reject a request for authorization of leave in view of a religious holiday. For instance, an employee can legitimately be dismissed for a non-authorized absence during the day of the *Aïd*; in one case,

---

[72] *J. Mouly*, "Le voile dans l'entreprise: nouveaux rebondissements sous l'angle de la discrimination", Recueil Dalloz, 2015, p. 1132.

[73] See Association française de Droit du travail, "Le fait religieux en entreprise", Synthèse des travaux du groupe AFDT, 22 January 2016. http://www.afdt-asso.fr/wp-content/uploads/2016/01/AFDT-Le-fait-religieux-au-travail-groupe-AFDT.pdf.

[74] *Ph. Auvergnon*, "L'expression des convictions religieuses sur le lieu de travail", in Droit et religion en Europe, Etudes en l'honneur de Francis Messner, Strasbourg, Presses universitaires de Strasbourg, 2014, p. 61.

this absence was prejudicial since the employer was not able to cope with an important order that day[75]. It should be acknowledged that the employee, by signing a contract, accepts the collective discipline of the enterprise. However, the employee can present to the employer a request for authorization of leave in view of a religious holiday and the employer should deal with this request in good faith,

> "this means to agree with the request if this is feasible with regards to the requirements of the enterprise. In the opposite case, the religious reason does not grant the employee the right to impose upon the employer a modification of the conditions of employment"[76].

A refusal by an employer may amount to potential indirect discrimination, as it may put religious individuals at a disadvantage compared to others (but this hypothesis is debatable). The justification has to be in relation to the disturbance that the absence could create within the enterprise.

b) Conscientious objection to work tasks

Religious objection to certain work tasks raises problems similar to the time-off request for religious observance. Under the European Convention,

> "Freedom to manifest one's religion or beliefs shall be subject only to such limitations as are prescribed by law and are necessary in a democratic society in the interests of public safety, for the protection of public order, health or morals, or for the protection of the rights and freedoms of others"[77].

If an employee refuses to perform or not to perform a task for religious motives, the employer, for safety and security reasons, can punish this behaviour. Under French labour law, employers have to abide by a "safety obligation of result". An employer can require his employees to remove any religious symbols they wear for reasons related to safety and security. Moreover, an employee is not entitled to be excused from obligations for religious motives, especially when his safety is at stake. Given the imperative nature of the legal provisions governing the medical examination in a work context, the Court of Cassation has confirmed the dismissal of an employee who refused to go to a medical examination for religious reasons[78].

Another issue is the question whether an employer should deal with the requirement of an employee to be excused from tasks such as handling meat products. Through the lens of the employment contract, religious beliefs are not part of it and "the employer does not commit any mistake in asking the worker

---

[75] Cass. Soc., 24 May1981.

[76] *F. Gaudu*, "Labor law and religion", Comparative Labor Law and Policy Journal, 2009, vol. 30, p. 524.

[77] Article 9 of the European Convention on Human Rights.

[78] Cass. soc., 29 May 1986, n° 83–45.409.

to implement the task he was hired to execute as long as this task is not contradictory with a rule regarding a matter of public policy"[79]. This line of reasoning implies that the employer should not take into account religious beliefs of his employee as this was not part of the employment contract.

However, the requirement to undertake the task may put the religious individual at a disadvantage in comparison with others. Although there is a duty to perform the labour contract in good faith, there is no general duty to accommodate religion at work in France. In private enterprises, except for occupational health and safety reasons, employers could hardly impose on staff not to express religious beliefs. Currently, it is unlikely for employees to not be allowed to claim religious freedom in the workplace. Employers should act in good faith: this implies that the "employer should consider sincerely the request, with the intention to grant it if there is no substantial inconvenience, with regard to the legitimate business interest. Then, good faith implies that the request is treated seriously, without negligence"[80]. Staff could expect that religious beliefs would be accommodated at work so long as the request is compatible with the operational requirements of the business. Employees could not impose upon their employer a modification of the conditions of employment, given that "these beliefs are not part of the employment contract framework"[81]. In such situations, it is almost impossible to predict the outcomes, as it would require a careful analysis of different factors and context.

Questions have arisen as to the potential indirect discrimination of employees on grounds of religious beliefs. The failure to make reasonable accommodations may create a specific disadvantage for employees with religious beliefs. Indirect religious discrimination is rooted in

> "an apparently neutral provision, criterion or practice [that] would put persons having a particular religion or belief, a particular disability, a particular age, or a particular sexual orientation at a particular disadvantage compared with other persons"[82].

The solution would be problematic if an employer could reject a request of religious accommodation only if it is justified on grounds of non-discriminatory objective criteria. The opposite end of this solution would be to require the employee to prove that a refusal to accommodate religion at work is discriminatory. It would then be up to him to present the facts leading to the assumed discrimination.

[79] Cass. Soc., 24 March 1998, n° 95–44738.

[80] *F. Gaudu*, "La religion dans l'entreprise", Droit social, 2010, p. 69.

[81] Cass. Soc., 24 March 1998, n° 95–44738.

[82] Art. 2§ 2, Directive 2000/78/EC of 27 November 2000 establishing a general framework for equal treatment in employment and occupation.

c) Proselytising

Proselytising is defined, in the dictionary, as "being zealous in spreading the faith". Individuals may be involved in the promotion of religion in the workplace through, for instance, the distribution of literature and prayers. Proselytism may be perceived by other individuals as a breach of the neutrality of the workplace. However, such behaviours are not strictly prohibited[83]. They could be considered as the manifestation of religious beliefs and be protected under Article 9 ECHR recognizing that freedom of religion includes the right to manifest religion "and to change [one's] religion or belief and freedom either alone or in community with others". According to the European Court, this also includes "the right to try to convince one's neighbour, for example through "teaching", failing which, moreover, "freedom to change [one's] religion or belief", enshrined in Article 9 (art. 9), would be likely to remain a dead letter"[84]. The solution put forward by the former French equality and anti-discrimination authority (HALDE)[85] was not in accordance with this ruling. It held that "the first limit to an employee's religious beliefs is the ban on proselyting in the workplace"[86].

If proselytising is protected under the right to manifest religion, it is also a behaviour, which sometimes goes beyond religious expression. The right of individuals to try to persuade others of the validity of their beliefs does not entitle them to harass other employees. "Improper proselytism" may take the form of "improper pressures on people"[87]. By creating an intimidating environment for the staff, such a behaviour could be qualified as moral harassment, pursuant to Article L. 1152–1 of the French Labour Code providing that: "No employee shall suffer repeated actions which have for object or for effect a degradation of his working conditions likely to violate his rights and his dignity, to alter his physical or mental health or to compromise his professional future".

The focus is on the consequences of the behaviour of the individual, not on the expression of the religion of the latter. In such circumstances, religious freedom is not at stake. Judges take into account the behaviour of the individual with regard to the obligation to perform the employment contract in good faith. For example, a Court of Appeal found that the dismissal of an employee with proselytist behaviour was justified by a real and serious reason given the objective facts showing the "exasperation of colleagues", and "service perturbations" threatening the running of the business[88]. Judges consider the contractual

[83] *Ph. Auvergnon*, "L'expression des convictions religieuses sur le lieu de travail", in Droit et religion en Europe, Etudes en l'honneur de Francis Messner, Strasbourg, Presses universitaires de Strasbourg, 2014, p. 31.

[84] ECHR, Kokkinakis v. Greece, 25 May 1993, n°14307/88, § 31.

[85] Now Le Défenseur des droits.

[86] HALDE, 6 April 2009, Délibération 2009–117.

[87] ECHR, Kokkinakis v. Greece, 25 May 1993, n°14307/88, § 48.

[88] CA Basse-Terre, 6 November 2006, n°06/00095.

fault of the employee to validate the measure adopted by the employer in such a situation. The reasoning was, for example, quite the same in a situation where a termination of contract of a self-employed worker was grounded on proselytist behaviour on the part of the latter. Belonging to the scientologist movement, the worker had tried to persuade people he was in charge of the training to become part of the Church. Judges held that the termination of the contract was lawful pursuant to Article 1135 of the Civil Code providing that the work agreement was to be performed in good faith[89].

---

[89] CA Versailles, 21 January 1998, n°95/00009736.

The Significance of Religion for Swedish Labour and Social Legislation

Reinhold Fahlbeck

I. Overture

What is the significance of religion for Swedish labour and social legislation?

Bluntly speaking, the answer is that religion is of negligible overall significance for labour and social legislation in Sweden. The cynic might even feel tempted to say that there is no justification for attributing any significance at all to religion in these two fields of the law. The realist would not really disagree.

In the decades after World War II, religion gradually disappeared from the public room. Ironically, the enactment in 1951 of the Freedom of Religion Act can be seen as the harbinger of that disappearance. By and large, religious organizations took on a defensive attitude or even went into quasi-oblivion. Public education was purged of its previously strong Christian character with mandatory confessional teaching and likewise mandatory attendance at confessional morning prayers. The judicial system was gradually cleared of religious elements, e.g. bibles in court rooms and oaths of a religious character. By and large, religious manifestations became limited to the privacy of churches and other places of worship. A leading Swedish daily triumphantly proclaimed: "God is dead".[1] The newspaper and large segments of Swedish society agreed that God as a being – if such a being had ever existed or could even be envisaged – was indeed dead. Religion exited from the public room.

The decades after World War II saw the coming into existence of the Swedish social welfare system and its modern employment law system. This happened in a social and existential environment where religion by and large had become non-existent or at least politically and socially irrelevant.

The last two decades have seen the resurrection of God, as it were. Not only that but also a return of religion to the public room. Religion is again at the focus of attention. Immigration of Muslims predominantly accounts for that. Overt Muslim religious practices have raised awareness not just of Islam but also of the Christian foundation of our society. Prevailing Western notions and practices concerning freedom of religion and thought as well as freedom of speech have come under attack by Muslims. Freedom of conscience based on religious or secular ideas has become one of the hottest topics in recent years, primarily in connection with medical practice; cf. Section 5 below.

Still, despite the return of religion as a factor of importance in social life, religion continues to be a factor without any significance in the legislative process. Its role is rather to be eliminated wherever it still has a role!

The pivotal example in this particular respect is the 2010 School Act with its radical removal of anything that smacks of religious confession from the curriculum in public schools. However, one significant exemption to this tendency of removal of religion from statutory law is the 2008 Discrimination Act.[2] Religion is one of the protected grounds of the act. The Discrimination Ombudsman has proved very zealous indeed in bringing offenders (actual or purported) to justice.

II. Sources of the Law on Religion

Religious law in Sweden has two basic sources: external and internal. External sources are of international origin, primarily the Convention for the Protection of Human Rights and Fundamental Freedoms (henceforward the *European Convention* or *ECHR*), adopted in 1950 by the Council of Europe. Internal

[1] The liberal newspaper *Dagens Nyheter* (Today's News). The proclamation did not accord with Nietzsche's identical statement since it lacked all metaphysical content, being meant as a statement of a simple, literal fact.

[2] The official Swedish designation of the 2008 Act is in fact the "Discrimination Act". The agency in charge of implementing the legislation is called the "Discrimination Ombudsman". Both designations can easily lend themselves to confusion and misunderstanding. What is meant is the opposite, i. e. anti-discrimination. The act aims at preventing discrimination and to remedy acts of discrimination.

sources are domestic – national – law, i. e. constitutional and sub-constitutional, ordinances by competent administrative agencies (e. g. the Work Environment Agency), court-made case law and, finally, decisions by administrative agencies (e. g. the Discrimination Ombudsman).

The European Convention is binding upon Sweden in three ways, (1) as a ratified international convention under public international law, (2) as part of the law of the European Union and (3) as a Swedish statute, transposed and incorporated into Swedish law in 1994. The Convention has primacy over domestic national Swedish law, including constitutional law.[3] The European Union (EU) also has legal rules on religion. However, the ECHR is part of EU law. Furthermore, a process is under way for the EU to become a member of the Council of Europe and consequently a formal signatory to the ECHR. If and when that happens, rulings by the European Court of Human Rights (henceforward the *European Court*) will be legally binding upon the EU.

The Swedish 1951 Freedom of Religion Act was repealed in 1998, effective from 2000, with no substantive replacement. The vacuum thus created was remedied by the simultaneous adoption of the 1998 Communities of Faith Act. The act points at the freedom of religion regulation in the core Swedish constitutional act (the 1974 Instrument of Government) and the ECHR. Those are, today, the two legal instruments for freedom of religion in Sweden.

Included in its chapter on fundamental rights and freedoms, the 1974 Instrument of Government contains articles on the freedom of religion, positive and negative.[4] The articles are limited to the relationship between the public realm and members of society. Though they can be invoked in legal proceedings, they

---

[3] The 1974 Instrument of Government (the core Swedish constitutional law):
Chapter 2, Article 19: "No act of law or other provision may be adopted which contravenes Sweden's undertakings under the European Convention for the Protection of Human Rights and Fundamental Freedoms".
Chapter 12, Article 10: "If a public body finds that a provision conflicts with a rule of fundamental law or other superior statute, or finds that a procedure laid down in law has been disregarded in any important respect when the provision was made, the provision shall not be applied".

[4] The 1974 Instrument of Government:
Chapter 2, Article 2: "No one shall in his or her relations with the public institutions be coerced to divulge an opinion in a political, religious, cultural or other such connection. Nor may anyone in his or her relations with the public institutions be coerced to participate in a meeting for the shaping of opinion or a demonstration or other manifestation of opinion, or to belong to a political association, religious community or other association for opinion referred to in sentence one".
Chapter 2, Article 1: "Everyone shall be guaranteed the following rights and freedoms in his or her relations with the public institutions: [...]
6. Freedom of worship: that is, the freedom to practise one's religion alone or in the company of others".

are of little impact in actual life. They are only rarely referred to in legal affairs and no body of case law exists on it.[5]

Of importance in national law is any legislation aimed to combat discrimination. The focal statute is the 2008 Discrimination Act. One of the grounds for discrimination is "religion". However, the Act and its *travaux préparatoires* do not elaborate on the meaning of the word "religion". They limit themselves to stating that the word "religion" shall be used in accordance with its customary meaning without elaborating on what that meaning is!

The Discrimination Ombudsman is in charge of the implementation of the Discrimination Act. A very substantial body of administrative case rulings exists, including religious discrimination. However, so far no decision by the Discrimination Ombudsman regarding purported religious discrimination has been examined by a court of final instance. Employers found guilty of discrimination on grounds of religion have preferred to pay the penalty imposed by the Discrimination Ombudsman, thus getting rid of the matter once and for all. As a consequence, it is not clear whether the legal standards and practices adopted by the Discrimination Ombudsman in cases involving religion would pass scrutiny by the courts of final instance. The Discrimination Ombudsman applies a definition of and standards for "religion" that seemingly go beyond what is protected as "religion" and "religious discrimination" under the European Convention.[6]

Thus, the European Convention, the ECHR, is *the* legal basis in Sweden for freedom of religion and religious practices. The ECHR is a living legal instrument. A body of case law exists and it grows as the European Court tries new cases.

Religious communities create internal rules and regulations of a legal character for their activities. Examples are Catholic Canon law and Islamic Sharia law. Such rules and regulations fall outside the scope of this article. They are distinct from Swedish national law. The reason is that they have no legal standing or authority *per se* under Swedish national law. They may be invoked in legal proceedings but they have no specific legal authority.

---

[5] One exception is the much publicized ruling by the Swedish Supreme Court in 2005 in a case dealing with a sermon by a pastor. He spoke very negatively of homosexual people and of homosexual practices. Prosecuted for hate speech under the Swedish Criminal Act he was acquitted by the Trial Court but found guilty by the Court of Appeal. The Supreme Court also found him guilty under that statute. The Court found no basis for acquittal in Swedish constitutional law, i.e. the 1974 Instrument of Government as quoted in the previous footnote. Ultimately, the Court turned to the ECHR for guidance. It studied Articles 9 (freedom of religion) and 10 (freedom of speech). It came to the conclusion that a verdict of guilt would probably constitute a non-acceptable infringement of the pastor's rights under the ECHR, so he was acquitted.

[6] In the one and so far only court case concerning discrimination on religious grounds a district court of first instance deliberately set aside the ECHR and fashioned a definition of its own of "religion"; Hässleholm trial court, case T 1370–13, judgement of 4 April 2015. The ruling looks like an archetypical example of "armchair law"!

This is also the case with the rules and regulations of the Church of Sweden. Until 2000 a state church, it is now separated from and independent of the State.[7] It no longer enjoys a special position under constitutional law. However, as distinct from other religious communities, it is dealt with in a statute separate from the 1998 Communities of Faith Act for all other religious communities. To a very limited extent, that separate statute equals the Church of Sweden with public law bodies. Apart from that, its rules and regulations are of private law character. Membership is now radically voluntary but a majority of Swedes still belong to it. Membership entitles members to certain coveted church services, e. g. marriage ceremonies and baptism.

III. The Judiciary and Religion

When the then newly enacted Common Law of the Realm of 1734 went into effect in 1736 it was decided that it should be prefaced with a set of moral rules. To some extent, the rules form the religio-philosophical basis of the 1734 Statute Book. Generally referred to as the *Rules for Judges* (*Domarregler*), they are commonly ascribed to Olaus Petri, one of the persons that brought Protestant Christianity to Sweden in the first part of the 16th century.[8] They are thought to have been written – or compiled – in their present form around 1540 but go back to medieval times. To a great extent, they are based on canon law. Some 43 maxims spell out the norms of proper judicial behaviour. The initial statement starts with the following:[9] "A judge shall first consider that he holds God's command and that his office belongs to God and not him and for that reason the judgement that he pronounces is God's ... and is for sure God's judgement and not that of men".

These rules are still printed in the annual, semi-official, publication of core Swedish statutes.[10] Though reference to them by courts is very rare today and has been so for decades, the rules are nevertheless known by all legally trained people in Sweden. They enjoy a prestige that borders reverence.

What is of importance in the present context is that these rules point at the close historical relationship between religion, the law and the judiciary. Today that relationship has been severed virtually in its totality, but that is of fairly recent date.

---

[7] Beginning in the 1520s, the Protestant Reformation took hold in Sweden. The country became firmly rooted in Lutheran Protestantism. The principle that all subjects should follow the religion of the Head of State (*cujus regio ejus religio*) was enforced with the utmost severity.

[8] See, e. g., *Gerhard Schmidt*, Die Richterregeln des Olavus Petri (Vandenhoeck & Ruprecht, Göttingen, 1966).

[9] My translation. For a German version see op. cit. previous note.

[10] Sveriges Rikes Lag (The Law of the Realm of Sweden), published since the 1860s by Norstedts Publishing House (now Norstedts Juridik, part of Kluwer). The publication is traditionally edited by a judge of the Swedish Supreme Court (serving or retired).

The Christian cross has not been part of the fittings of Swedish court rooms, at least not in modern times.[11] Prayers or other acts of faith have not been part of court procedures in modern times either, but bibles were present in court rooms until quite recently.

Religious oaths were very much indeed part of court room procedures until quite recently. Two examples: Judges took an oath upon being sworn in as judges. That oath resonated of the *Rules for Judges* – and still does today. Witnesses also had to take an oath. In both instances this was done with one hand on the Bible and with express reference to "Almighty God and His Holy Word".[12] Both oaths were secularised as recently as in 1975. Oaths are "taken", not "sworn". [13]

Another remnant of previous customs was "the court divine service", also known as "the court sermon". The 1686 Church Act prescribed that each year of the district court procedures was to begin with a divine service. The prescription was in force until 1990. A divine service still takes place in various courts on a voluntary basis. The Svea Court of Appeal, the oldest (1614) and most prestigious of the courts of appeal, discontinued the custom as recently as in 2008.

IV. Working Time

1. The ecclesiastical year and the secular year

As in all "Christian countries" the secular year has been heavily influenced by the ecclesiastical (or liturgical) year, even mirroring it. First and foremost, the Chris-

[11] Cf., e.g., the ruling by the German Constitutional Court (*Bundesverfassungsgericht*), BVerfGE 35, 1 BvR 308/69, 17 July 1973, in a case dealing with complaints by Jewish persons that the presence of a Christian cross in the court room violated their rights under Article 4 (freedom of religion) of the German Federal Constitution since it forced them to conduct their case "under the Cross" ("Verhandlungen unter dem Kreuz", on p. 376). The Court agreed. See also e.g. BVerfGE 93, 1 BvR 1087/91, 16 May 1995 (C II.2 a) on p. 18, ("einen Rechtsstreit unter dem Kreuz zu führen"). No similar case is recorded in Sweden.

[12] An illustration: During my time as clerk of a district court ("Referendar") in the mid-1960s I often administered the swearing of oaths. It was done in the most formal and solemn way imaginable. We – my fellow recording clerk and I – were formally dressed, stood at attention in front of the witness, asked the witness to reciprocate, looked the witness straight in the eyes and ordered the witness to reciprocate, ordered the witness to lay his/her right hand on the Bible and take the oath as pronounced by me. Not a few witnesses found it difficult to do so in a clear and strong voice!

[13] The admonition by Christ in the Sermon on the Mount (Matthew 5, verses 33–37), not to "swear" any oaths was discussed when the religious reference was abolished in 1975. However, Swedish case law has no equivalent to the 1972 decision by the German Constitutional Court on refusal to "swear" oaths; Bundesverfassungsgericht, 11 April 1972, 2 BvR, 75/71 (Eidesverweigerung aus Glaubensgründen). The 1734 Common Law of the Realm obliged judges to "swear" the oath and to "promise and swear" to follow the commandment of the oath but today the obligation is secularised and only obliges to "promise and assure".

tian seven-day weekly calendar is also the secular calendar. Second, the Christian Sunday celebration-*cum*-rest is reflected in Sunday as the traditional secular rest day. Third, Christian religious feasts have traditionally been celebrated as secular holidays as well, often as days off from work. In previous centuries the number of holy days was quite substantial. A gradual reduction has been in progress since at least the Church Ordinance of 1571 and in particular the holiday reform of 1772. The latest holiday to be thus de-sanctified was the Whitmonday, i.e. Monday following Whitsunday (2005). Other holidays have been moved to the nearest Saturday, e.g. All Saints Day (1953).

As of 2015, only a few Christian feast days fall on weekdays (Christmas Day, if it falls on a weekday, Good Friday, Easter Monday and Ascension Day). They are observed as secular holidays in the sense that they are days off from work. In addition, work on the days before these religious feast days often ends at noon or in the early afternoon.

Unless compensatory time off from work is introduced, the de-sanctification of holidays results in an increase in the total yearly working time. This was avoided in 2005 when Whit-Monday ceased to be a work-free Christian feast day. It was replaced by June 6, the National Day, which became a work-free holiday.

The Christian Lent is not reflected in statutory rules or in collective agreement regulations. One reason probably is that strict fasting is no longer practiced by Christians at large.

2. *Working time legislation*

The 1977 Annual Holidays Act is strictly religion-neutral. Religion is not a factor in any sense in the structure of the act or its administration.

The 1982 Working Time Act is a piece of framework legislation. The Act represents something of a hybrid between public and private law since it can be replaced wholly or in part by collective agreements. This has also happened to a great extent. Of interest in the present context is whether and to what extent religion has influenced the legislation (and collective agreement regulations).

The ecclesiastical year to a great extent rules the Working Time Act, though religion *per se* has no impact whatsoever on present-day working time legislation. The seven-day week is the unit for computing standard (normal) working time. Overtime work computation depends to some extent on the seven-day week as well (though the month – non-ecclesiastical unit – is of greater importance).

In accordance with EU law – but antedating it by decades – employees are entitled to a weekly rest period. Under the 1982 statute (and its predecessors) that rest period must be at least 36 hours. As far as possible, this weekly rest shall be scheduled for weekends. Derogation by means of a collective agreement is possible. However, weekly rest falls on weekends for the overwhelming majority of employees.

Of course, the fact that the weekend and the Christian Sunday coincide is not coincidental. However, that concurrence has by and large lost its religious character. Social life at large today explains why the weekend is still the weekly rest period for most employees. This lost connection between religion and the weekend rest is vividly illustrated by the legislative history of the 1982 Working Time Act. In its bill to Parliament (1981/82:154) proposing a new working time legislation, the government discusses working time issues at great length. However, not even one single time are words like "religion", "church service, "church attendance" or "prayer" found. The bill is clinically free of any religious allusions.[14] On the other hand, the word "veckovila" ("weekly rest") figures no less than 99 times.[15] A person not privy to knowledge of Sunday as the Christian day of worship can find no explanation why the weekend has been chosen as the period for the weekly rest!

Unless limited by rules in collective agreements, employers are at liberty to order work on Sundays. What would happen if an employee refuses to perform work on a Sunday (or any other day considered holy by the employee)? To the best of my knowledge, no Swedish court has ever been faced with this situation. By all likelihood the refusal would constitute just cause for dismissal under the 1982 Employment Protection Act, unless legally mitigating factors would dictate otherwise. The reason is that the employee would be held to be in breach of his/her contractual obligations. Furthermore, Article 9 of the ECHR has been held not to protect such refusals and a Swedish court – if it were aware of the holdings in question – would no doubt consider domestic Swedish law corroborated by those holdings.[16]

[14] The same is true for all subsequent bills with changes and amendments to the statute. That includes the implementation of Working Time Directive 2003/88/EC; see 3 below.

[15] It is tempting in this connection to refer to case C-84/94 United Kingdom v. Council of the European Union, concerning Council Directive 93/104/EC (ECR I-5755, 1996). The case dealt with aspects of the organization of working time, e.g. the weekly rest. The directive required that the rest period had to, in principle, include Sunday. That requirement was questioned by the UK. The Court concurred, stating that "the Council has failed to explain why Sunday, as a weekly rest day, is more closely connected with the health and safety of workers than any other day of the week" (para. 37). Similarly, the Swedish government failed to explain why it was necessary, in principle, that the weekly rest under the 1982 Working Time Act be scheduled to fall on weekends, i.e. primarily on Sundays. However, as the Government Bill to Parliament indirectly makes clear, it can be stated for certain that in 1982 such scheduling was not considered necessary for reasons relating to religion!

[16] See in this respect two cases dealt with by the (former) European Commission of Human Rights under Article 9 of the ECHR. The first case is Application No. 24949/94, (unpublished) decision of 3 December 1996, Konttinen v. Finland concerning a member of the Seventh-Day Adventist Church. Citing religious concerns, Mr Konttinen refused to work after sunset on Friday. His dismissal was considered to be caused not "because of his religious convictions but for having refused to respect his working hours". The second case is Application No. 29107/95, decision of 9 April 1997, D&R 104 (1997), Louise Stedman v. the United Kingdom. Ms Stedman was ordered to work on Sundays. She declared that she was not willing to work on Sundays,

3. Leave of absence/time off

Some twenty statutes grant time off to employees, e.g. parental leave, friends and family care, family reasons and studies. No statute provides for time off for reasons related to religion.[17]

EC Working Time Directive 2003/88 specifically points at "workers officiating at religious ceremonies in churches and religions communities".[18] Swedish law has no equivalent provision. The 1982 Working Time Act is silent in this respect. So are the *travaux préparatoires.*[19]

The liturgical year of other religions has so far had no influence on Swedish labour law or social legislation. No statutory rules have been introduced to accommodate the faithful of other religions and no such rules are envisioned. Also, there is no generally accepted practice for dealing with requests by employees of such religions for leave from work in order to meet the requirements of their religion. Calls for the introduction of statutory (or case law) rules to that effect are unheard of. Collective agreements sometimes contain provisions but only rarely so. The ECHR imposes an obligation on employers to try to accommodate employee wishes. Under the ECHR, employers are obliged to observe the positive obligation to promote the exercise of freedom of religion.[20] However, it is definitely true that most Swedish employers are unaware of that obligation. By

which she – as a Christian – considered "should be devoted to non-commercial, family and religious activities". She was dismissed. However, the Commission declared that Ms Stedman "was dismissed for failing to agree to work certain hours rather than her religious belief as such".

[17] See generally *Fahlbeck, Reinhold*, Bed och arbeta. Om religionsfrihet i arbetsliv och skola (Liber förlag, 2011), subsection 6.3.4. See very succinctly also *Fahlbeck, Reinhold*, Ora et Labora – On Freedom of Religion at Work Places. A Stakeholder cum Balancing Factors Model, International Journal of Comparative Labour Law and Industrial Relations, volume 20, 2004, p. 57 et seq.

[18] Article 17(1) (c).

[19] See e.g. Government Bill 1995/96:162 and Government Bill 2003/04:180, both on the implementation of the EC Working Time Regulation. The Government Report SOU 1995:92 preparing for the 1995/96 Government Bill refers to Article 17 of the Directive. However, it does not mention the provision concerning religious ceremonies. This omission conveys the impression that that provision was deliberately ignored. Disregarding the need for time off of non-Christian religious officiating persons at days other than Sundays is remarkable, perhaps reprehensible.

[20] See in this respect ECHR Commission case X v. The United Kingdom, Application No. 8160/78, decision of 12 March 1981, D & R 22, "the Muslim teacher's case". It illustrates the situation under Article 9 ECHR. A Muslim teacher at a public school applied for time off to attend Friday prayer. Under its obligation to promote the exercise of freedom of religion of its employees, the school had actively tried to accommodate the teacher. The Commission found that the teacher's absence to attend prayers caused "serious difficulties" for the school to fulfil the statutory requirements of the education system. For this reason and because the teacher had accepted employment without reservation for his wish to attend Friday prayer, the Commission came to the conclusion the school had not failed to "give due consideration to his freedom of religion". The ruling and its underlying legal premises is virtually unknown in Sweden.

all likelihood, the Work Environment Agency, in charge of overseeing working time legislation, also lives in benign ignorance of any such obligation!

The Jewish community is partly accommodated since Saturdays are work-free at most places of work. Time off for the Muslim Friday prayer is de facto granted only at the discretion of employers. Still, collective complaints by Muslims concerning the absence of provisions for time off for Friday prayer are not heard of. The Muslim *Ramadan* is a factor of practical importance at many places of work. Strict fasting during all day-light hours may pose a work safety problem. *Ad hoc* solutions will have to be found. One possibility is to schedule the annual holiday to coincide with *Ramadan*.

4. Store opening hours

Under the 1966 Store Opening Hours Act (and its predecessors) commercial retail was allowed only within specified time limits. The act elapsed by the end of 1971 and was not replaced by new rules. This had the deliberate consequence of introducing full freedom for retailers. Thus, no particular days, no particular hours of the twenty-four-hour day and no particular period of the year were exempted. Critics talked of the substitution of "the law of the jungle" for "the rule of law". During the 1971 deliberations in Parliament references to religion as a factor weighing against complete freedom were virtually non-existent. The report of the parliamentary committee in charge of the matter did not discuss it at all, limiting itself to mentioning in passing hesitation by some political groupings.[21]

The radical deregulation by the 1971 act persists. Today no one seriously advocates statutory limitations. Collective agreements specify additional pay for working hours considered inconvenient, such as evening and night hours as well as work on weekends. Such payment makes these working hours attractive to many employees. For that reason there is no general employee opposition to Sunday work, not even work on days such as Christmas Day or Good Friday. Nor are there any qualms of ethical or religious character about work being performed on Sundays among the population at large, not even work on Sunday mornings when church services are customarily held.[22] No restrictions – voluntary or oth-

[21] Trade and Industry Committee (*Näringsutskottet*) report 1971:53.

[22] As is well known, the German Constitutional Court (*Bundesverfassungsgericht*) in a ruling of 1 December 2009 (1 BvR 2858/07), found regulations in the Federal State of Berlin (*Bundesstaat Berlin*) allowing stores to stay open for certain hours on all four Sundays in Advent in violation of the 1949 Federal Constitution. The 1949 Federal Constitution in this respect has taken over Article 139 of the 1919 Weimar Constitution. It states: "Der Sonntag und die staatlich anerkannten Feiertage bleiben als Tage der Arbeitsruhe und der seelischen Erhebung gesetzlich geschützt". Swedish working time regulation knows of nothing like "seelische Erhebung". The very notion of *spiritual edification* is utterly alien to present time public mentality and thinking in Sweden and has been so for several decades, probably for the entire post-World War II period.

erwise – exist on the sale of food, beverage or other merchandise that might be considered offensive on Sundays or religious holidays, such as Good Friday.[23]

In actual practice most stores are closed on Sundays. However, shopping malls tend to be open on weekends as are most stores selling food and beverage.

V. The Duty to Work. Work Tasks. Conscientious Objections

The main aspects of an employee's duty to work relate to *what*, *when*, *where* and *how* work is to be performed. Of interest in the present context are the issues of *when* and *what*. The *when* issue relates to working time. It has been discussed supra. The *what* issue relates to the work tasks that employees can be assigned and are obliged to perform. By and large this issue has no religious implications. Most work tasks have no moral implications.

However, certain work tasks may have moral and religious implications. The issue in this respect is to what extent moral or religious misgivings can serve as excuses to perform certain work tasks. This is an issue that has attracted little attention in Swedish labour law and social security regulation.[24] The traditional legal response has been that employees (and social security applicants) are obliged to perform all work which meets two criteria: it must fall within the employer's natural area of activity and within the employee's (applicant's) professional ability. This *litmus test* affords little or indeed no room for religious misgivings.

A well-established, unwritten, principle of general application is that employees are not obliged to perform work contrary to public policy, *contra bonos mores*. This principle would easily lend itself to the area of ethical or religious misgivings. So far, however, no instance where that has happened has been recorded.

As was mentioned in Section 1, the last decades have seen the return of religion to the public room. One consequence of this is a development resulting in religious misgivings being increasingly voiced. However, nothing substantial has been attained to clarify the legal consequences of such misgivings at places of work or within the social security system. No domestic statutory or case law exists.

Article 9 of the ECHR presents the overriding norm. That norm is directly applicable at places of work, even private ones. Under Article 9, paragraph 2, a balance must be struck between the competing interests at stake, primarily the employee's interest not to have to perform work that infringes upon his or her

[23] The one and only exception is the sale of alcoholic beverages in the State liquor monopoly stores. Opening hours are limited by statute, late Saturday afternoons and evenings as well as Sundays being precluded as a rule. However, that regulation is exclusively based on considerations concerning public health. Religion is of no import.

[24] See generally a discussion regarding Sweden in *Fahlbeck, Reinhold*, op. cit. note 17, subsection 6.3.5. See very succinctly also *Fahlbeck, Reinhold*, Ora et Labora article note 17, p. 58 et seq.

ethical or religious beliefs, the employer's interest to have all workplace work tasks performed and the interests of the persons affected by the work performance refusal of the employee, be they clients, customers, patients, students or other persons concerned.

No domestic regulation exists, statutory or otherwise. Case law is non-existent as well. Article 9 ECHR rules. Consequently, the legal situation in Sweden does not differ from any other member state of the Council of Europe. Case law is scarce under the ECHR.[25] It is non-existent under the Swedish application of the ECHR. A few cases have been decided without reference to the ECHR.[26] The decisions are of an *ad hoc* character. No principles have been established.

The notion and reality of "conscientious objection" was part of the social fabric during the Cold War as conscientious objection to military service occurred, albeit fairly rarely. With the end of the Cold War awareness of the notion subsided. Today the situation is completely different. The issue has attracted enormous attention in recent years. That attention has focused almost solely on medical work, virtually exclusively on abortion. Unlike most European countries Sweden today does not allow for medical personnel being excused from participating in work relating to abortion. The *travaux préparatoires* to the present 1974 Abortion Act specifically provide for conscientious objection and so do several subsequent parliamentary reports.[27] However, the statements to that effect seem to have been forgotten or are being deliberately overlooked. The 2010 Resolution (1763) by the Parliamentary Assembly of the Council of Europe on "[t]he right to conscientious objection in lawful medical care" is well known but derided and

[25] Case of Eweida and others v. the United Kingdom, Applications Nos. 48420/10 (Ms Eweida), 59842/10 (Ms Chaplin), 51671/10 (Ms Ladele) and 36516/10 (Mr McFarlane), judgement of 15 January 2013, provides the best illustration. Ms Ladele refused, for reasons of her Christian faith, to be designated as a registrar of civil partnerships and Mr McFarlane for the same reason refused to provide psycho-sexual counselling to same-sex couples. The European Court found the opposing interests of others to be outweighing their religious misgivings. Also, since the policy pursued by the employer was considered to have a legitimate aim and to be proportionate there was no indirect discrimination under Article 14 either. No corresponding court cases exist in Swedish case law The Ms Eweida and Ms Chaplin cases concern the wearing of a visible Christian cross; cf. Section VI below.

[26] E. g. Labour Court case 2005 No. 21, the eldercare case. A Jehovah Witness refused to perform certain work that was part of her regular work assignment. She was dismissed. She claimed that she had been indirectly discriminated against. The Court disagreed. It took the position that any person with the same work assignment, who, regardless of reason, was to refuse to perform the specific work in question, would be treated in the same way. Refusal to perform the work, not religion, was the reason for her dismissal, according to the court. Cf. rulings by the (former) European Commission based on the same rational quoted in note 16.

[27] See e. g. Government Bill to Parliament 1974:70 proposing what became the 1974 Abortion Act, on p. 76 et seq. See also the report on that Government Bill submitted by the Social Committee of Parliament 1974:21, on p. 40. For reiterations see e. g. reports by the same parliamentary committee 1983/84:3, on p. 16, 1984/85:11, on p. 17, 1986/87:5, on p. 11, or 1987/88:2, on p. 2. More recent reports by the committee ignore those previous statements and take the position that there is no excuse for conscientious objectors.

belittled as non-binding.[28] The call in Parliamentary Resolution 1928 (2013) to "ensure the right to well-defined conscientious objection in relation to morally sensitive matters, such as [...] services related to health care" is ignored.[29] A much publicised case concerning conscientious objection is now before a district court. It concerns a midwife who refuses all participation in work related to abortion.[30]

Feelings are running very high indeed on the subject, in particular among those opposing conscientious objection. It has even gone so far in some circles as to hail unhindered availability of abortion as something of a higher moral order than conscience generally. There is an urgent need for a cooling down of sentiments. A ruling by the ECHR might settle the issue, perhaps in favour of conscientious objection in accordance with the 2010 Resolution 1763.

VI. Religious Dress and Ornaments at Places of Work

Religious dress (or "religious garb") and religious ornaments have emerged as legal issues only recently. Immigration accounts for that, primarily of Muslims. In the three or four decades after World War II, dress and religious ornaments were considered private matters. Apart from places of work specifically calling for dress codes, employees were at liberty to dress as they chose, all within the boundaries of decorum. No statutory rules existed and case law dealt with practical matters, such as the necessity at specific places of work for special clothes, e. g. for safety reasons, and the responsibility to provide and pay for such clothes.

Today the situation is totally different. Religiously motivated garb and ornaments have become common. The situation has become very sensitive indeed.[31]

The European Court once declared that "[s]chools should not be the arena for missionary activities or preaching".[32] Though the Court has not been called

[28] Ironically, the initiative to a resolution on the issue came from Swedish assembly members. Their intention was to attain a resolution banning conscientious objections to participating in abortions. The initiative backfired. Sweden has actively – but so far unsuccessfully – worked to have the resolution revoked.

[29] Resolution 1928 (2013), Safeguarding human rights in relation to religion and belief, and protecting religious communities from violence, para. 9.10.

[30] Örebro tingsrätt (Örebro District Court), case T 1781–14, Ellinor Grimmark v. the Administrative Board of the County of Jönköping (Landstinget i Jönköpings län). The District Court ruled against the midwife. The case is now before the Labour Court (a court of final instance).

[31] For a thoughtful discussion on religious garb see e. g. *Robson, Ruthann*, Dressing Constitutionally. Hierarchy, Sexuality, and Democracy from Our Hairstyles to Our Shoes (Cambridge University Press 2013), in particular Chapter 6, Dressing Religiously. Though the discussion is limited to the US, the issues and problems discussed are universal. For a discussion regarding Sweden see *Fahlbeck, Reinhold*, op. cit note 17, subsection 6.3.8. See very succinctly also *Fahlbeck, Reinhold*, article Ora et Labora, note 17, pp. 60 et seqq.

[32] Lautsi v. Italy, Application No. 30814/06, unanimous Chamber ruling, 3 November 2009, para. 47(c). The ruling was reversed on appeal by the Grand Chamber, 18 March 2011. Though

upon to pronounce itself on the role of religious garb at workplaces, it seems fair to believe that the Court would come to the same conclusion.

On the other hand, freedom of religion and the concomitant right to manifest one's religion under Article 9 of the ECHR applies to workplaces as well. A recent case concerned a private workplace in the UK (British Airways). An employee wished to wear a cross visibly on a necklace and to deliberately manifest her religious beliefs in that way. The European Court stated:

> "As previously noted, this is a fundamental right: because a healthy democratic society needs to tolerate and sustain pluralism and diversity; but also because of the value to an individual who has made religion a central tenet of his or her life to be able to communicate that belief to others".[33]

A body of ECHR case law on the matter has emerged. It primarily concerns Muslim attire, the Muslim headscarf and the Muslim burka. The European Court has always found bans on such attire acceptable, despite the infringement on the religious freedom of the bearer that such bans (might) represent.[34] The *Eweida case* just referred to dealt with a Christian cross. The Sikh turban and the Jewish kippa have not been dealt with under the ECHR in a workplace context (or in the context of social security).

Sweden has not developed any rules of its own regarding religious attire or ornaments at workplaces. Case law is non-existent. So is regulation in collective agreements. No labour market standards have developed either.[35] This means that the case law of the European Court is the prime source of law. At the same time, Sweden enjoys a wide margin of appreciation to fashion its own rules. The reason is that there is no consensus among the member states concerning religious attire and religious ornaments at the workplace.[36]

---

the statement of the Chamber has not been repeated by the Grand Chamber, the general character of its ruling conveys the same message.

[33] Eweida and others, note 25 supra, para. 94.

[34] The rulings concern primarily France and Turkey. In these countries secularism – or *laïcité*, as it is referred to in France – is part of basic national law. It is not at all certain that the outcome will be the same if and when the European Court is confronted with the same issue in countries with no or little similar basic traits, for example Sweden. Cf. in this respect the much publicized ruling by the German Constitutional Court (*Bundesverfassungsgericht*) concerning Ms Feresta Ludin, a teacher; BVerfGE, 2 BvR 136/02, 24 September 2003. Ms Ludin had been refused employment at a public school since she insisted on wearing a Muslim headscarf even in the classroom. The Constitutional Court found the refusal unacceptable since it lacked the necessary legal authority in the law of the federal state in question (Baden-Württemberg). Thus, the Court did not rule out a ban as an unconstitutional infringement *per se* of the constitutionally protected freedom of religion.

[35] Swedish school authorities have been quite permissive with regard to student attire but no similar development can be recorded for universities. The issue of attire by teachers in public schools has not been addressed.

[36] For comments by the European Court concerning the margin of appreciation in matters of religious attire and ornamentation see e.g. S.A.S. v. France, Application No. 43853/11, judgement of July 1, 2014, para. 129.

Public opinion is divided and vacillating between acceptance, reluctance or downright hostility. However, that does not apply to the treatment of women. Unequal treatment of women *vis-à-vis* men and female oppression is very much indeed frowned upon. Most Swedes would wholeheartedly agree with the European Court when it stated the following in a 2001 ruling:

"In those circumstances, it cannot be denied outright that the wearing of a headscarf ..., as the Federal Court noted, is hard to square with the principle of gender equality. It therefore appears difficult to reconcile the wearing of an Islamic headscarf with the message of tolerance, respect for others and, above all, equality and non-discrimination that all teachers in a democratic society must convey to their pupils" and "the advancement of equality of the sexes is today a major goal in the member States of the Council of Europe. This means that very weighty reasons would have to be advanced before a difference in treatment on the ground of sex could be regarded as compatible with the Convention".[37]

Most Swedes would also wholeheartedly agree with the blistering criticism expressed in the Council of Europe Resolution 1464 (2005), *Women and Religion in Europe,* on the way religion is sometimes invoked to justify differing treatment of women. Paras 5 and 6 *inter alia* state the following:

"Freedom of religion cannot be accepted as a pretext to justify violations of women's rights, be they open or subtle, legal or illegal, practised with or without the nominal consent of the victims – women" (para. 5).

"It is the duty of the member states of the Council of Europe to protect women against violations of their rights in the name of religion and to promote and fully implement gender equality. States must not accept any religious or cultural relativism of women's human rights" (para. 6).

On the other hand, there is also a widespread reluctance to interfere with the behaviour of others. This is particularly the case with regard to immigrants. There is a widespread fear of being considered hostile to immigration or even racist if reacting in a negative or condescending way to the customs and behaviour of immigrants. Coupled with this is an attitude of indifference to all things religious prevailing among large segments of the Swedish population. This indifference is probably the main reason why the public attitude towards religious attire and ornamentation – though by and large loathed – is very permissive.

This all would point in the direction of permissiveness to religious attire and other religious manifestations at workplaces. However, by and large this is not the case. Religious manifestations at workplaces are quite rare. One reason for this is perhaps that many feel embarrassed and uncomfortable, even annoyed,

[37] Dahlab v. Switzerland, Application No. 42393/98, judgement of 15 February 2001, ECHR Reports 2002, p. 43 et seq. The reference to the Federal Court concerns Switzerland. Statements to the same effect as in Dahlab are common in the case law of the European Court. For a recent statement see e. g. S. A.S v. France, previous note, upholding the ban on wearing a burka in public places in France. The Court reiterated in this connection "[...] that the advancement of gender equality is today a major goal in the member States of the Council of Europe [...]."; para. 119.

by overt religious manifestations regardless of what religion is manifested. They are frowned upon. By and large, religion is still considered a private matter and should be kept private. Another reason – and perhaps the strongest – is the marked reluctance on the part of employers to accept religious manifestations at their workplaces. The prevailing employer attitude is that workplaces are no arenas for religions manifestations and should not be.

All things considered, religious manifestations have so far given rise to precious little public discord in actual working life. As far as is known, open workplace conflicts are very rare indeed. Resort to the courts is unheard of. No court case is recorded. Still, the situation is very sensitive indeed.

The conclusion so far is that from a domestic legal regulatory point of view the whole area of religious manifestations at workplaces is something of a *terra incognita,* and has been so for the entire post-World War II period.

However, returning to overriding international norms the picture is changing somewhat. Article 9 of the ECHR applies. Case law from the European Court provides guidance on the principal level. As was said in Section 5 a balance must be struck between the legitimate wishes of the employee concerned and legitimate opposing interests. The methodology presented by the European Court in the *Eweida case* applies.[38] As the reasoning of the Court in that case demonstrates, no simple yardsticks are available. The necessary balance has to be struck on an *ad hoc* basis, taking into account the circumstances of the situation at hand.

As was pointed out in Section 2, the 2008 Discrimination Act deals with religious discrimination. The Discrimination Ombudsman is very active in combating discrimination. This also applies to religious discrimination. As was also pointed out, employers found guilty by the Ombudsman have consistently refrained from taking those decisions to court, preferring to pay the penalty imposed by the Ombudsman, thus getting rid of the matter once and for all. As was also pointed out, it is far from certain that decisions by the Ombudsman would always be upheld by courts if brought before them. It seems fair to say that a legal sub-culture exists here that ought to be tested by the courts. The sub-culture is characterized by a very permissive attitude towards religiously motivated attire and behaviour. This is in particular the case with regard to Muslims. For example, the Muslim scarf is consistently considered to be a religious manifestation. No attention is paid to the possible infringement of the negative freedom of religion of others that such wearing might constitute or to other effects that the wearing of such a scarf might have, e.g. the employers' interest to create and convey a

[38] Note 25 supra.
Reference can also be made to a ruling by the German Federal Labour Court (*Bundesarbeitsgericht*), 2 AZR 472/01, 10 October 2002, (Vol. 103, 2004, p. 111), It concerns the dismissal of a saleswoman who wished to wear a Muslim headscarf. The Court here presents a well thought-out model for striking the necessary balance. The model is in perfect harmony with the ECHR and the subsequent Eweida *case* but it is more elaborate than Eweida.

certain corporate image. Nor is any attention paid to the highly controversial issue whether the scarf is the result of female oppression. The 2010 Council of Europe Resolution 1464 (2005), *Women and Religion in Europe,* with its blistering criticism of religions for the subjugation of women has never been referred to. It is taken for granted that female attire is based on genuine rather than nominal consent. The stated policy of the Discrimination Ombudsman is that religious manifestations take precedence over gender equality, at least as far as Muslim manifestations are concerned. This policy is justified as a means of promoting integration into Swedish society. Some observers are critical to this policy since, in their view, it represents integration by means of segregation.

VII. Employment Policy Programs and Employment Policy Measures

Full employment is a cherished social value. It has been a lodestar of public policy throughout the entire post-World War II period.

The Socialdemokratiska Arbetarepartiet (SAP, the Social Democratic Party) defined itself as "the workers' party" and was originally built on a constituency of manual workers. Full employment has been the mantra of the SAP for the entire post-World War II period. Since the SAP had been in power uninterruptedly between 1945 and 1976 (and again for approximately half of the time since then), the full employment idea has been the single strongest feature of post-World War II labour politics and social engineering. Enormous administrative efforts have been undertaken to achieve the goal and enormous amounts of money have been spent. Active labour market policy has been a hallmark of post-World War II Swedish society and one of the most prominent features of Swedish social fabric.

The National Labour Market Board was in charge of implementing efforts to achieve that goal. Various unemployment benefit schemes have been available for the unemployed. Robust, voluntary and active public employment exchange has been an important ingredient. So have various schemes for work-experience placement of the unemployed and referral to specific jobs that are available.

The reverse side of all these schemes is – and has consistently been – the obligation of the unemployed to participate in efforts to find and accept work and/or work-experience placement. Central in this respect is the obligation to accept "suitable work" or "suitable work-experience placement".

General reference in this respect can be made to rules adopted by the ILO, namely the 1988 Convention No. 168 concerning Employment Promotion and Protection against Unemployment.[39]

[39] Article 21, para. 2 of the Convention reads: "In assessing the suitability of employment, account shall be taken, in particular, under prescribed conditions and to an appropriate extent,

The overriding Swedish statute is the 1997 Unemployment Insurance Act. The statute replaced a 1973 predecessor. Words such as "religion" or "faith" are non-occurring in the *travaux préparatoires* of either of them.

At present, a public Directive of 2012 on what constitutes "suitable work" is in force.[40] It has several predecessors. Section 4 of the 2012 Directive states that if the person in question "cannot accept available work due to personal conditions or circumstances that are acceptable under this Directive, such person must as soon as possible take measures to eliminate such obstacles, whenever possible".[41] Failure to do so will result in the withdrawal of benefits. To some extent the Directive specifies acceptable excuses. They all deal with practicalities. The labour market authorities retain a wide margin of appreciation and have done so during the entire post-World War II period. It seems justified to say that the present Directive is very strict indeed. In this respect it does not differ in principle from its post-World War II predecessors, although the strictness of predecessors has differed somewhat depending on the economic situation.

What is of relevance here is that the 2012 Directive does not make any reference to conscientious objections or objections of a religious nature. This may seem reprehensible, perhaps even shocking. No room for spirituality, no room for conscience? However, the structure of the Directive is perhaps not surprising after all since Article 21 of the 1988 ILO Convention (see note 39) makes no reference to religion or conscience either.

An on-going court case at the time of this writing illustrates the situation.[42] A Jehovah's Witness refused, for religious reasons, to come to a work-experience placement interview at a company that promotes and sells lotteries to private organizations. His refusal was considered non-acceptable by the labour market authority so he was barred from further assistance. He appealed. The Administrative Court of first instance ruled in his favour, citing freedom of religion. The labour market authority appealed. The Administrative Court of second instance upheld the bar. The Court took the position that the refusal did not enjoy protection in terms of "religion" under Article 9 of the ECHR. Nor was it justified for any other reason. The position offered was considered to be "not unsuitable" so the refusal was unacceptable. That ruling by the Administrative Court of second instance stands since the Supreme Administrative Court in 2015 declined to hear the case.

---

of the age of unemployed persons, their length of service in their former occupation, their acquired experience, the length of their period of unemployment, the labour market situation, the impact of the employment in question on their personal and family situation and whether the employment is vacant as a direct result of a stoppage of work due to an on-going labour dispute". The 1988 Convention replaced several predecessors, e.g. the 1934 Unemployment Provision Convention and Recommendation.

[40] Directive on suitable work, issued by the Inspectorate for the Unemployment Insurance, IAFFS 2012:1.

[41] My translation of the Swedish original.

[42] The Administrative Court of first instance (Förvaltningsrätten i Göteborg), case No. 6207–14, judgement of July 4, 2014. The Administrative Court of second instance (Kammarrätten i Göteborg), case No. 4254–14, judgement of 22 April 2015.

To conclude: Neither religion nor faith has played any role whatsoever for the structure and administration of the single most important work-related social security system in Sweden.

VIII. The Social Security System at Large

The concluding remark in Section 7 on employment policy was that neither religion nor faith had played any role whatsoever for the structure and administration of the single most important work related social security system in Sweden.

What about other social security systems? The Swedish social security system has attracted world-wide attention. Sweden has even been looked upon as something of a model. The notion that Sweden is the *People's Home* is cherished and is indeed often used to characterize Sweden as a nation. Swedes are supposed to take pride in that and it seems fair to say that during the first three to four decades after World War II – the heydays of "the Swedish Model" – a good proportion of the population actually did feel this way.

Examples of social security systems other than the employment policy system are schemes for financial social assistance to individuals in need, housing allowance (rent allowance), free medical care (including free-of-charge abortion) and family/child allowances. These schemes all cost huge amounts of money.

What is the role of "religion" or "faith" – positive or negative – in the structure and administration of these schemes? The answer is that religion plays no role whatsoever in any of these schemes. It is true that they are all built on notions of solidarity and brotherhood. However, confessional religion or creed played no role whatsoever.

IX. Collective Labour Law

The law on collective bargaining, freedom of association, the right to organize, labour market unions, collective agreements, industrial actions and industrial democracy/co-determination forms the core of collective labour law. Sweden has a mighty body of collective labour law. Its origins and basic legal structures date to times before World War II but its present statutory dress dates primarily from the 1970s. Has religion played any role in the formation of this body of law?

The answer is negative. Collective labour law as a social and legal phenomenon has deep roots in the Swedish social fabric. That fabric lost most of its confessional religious character already before the advent of the collective labour movement. The labour movement distanced itself from religion, indeed by and large repudiated it. No Christian unions were formed. No overtly Christian political party emerged until long after the formation of collective labour law.

Mainly for these reasons, confessional religious elements were never part of the development of collective labour law.

Religious communities such as churches or parishes have always enjoyed the same rights under collective labour law as all other collective legal entities. The degree to which they have taken advantage of it has depended on the internal policies of those very communities and not on the legal system per se. No vestiges of religious communities can be found in collective labour law.

Religious bodies acting as employers have always enjoyed the same rights as non-religious employers. They have also always been subjected to the same requirements as non-religious bodies, e.g. the duty to bargain. They have never enjoyed any immunities, e.g. from industrial actions.

Collective labour law cases with religious elements involving religious bodies are virtually non-existent. Some rare exceptions do exist.

One much publicized case concerned the Plymouth Brethren. Part of the religion is a refusal to sign agreements. A company owned by members of the religion refused to sign a collective agreement. The union decided to boycott the company in order to force the company to sign such an agreement. The Labour Court ruled against the union. However, the reason had nothing to do with religion. The word "religion" does not even figure in the ruling. The Court found that the company enjoyed immunity from industrial action with the declared aim under the 1976 Co-Determination Act for the one and only reason that it was a family business. As such it was protected from industrial actions of the kind under investigation.[43]

X. Concluding Remarks. Religion and Swedish Society in the Post-World War II Period

As said in Section 1, the decades after World War II saw the coming into existence of the Swedish social welfare system and its modern employment law system. In both respects, Sweden has often been looked upon as a model. In both respects, the build-up represents a mighty feat of social engineering. That engineering was very determined. It was primarily conducted by the ruling Social Democratic Party (SAP) in power in the forming decades of "the Swedish Model".[44] The survey of the significance of religion for Swedish labour and social legislation presented here amply demonstrates that religion has played virtually no role whatsoever in that social engineering.

Would it be appropriate to finish this survey on that note? No, most definitely not, I would say. This is my answer.

---

[43] Arbetsdomstolen (Labour Court) 2008 no. 5.

[44] The party was in power uninterruptedly between 1945 and 1976 and much of the time since then.

It is true, as was said in Section 1, that the post-World War II body of labour and social legislation was created in a social and existential environment where religion by and large had become non-existent or at least politically and socially irrelevant. It should be pointed out that no party of a Christian character existed, quite unlike in Central and Southern Europe. It should also be pointed out that Sweden was not exposed to the social thinking of the Catholic Church.

It is equally true that the very idea that religion should be of significance in the build-up of the welfare-*cum*-employment law systems was frowned upon, if such an idea was at all considered (which, by and large, it most definitely was not).

However, this ascertainment is not the appropriate endnote. One has to consider the social ethics prevailing in post-World War II Sweden. The efforts of the ruling Social Democratic Party (SAP) were based on ideas such as equality and solidarity between all members of society, equal rights for and equal treatment of women and men, social security for all members of society, collectivism in solidarity and equal sharing, the right to work and the right to enjoy a meaningful working life. Though little or no reference was made to ideas of a religious nature the prevailing social ethics had a strong flavour of secular religiosity akin to confessional religion. Catholic social thinking played no overt part but the ruling SAP was familiar with it, primarily through its contacts with the German trade union movement.

A present-day observer might in fact be tempted to say that the building stone of the social engineering in the first post-World War II decades was "The Golden Rule". In biblical terms, that rule is phrased as an exhortation to "[d]o to others whatever you would like them do to you".[45]

---

[45] Luke chapter 6 verse 31, *Matthew* chapter 7 verse 12. A German observer might be tempted to recall what Der Herr said to Mephistophles in the opening Prolog im Himmel in *Goethe's* Faust: "Ein guter Mensch in seinem dunklen Drange / Ist sich des rechten Weges wohl bewusst". This is not to say that the architects of the post-war social engineering worked in the dark. Quite the contrary. They were most conscious about what they were doing. It can, however, perhaps be said that they did so in their "dunklen Drange" from the point of view of a confessional religious perspective!

The Significance of Religion for US-American Labor and Social Legislation

Thomas C. Kohler

I. Introduction

Writing in 1933, two years before the enactment of the landmark National Labor Relations Act, the economist and labor historian, David Saposs, noted that, "The significant and predominant role of the Catholic Church in shaping the thought and the aspirations of labor is a neglected chapter in the history of the American labor movement. Its influence explains, in part at least, why the labor movement in the United States differs from others, and why it has become more and more reactionary." Saposs proceeds to remark that the part the Catholic Church has played in the American case "can best be understood by providing a brief resumé of the historic attitude of the Church towards labor in Europe and the world."[1]

More than eighty years after he wrote those words, the significance of religion in both shaping the attitudes of those in the labor movement, as well as the form American labor, social, and civil rights legislation has taken (for civil rights in the American case involves both labor and social legislation) remains a largely neglected topic. A number of factors may explain this lack.

We typically understand labor and social legislation solely through the categories of modernity. To some, such legislation exemplifies the operation of a sort of inexorable historical force moving humankind toward equality, in the

[1] *David Saposs*, "The Catholic Church and the Labor Movement," The Modern Monthly, vol. VII, No. 4 (May, 1933) p. 225.

way described by Alexis de Tocqueville in *Democracy in America*, or, in a much different manner, by Marx and his epigones. Others, perhaps most, regard such legislation, and the activity of labor organization generally, solely in terms of economic self-interest. Workers, as a class or as otherwise unaffiliated individuals bound by a limited set of ultimately egotistic goals, engage in collective action and demand protective legislation to shift income to themselves. Society, in response and acting in its own interest to promote social peace and to secure property and capitalist economic arrangements, makes concessions through labor and social legislation to mollify demands of pressure groups by ameliorating "market failures" or because rent-taking has been coerced by concerted collective action. The legitimacy of such legislative concessions and the resulting interference in the operation of markets remain topics of hot debate, perhaps particularly in the United States.

In accounting for this lack, one must also take account of rather widespread attitudes among academic commentators and researchers that range from a general queasiness with questions relating to religion to incredulity if not outright contempt for the notion that religion might have any role here. These tendencies often become more pronounced when issues touching on Catholicism come into play. As the distinguished historian, Anthony Grafton, has remarked, matters involving Catholicism past the medieval period, "have rarely if ever seemed a proper object of study for scholars in elite universities." The study of "modern Catholic culture – like most Catholics – was usually disdained, as the province of lesser breeds fit only for the legendary parochial schools where nuns told their charges never to order ravioli on a date, lest their boyfriends be reminded of pillows. Stereotypes and prejudices of this kind, as nasty as anything fastened on the Jews, persisted in American universities until an uncomfortably recent date,"[2] a date which the American writer, Thomas Cahill, observes "may be only the day before yesterday."[3] Such attitudes hardly represent a strictly American phenomenon. Manuel Borutta points out, "In Germany, as early as the *Vormärz* period, Catholicism served as a term of stigmatization connoting both religious orthodoxy and reaction, and in fact both within Protestantism as well as within Judaism."[4]

None of this suggests that religion in general, or Catholicism in particular, alone accounts for American labor and social legislation. Like all complex social developments, such legislation represents the product of numerous social and

---

[2] *Anthony Grafton*, "The Soul's Entrepreneurs", The New York Review of Books, March 3, 1994, pp. 33–37.

[3] *Thomas Cahill*, How the Irish Saved Civilization: the Untold Story of Ireland's Heroic Role from the Fall of Rome to the Rise of Medieval Europe (New York, Anchor Books 1995), p. 7.

[4] *Manuel Borutta*, Antikatholizismus: Deutschland und Italien im Zeitalter der europäischen Kulturkämpfe (Göttingen, Vandenhoeck & Ruprecht 2011), p. 15.

historical forces. Nevertheless, religion has played a crucial if unappreciated role in the genesis of such legislation and in providing the motives to the movements that urged their passage. One cannot fully appreciate the purposes or the significance of such legislation, and the values that such legislation in part embodies, without taking those religious influences into account. What labor, social and civil rights activists understood themselves to be doing, the goals they intended, and the values that motivated their activities, struggles and sacrifices in many cases may not be those ascribed to them by most scholars. A failure to understand the religious influences that motivated their undertakings delivers a stilted and incomplete, if not misleading comprehension of labor and social legislative regimes. The topic represents a surprisingly complex and capacious one and we can touch only on a few of its facets here.

David Saposs' valuable article provides a useful way of proceeding. Given the Catholic Church's role in "shaping the thoughts and aspirations of labor," and its role in influencing the shape of our labor legislation, in the first part of this paper, I will set out a very brief "resumé of the historic attitude of the Church toward labor in Europe." In the second part, I will sketch how both Catholic and Protestant social thought influenced the shape of our key labor and social legislation, a great deal of which stems from the "New Deal" era. I will also discuss the absolutely indispensible role of the African American Protestant Churches in the passage of our landmark Civil Rights Act of 1964.

Recently, much has been made of the fact that religion, at least in its traditional embodiment in the so-called Mainline Protestant Churches, in the Catholic Church, among our "Evangelical" churches (not to be confused with the German "evangelische Kirche"), and in Jewish practice and observance, may exercise less influence today than it has historically in the United States. If "religion," broadly described, played such an important role in the enactment of American and social legislation, what might the future hold for us? At present, American exceptionalism seems quite vibrant and I think it most unlikely that we anytime soon will follow a social state model. I will try to touch on a few of the factors that I believe make us so distinct, and to speculate a bit on the future of labor and social legislation in the U.S., and its possibilities in a time when employment, as a ongoing relationship, seems to be disappearing and all social ties appear fragile and ever more evanescent. Sir Henry Maine famously observed that, "the movement of progressive societies has hitherto been a movement *from Status to Contract.*"[5] In an age of "shrink-wrapped contracts," of the type to which users of computers must agree, without any possible negotiation, before downloading updated programs for their computers, or buying tickets for airline travel, to take just two common examples, the notion of "contract" is undergoing almost

[5] *Henry Maine*, Ancient Law: Its Connection with the Early History of Society and its Relation to Modern Ideas (n.p., Dorset Press 1986) (1861), p. 141 (italics in original).

unrecognizable transformation. At the same time, status, at least in the American case, increasingly refers to something measured on a moment-to-moment basis. Religion raises the most basic questions about our relations to ourselves and to others, about how we conceive reality, the purpose of our lives and what constitutes the just and the desirable. Perhaps the topic of this panel presents matters of more than historical curiosity?

II. The Catholic Church and Labor: Some Historical Notes

Although Saposs points us in a useful direction to understand the American labor movement and, thereby, American labor and social legislation, unfortunately, the "resumé" of the Church's "historic attitude toward labor" he provides falls badly short and significantly mischaracterizes a complex and surprisingly long tradition. Because his views typify those still broadly held, some comments upon them may prove useful.

As Saposs has it, the Church "made costly blunders" in the nineteenth century "by failing to interest itself in the material well being of the newly created industrial working class," but instead "siding with the upstart capitalists," leaving the "socialists as the sole champions of the downtrodden" in Continental Europe. One could say quite a bit about these observations, including the fact that the Church in its theology and its social teachings from the Enlightenment forward has encountered great difficulty in dealing with modern liberalism in general, and capitalism in particular – for some recent examples one might consider Pope Francis' observations on capitalist orders in his Apostolic Exhortation, *Evangelii Gaudium* [*The Joy of the Gospel*], which he published in 2013 and which undoubtedly strongly reflects the views of Pope Benedict, as well his many recent, and more informal observations. As an aside, one can point out that these observations have produced more anxiety, if not outright anger, than joy among some self-described American Catholic "conservatives."

Saposs' views reflect what our colleague, Michael Kittner, has referred to as the "myth of the nineteenth century." According to it,

> "workers suffering under the abuses of early factory work stand unchallenged on the pedestal as pioneers of a social movement, as those who plucked up their courage in the face of repression from the factory owners and the state and founded unions and social democratic parties and took up the fight for the betterment of their living standards."

Everything that came before, he notes, according to the myth appears "small, trivial or simply measly."[6]

---

[6] *Michael Kittner*, Arbeitskampf: Geschichte-Recht-Gegenwart (München, C.H. Beck 2005) pp. 33–34.

Widely held, the myth falls every bit as widely from the facts. Kittner points out that the journeymen (*Gesellen*) early began organizing their own associations, variously referred to as "brotherhoods," guilds (*gilda*, or *gildonia*, which since the eighth century referred to a society or band of persons bound together by mutual oaths), or associations (*Verbände*) very early, the first documented in Berlin in 1331.[7] By the fifteenth century, journeymen's associations existed in nearly all large German cities, and even in Nürnberg, which had forbidden the existence of guilds of maters, but did – and indeed was forced at the cost of not being able to attract them – tolerate the societies of journeymen.[8] These associations dealt with the masters to establish the regulation of their relationships, but the journeymen's associations, as well as the guilds of the masters, performed far more than economic functions. In a study published in the late nineteenth century, Lujo Brentano observed that:

> The Gild, which, as we have shown, stood like a loving mother, providing and assisting, at the side of her sons in every circumstance in life, cared for her children even after death. [...] In this respect, the Craft-Guilds of all countries are alike; and in reading their statutes, one might fancy sometimes that the old craftsmen cared only for the well being of their souls. [...] We find innumerable ordinances also as to the support of the sick and poor; and to afford a settled asylum for distress. [...] The chief care however of the Gildmen was always directed to the welfare of the souls of the dead.[9]

Among their many other functions, their guilds afforded journeymen with assistance in traveling, in securing positions, settling disputes, enforcing agreements, providing support for the ill and infirm, and by supplying fellowship, spiritual and otherwise. Their existence established an effective network for information, communication and action across the German territories and beyond.

From the start, Kittner notes, the new mendicant orders, which had just begun to make their appearance in this era, particularly the Franciscans and the Dominicans, played an essential role in helping to organize and in sponsoring the journeymen's associations. In fact, he reports, more than two-thirds of the journeymen's associations had established organizational relationships with the mendicant orders, with the Franciscans in the lead. These relations also provided "a platform" for discussions and resolving disputes between the journeymen and their masters. Institutionally, Peter Moraw notes, the mendicant orders and the corporate town and its related bodies were closely bound and consequently, "The Franciscan Church could become the headquarters in town conflicts." He adds that in situations where "an interdict was imposed, the mendicants" typically took the side of the citizens and remained with them, to provide them

---

[7] *Kittner*, p. 19.

[8] *Kittner*, p. 32.

[9] *Lujo Brentano*, On the History and Development of Gilds, and the Origin of Trade-Unions, pp. 69–70 (London, Trübner & Co. 1870).

with spiritual care and other support, rather than siding with the bishop or pope imposing the punishment. This was true, he notes, even though the leadership of these orders usually came from the upper social and economic classes.[10]

The journeymen's associations, Peter Bossy tells us, represent only a part of the great lay fraternity movement that, like the journeymen's guilds themselves, could be found across all of Latin Christendom until the onset of the Reformation. [11] Wolfgang Hardtwig remarks that, "the religious motive has played a substantially greater role in the shaping and development of the character of modern associations than has been previously assumed."[12]

The Church's consistent concern with support and maintenance for mediating institutions of all types became particularly acute in the wake of the French Revolution. The first sentence of Article 1 of the famous "August Decrees" of 1789 succinctly states the challenge: "The National Assembly entirely destroys the feudal regime." The great French historian, François Furet, has observed that the Decrees and subsequent legislation furthering their program, such as the 1791 *Loi le Chapelier*, which suppressed guilds, workers' associations, and other corporate bodies, amounted to "philosophy's destruction of a world"[13] These enactments swept away an entire "juridical and social order, forged over the centuries, composed of a hierarchy of separate orders, corps, and communities ... leaving in its place a social world conceived in a new way as a collection of free and equal individuals subject to the universal authority of law."[14] The creation "without concessions" and within a very short period of time, "of a wholly modern, individualistic society," Furet notes, posed a novel and deeply troubling problem. "What had to be worked out now" for this unprecedented "society of free and equal individuals," he points out, would be the way in which they might be related to and united with one another.[15] In a similar vein, in his *Reflections on the Revolution in France,* Edmund Burke, the great defender of what he called the "little platoons" in which society consists, demanded to know how it was, in light of the changes the Revolution wrought, that "three or four thousand democracies should be formed into eighty-three, and that they may all, by some sort of unknown attractive power, be organized into one?"[16]

---

[10] *Peter Moraw*, Von offener Verfassung zu gestalteter Verdichtung: Das Reich im späten Mittelalter 1250–1490 (Berlin, Propyläen Verlag 1985), p. 143.

[11] *John Bossy*, Christianity in the West, 1400–1700 (Oxford, Oxford Univ. Press 1985), p. 58.

[12] *Wolfgang Hardtwig*, Genossenschaft, Sekte, Verein in Deutschland, Band I: Vom Spätmittelalter bis zur Französischen Revolution (München, C.H. Beck 1997), p. 30.

[13] *François Furet*, The Night of August 4, in: A Critical Dictionary of the French Revolution, p. 266 (François Furet & Mona Ozouf (eds.), Arthur Goldhammer, trans., The Belknap Press of Harvard Univ. Press 1989).

[14] Id., p. 107.

[15] Id., p. 113.

[16] *Edmund Burke*, Reflections on the Revolution, in: France 135 (Conor Cruise O'Brien, ed. Penguin Books 1986) (1790), p. 144.

That problem, which Furet and Burke highlight, represents the core of what Napoleon Bonaparte, of all people, would first refer to as the "social question." This seemingly intractable problem bedeviled the nineteenth century and the contests over its possible resolution involved thinkers as diverse as Karl Marx, John Stuart Mill, Alexis de Tocqueville, Herbert Spencer, Émile Durkheim, Max Weber and the holders of the Chair of Peter, to name but a very few. We hardly need reminding that the problem remains every bit as pressing for us.

Because of their numbers and their dire need, those "freed" or displaced from the land as peasants or as small holders, along with day laborers, weavers, small tradesmen and others subject to what Marx called "de-skilling" and who lived at the edge of economic survival – which one survey states accounted for about 65 % of the population of Prussia in the mid-nineteenth century[17] – quickly became the focus of those considering the social question. A good decade and a half before Marx adopted the term, the Catholic philosopher and social theorist, Franz von Baader, referred to this rapidly expanding group as the proletariat. This class of people had no legal standing, no voice in government, few if any resources, and the ties that once gave structure to their lives and relationships had been dissolved. They literally constituted those without a place in society.

The development of the notion of solidarity at the hands of those who would form the Catholic social thought tradition represents one key response to the social question and to the problems it raised. The political theorist, J. E. S. Hayward notes that, "it was amongst the Roman Catholic social theologists ... that the idea of solidarity first achieved its pivotal social significance and underwent an evolution that prefigured its subsequent philosophic prominence and temporary political preeminence."[18] The attempt to find what I might call "structures of solidarity" through which to integrate those at the margins, and to replace the compact social unity and the social institutions that the August Decrees and the "revolution from above" introduced by the Prussian bureaucracy had swept away, became the focus of the activists and theorists in the Catholic social thought movement.

This movement involved a rather large and quite diverse, if not to say motely group of people over the decades, and the laity played a leading role in developing its thought. Some of its early figures include such leading German Romantic thinkers as Adam Müller (1779–1829), Franz von Baader (1765–1841) and Josef Görres (1776–1848). Other prominent if not always unproblematic thinkers

[17] *Ilja Mieck*, "Preußen von 1807 bis 1850: Reformen, Restauration und Revolution" in: Handbuch der preussischen Geschichte, Band II, Otto Büsch (Hrsg.), p. 153, (Berlin, New York, Walter de Gruyter 1992).

[18] *J. E. S. Hayward*, The Idea of Solidarity in French Social and Political Thought in the Nineteenth and Early Twentieth Centuries, pp. vi–vii (1958) (unpublished Ph.D. dissertation, University of London), p. xl.

include Félicité Lamennais, whose writings such as *Paroles d'un croyant* [*Words of a Believer* 1834] and *Le Liver du peuple* [*The Book of the People* 1838] give a taste of his concerns. The first decried political tyranny and the oppression and exploitation of the working classes, and called on these groups to organize. Throughout it, he also repeatedly reminds his readers of the obligations of mutual help and love that everyone owes each other. The book was a sensation – and also earned a "perpetual" condemnation from Pope Gregory XVI in the 1834 encyclical, *Singulari nos* [*On the Errors of Lamennais*]. The latter work by Lamennais insists that while the "class struggle" unquestionably reflects the conditions of individual and social justice, it does not constitute some fundamental or existential clash among humans. The character of human work, he asserts, mirrors the basic condition of human solidarity. Work requires reciprocity, Lamennais argues, it is communal by nature, and links us not only to our contemporaries, but those who both proceeded and will succeed us.

Throughout his life, Lamennais remained deeply engaged in the social question and in trying to remedy the situation of those on the social and economic margins. The poet and critic, Kenneth Rexroth, testifies to the sway of Lamennais' ideas: "We should not forget," states Rexroth, "that Marx and Engels and Bakunin read everything they could get of Lamennais – enthusiastically – no matter how much they might disagree with him, and in the Revolution of 1848, he was incomparably more influential than the three of them put together."[19]

A broader account of the Catholic social tradition would exceed the bounds of our topic. For present purposes, the line runs from those mentioned here to important mid- and late nineteenth century figures like Franz Hitze (1851–1921), William Emmanuel Freiherr von Ketteler (1811–1877), the bishop of Mainz, a leading proponent of worker self-organization and of the idea that the state has positive obligations through legislation to promote self-help through promoting the formation of mediating groups and the extension of assistance to those in need. Pope Leo XIIIth, who propounded the first social encyclical, *Rerum novarum* [*On the New Things*], in 1891 referred to Ketteler as his "great predecessor in the defense of the rights of Labor against the abuses of Capital."

Ketteler, incidentally, admired the thought of the great socialist, Ferdinand Lassalle (1825–1864) and (ultimately unsuccessfully) attempted to collaborate with him in establishing a group of worker co-operatives, which included a special provision for women.[20] An extensive network of Catholic societies, study

---

[19] *Kenneth Rexroth*, "Lamennais", in: The Elastic Retort: Essays in Literature and Ideas (New York, Seabury Press 1973), p. 196.

[20] For some evaluations from rather different standpoints, see, "Ultramontaner Sozialismus", in: Die Neue Zeit: Wochenschrift der deutschen Sozialdemokratie, redigiert von *Karl Kautsky*, 21. Jahrgang, Bd. I, p. 641 (Stuttgart, J. H. W. Dietz 1903), pp. 641–645; *Paul Gribe*, Die Arbeiterfrage bei Lange, Ketteler, Jörg, Schäffle: aufgezeigt an ihrer Auseinandersetzung mit Lassalle (Vaduz, Kraus Reprint, 1965); *George Metlake*, "Was Bishop Ketteler a Socialist?", America,

groups and worker's associations also came into existence in Germany in the latter part of the nineteenth century, and they would remain an important part of reflection upon and transmission of Catholic social doctrine, particularly as it affected the condition of workers, until their suppression by the National Socialists in 1933.[21]

The work of the Jesuits and the Dominicans would also play a significant role. Some of the key figures included the Jesuit economist and moral theologian, Heinrich Pesch, who had studied with Gustav Schmoller, Max Sering, and Adolph Wagner, leading members of the "younger historical school" of economics, and members of the "Kathedersozialist" (academic socialist) circle. Pesch's successors, the Jesuits Gustav Gundlach (1892–1963) and Oswald von Nell-Breuning (1890–1991), along with other members of the "Königswinter Circle" would play a major role in the promulgation of the 1931 papal encyclical, *Quadragesimo anno,* which would influence Senator Robert Wagner, the author of the 1935 National Labor Relations Act.

While German Protestantism never developed anything similar to the body of Catholic social doctrine, it did have a long and influential history of reflection and action on the social question, especially as it affected workers. Among important figures here are Johann Friedrich Oberlin (1740–1826), the founder of the home [domestic] mission movement and the man after whom the famous American liberal arts college is named; Johann Hinrich Wichern (1808–1881); Friedrich Wilhelm Raiffeisen (1808–1881) and Victor Aimé Huber (1800–1869), who carried on an extensive correspondence with Bishop von Ketteler and with Lassalle. Among other things, Huber supported the formation of producer (worker-owned) co-operatives, unionization and for worker co-determination, which social Catholics also long had supported. In 1890, Adolf Stoecker, Ludwig Weber, Adolph Wagner, and Adolf von Harnack founded the well-known Evangelical Social Congress in which scholars like Max Weber would play an active role.[22]

With this brief resumé in mind, we can now turn to consider the role of religion in American labor and social legislation. We will begin with the central piece of labor legislation, the National Labor Relations Act (NLRA) of 1935.[23]

---

vol. VI, no. 6, Nov. 18, 1911, pp. 126–127; *John A. Ryan* and *Joseph Husslein*, The Catholic Church and Labor (New York, Macmillan Co. 1924), pp. 24–57.

[21] On this theme, see, e. g., *Heinrich Krauss*, *Heinrich Ostermann*, Verbands Katholizismus? Verbände, Organisationen, Gruppen im deutschen Katholizismus (Kevelaer, Butzon & Bercker 1968).

[22] On this theme, see *Thomas C. Kohler*, "Rebuilding Democracy" in First Things, November 2014, pp. 337–42 (on the roots of the German social market model).

[23] 29 U.S.C. §§ 151–169.

III. Religion and American Labor and Social Legislation

1. The NLRA and related New Deal Era Legislation

One can fairly ask how some understanding of Catholic, and to a lesser extent, Protestant social thought in Europe pertains to an understanding of American labor and social legislation. The distinguished American labor historian, Nelson Lichtenstein helps to provide an answer to this question. "For more than 100 years,

> "he explains, the American labor movement has been heavily Catholic, both in its rank and file composition and top leadership. In the half century from the 1880s to the 1930s, waves of immigrant Catholic workers, first from Ireland and Germany, then from Poland, Italy, Hungary and Mexico swelled American trade union ranks. Before World War I and then again in the 1940s Catholics certainly composed a plurality, if not an outright majority of all organized workers. Top trade union leadership may well have been even more heavily Catholic during these years. But, unlike continental Europe the U.S. never had a separate Catholic labor movement; instead the hierarchy of the Catholic Church and a corps of "labor priests" long found the trade unions a social movement upon which the Church could have a distinct social and political impact, one designed both to moderate free market capitalism in the light of such Papal encyclicals as Rerum Novarum (1893) and also to stem the tide of socialism and secularism that seemed so dangerous during the first half of the 20th century.[24]

In the U.S., the earliest examples of unionization consisted of associations of skilled labor organized by trades such as the Cordwainers (shoemakers), whose patterns of organization, not surprisingly, mirrored the historical patterns of the guilds. A variety of factors hobbled their spread, including labor shortages in the U.S., which led to labor mobility, and the use of legal sanctions like criminal and civil conspiracy actions against the combined activities of workers. The Knights of Labor represent the first mass organization of workers in the United States. They had roots in the Molly Maguires, a secret society that had originated in Ireland in response to abuses practiced by landowners and others against the rural poor. The Molly Maguires were active in the anthracite coal regions of Pennsylvania where many Irish immigrants worked in the mines. The trials and executions of twenty young members of the organization remain in America's cultural memory.

Like the Molly Maguires, the Knights of Labor began as a secret and quasi-religiously based organization, which by the mid-1880s had over 700,000 members, and was predominantly Catholic in membership. The Knights, which was as much a social reform movement as a union in the more limited sense of the term,

---

[24] *Nelson Lichtenstein*, "Labor and Social History Records at the Catholic University of America", in: Labor History Archive in the United States: A Guide for Researching and Teaching, Daniel J. Leab and Phillip P. Mason (eds.), (Detroit, Wayne State University Press 1992), p. 121.

had a surprisingly broad and for the time, advanced agenda. It included the abolition of the wage system and its replacement by producer (*i.* e., worker-owned and managed) co-operatives; equal pay for equal work between the sexes; introduction of the eight hour day and the establishment of a Bureau of Labor Statistics; the replacement of strikes by binding interest arbitration ("in order that the bonds of sympathy between [labor and management] be strengthened"); and the abolition of child labor (federal legislation limiting child labor would not come into effect until 1938, as part of the Fair Labor Standards Act). The Knights also had a very large number of African-American members. The labor historian, Leon Fink, states that, "On the whole, it can be said that the Knights loomed in the mid-1880s as a beacon of racial enlightenment in a dark sea. In no other contemporary organization, it appears, was there such a quickening dynamic toward, rather than away from, racial equality."[25]

In 1884, the Archbishop of Quebec, Eleazer Taschereau, banned Catholics from membership in the Knights based on Rome's condemnations of membership in secret societies like the Masons, which dated to the 1730s. Cardinal Gibbons and several other American bishops successfully intervened with Rome to lift this ban, and to make clear that Catholics could maintain membership in the Knights without offending Church teachings.[26] Three years later, in 1891, Pope Leo XIII would issue the first social encyclical, *Rerum Novarum*. Among other things, the encyclical teaches that the right to form and join unions and other employee associations "is the natural right of man; and the State must protect natural rights, not destroy them."[27] The encyclical also encouraged the formation of such organizations, called for a family wage, the limitation of child labor, and emphasized the positive duty of the state to enact protective legislation, *e.g.*, "wage earners, since they mostly belong in the mass of the needy, should be specially cared for and protected by the government;" "the poor and the badly off have an especial claim to consideration."[28]

The Knights meteoric rise in membership, incidentally, was very short lived. Established in 1869, the Order by the mid-1880s had about 800,000 members, but in the wake of the Haymarket Riot, which combined with other organizational and internal difficulties, led to the group suffering prodigious losses. By the early 1890s, largely had been replaced by trade unions affiliated with the American Federation of Labor. Through the entire time period under consider-

---

[25] *Leon Fink*, Workingmen's Democracy: The Knights of Labor and American Politics (Urbana, Chicago, London, University of Illinois Press 1983), p. 169.

[26] *Gibbons* arguments, with some explanatory notes by the editors, are stated, in: "Memorial Presented to the Holy See by Cardinal Gibbons on the Knights of Labor", reprinted in, Ryan and Husslein, The Church and Labor, p. 145.

[27] Leo XIII, Rerum Novarum ¶ 38.

[28] Rerum Novarum, ¶ 37.

ation and beyond, the American labor movement would remain substantially, if not dominantly, Catholic in composition.

What accounts for the strange fact that the union membership and leadership rates among Catholics – and Jews – have been vastly disproportional to the rates of their representation in the American populace? One explanation that readily offers itself is that, as poor and marginalized immigrant groups, Catholics and Jews had more than sufficient economic incentives to organize themselves to improve their economic lot. Certainly, there is something to this line of thought. Until the mid-1960s, when these trends began to reverse themselves, Catholics did receive lower average incomes, they did hold lower-status positions in the workforce, and they were less likely to receive college educations than their Protestant fellow citizens.[29]

Nevertheless, and not unlike the situation in a place like Germany, Catholics constitute a small minority of the American population. At the time of the passage of the Nation's basic labor relations law, the National Labor Relations Act, in 1935, Catholics made up less than 15 % of the population. Today, and after years of unprecedented rates of Hispanic immigration, Catholics still make-up just over 20 % of the U.S. population.[30] If, as is typically assumed, economic advantage acts as the primary incentive to join a labor union, Catholics hardly constituted the only portion of the population with a substantial self-interest in acquiring union membership.

So, if it is not simple economics, what does account for the character of American unions? Labor historian David Montgomery points in an important direction, noting that, "as Mary K. Simkhovitch remarked in her 1916 commentaries on working-class religiosity, Protestantism may have provided the vocabulary for much nineteenth-century protest, but it lacked the organic and corporatist vision out of which a coherent social program for industrial society might be constructed."[31]

This point gets to the heart of the matter. Until the post-Vatican II era, when traditional symbology in the liturgy, in sacramental practice, and in other sectors of Church life changed, and disciplines such as the Friday abstinence from meat and other communal practices, such as processions to celebrate important feasts like *Corpus Christi* were loosened or retired,[32] Catholics, like Jews, understood

---

[29] On this, see *Thomas C. Kohler*, Religion in the Workplace: Faith, Action and the Religious Foundations of American Employment Law, 83 Chicago-Kent L. Rev. 975 (2008) (The Kenneth M. Piper Lecture).

[30] Pew Research Center, "10 Facts about Religion in America", (August 27, 2015) available at http://www.pewresearch.org/fact-tank/2015/08/27/10-facts-about-religion-in-america/.

[31] *David Montgomery*, The Fall of the House of Labor: The Workplace, the State, and American Labor Activism, 1865–1925 (Cambridge, Cambridge University Press 1987), p. 306, citing Simkhovitch "City Workers" World, pp. 221–231.

[32] On the importance of these seemingly trivial observances, see *Mary Douglas*, Natural Symbols: Explorations in Cosmology (London, Barrie & Rockliff, The Cresset Press 1970).

themselves as inextricably part of a community. Edmund Burke puts the point in his famous description of society as "a partnership not only between those who are living, but those who are living, those who are dead, and those who are yet to be born."[33] Burke carried such an understanding in his bones. Literary scholar, Thomas Copeland, characterized Burke as a man who "always marched at the head of a clan,"[34] an observation to which Conor Cruise O'Brien adds, "The clan at whose head Edmund Burke marched was shot through with Catholicism."[35] In its self-understanding, the Catholic Church is a "communion of saints,"[36] which included the living and the dead, who are bound in ties of intercessory prayer so "that the union of the wayfarers with the brethren who sleep in the peace of Christ is in no way interrupted."[37] "In this solidarity with all men, living or dead, which is founded on the communion of the saints, the least of our acts done in charity rebounds to the profit of all."[38] The distinguished anthropologist, Mary Douglas, has observed that, "Protestantism rejected mediation equally through the instrument of things as through the instrument of persons."[39] Protestants meet God – or any other sort of authority – face-to-face, in a direct encounter. Belief in direct and personal revelation permits Protestants to judge matters of faith and morals for themselves. Catholics, on the other hand, traditionally have understood themselves as situated beings. Grace, authority, understanding itself come through the mediation of community. As the sociologist, Andrew Greely, puts it, "For writers like Sherwood Anderson or Sinclair Lewis, the solution to one's problems with the local community is simply to move out of Winesburg or Gopher Prairie. The Catholic can never leave the neighborhood behind."[40] The "One's self, I sing – a simple separate person," celebrated by the great – and very American – poet, Walt Whitman, would constitute a contradiction in terms to the Catholic mind.

Another important element explaining the greater proclivity of Catholics, and again, Jews, to engage in union activity is the attitude they historically have taken toward human work. In work – authentic work – the Rabbis have taught

---

[33] *Edmund Burke*, Reflections on the Revolution in France, p. 194.

[34] *Thomas W. Copeland*, Our Eminent Friend Edmund Burke: six essays (New Haven, Yale University Press 1949), quoted in, *Conor Cruise O'Brien*, Introduction to Edmund Burke, Reflections on the Revolution in France, p. 23.

[35] *Conor Cruise O'Brien*, Introduction, p. 30.

[36] The term "communion of saints" is an inclusive, not a triumphalist one and embraces "all honest believers in Christ and honest seekers after God who may be said to be said to be members of the Church 'in desire' only". *Josef Pieper & Heinz Raskop*, What Catholics Believe, Christopher Huntington, trans. (New York, Pantheon Books 1951), pp. 39–40.

[37] Catechism of the Catholic Church, ¶ 955 (Vatican City, Liberia Editrice Vaticana, 2d ed., 2000).

[38] Id. ¶ 953.

[39] *Mary Douglas*, Natural Symbols: Explorations in Cosmology, p. 48.

[40] *Andrew Greeley*, The Catholic Imagination (Berkeley, Los Angeles, London, Univ. of California Press 2000), p. 117.

humans are given the unique privilege among all the creatures to co-operate in the completion of creation.[41] Catholic teachings follow this tradition: "by means of work, man participates in the activity of God himself."[42] This stands in stark contrast to modern thought, which sees human work only instrumentally, or as Protestantism in general typically has viewed it, as constituting "only or predominantly travail, affliction and vanity (*Vergeblichkeit*),"[43] the punishment imposed by God upon Adam and all his successors for the first sin ("By the sweat of your face you will earn your food, until you return to the ground, as you were taken from it," Gen. 3:19). Following the Jewish understanding, in the Catholic conception of it, work becomes a gift: "Only man is capable of work," Church teaching explains. "Work is one of the characteristics that distinguishes man from the rest of creatures whose activity for sustaining their lives cannot be called work." Work carries with it, "a particular mark of man and of humanity, the mark of a person operating within a community of persons. And this mark decides its interior characteristics; in a sense it constitutes its very nature."[44] Consequently, states the philosopher, Jósef Tischner, "Work is reciprocity, it is agreement, it is a multifaceted dependence. Work creates a communion."[45] In other words, work has a sacramental quality embedded in it. The monastic *Ora et labora* reflects a long held understanding of the character of human work.

With this as background, one can see how the labor movement in the U.S. assumed its Catholic character. To borrow Mary Simkhovitch's words, Catholicism did provide "the organic and corporativist vision out of which a coherent social program for industrial society" could and did arise. Their attitudes toward association and to work, combined with a long social thought tradition, disposed Catholics to union activities in a way that distinguished them from other Americans. David Montgomery points out, for example, that in the "wave of joint religious-revival/trade-union-recruiting campaigns known as the Labor and Religion forward movement that touched 150 cities between 1911 and 1916," Catholic unionists had been "conspicuous on the platforms of these Protestant rallies," which aimed "to recruit Protestant craftsmen, who had often been reluctant to unionize."[46]

Immigration stamped the period under discussion, with Ireland and especially Germany providing very large proportions of the new American population.

---

[41] For two useful reflections, see *Franz Segbers*, Die Hausordnung der Tora: biblische Impulse für eine theologische Wirtschaftsethik (Luzern, Edition Exodus 2002); Luise and Willy Schottroff (Hrsg.) Mitarbeiter der Schöpfung: Bibel und Arbeitswelt, (München, Chr. Kaiser Verlag 1983).

[42] *John Paul II*, Laborem exercens, ¶ 26.

[43] *Luise und Willy Schottroff*, Zur Einführung, Mitarbeiter der Schöpfung, p. 7.

[44] *John Paul II*, Forward, Laborem exercens.

[45] *Jósef Tischner*, The Spirit of Solidarity, Marek B. Zaleski and Benjamin Fiore, trans. (San Francisco, Harper & Row 1984), p. 98.

[46] *David Montgomery*, The Fall of the House of Labor, pp. 304–305.

These newcomers, especially from Germany, acted as something of a transmission belt, bringing with them both the attitudes and the social thought being developed in their homelands, and replicating them here.[47] One example is the German Catholic Central Verein, which was founded in 1855, which by the early 1900s had a membership of over 200,000. It became especially dedicated to the study of the social question and to the transmission of the Church's social doctrine.[48] In many ways, it represents this organization and its constitutive associations represent a replication of the Catholic *Verbände* culture that stamped Germany until their suppression in 1933 by the National Socialist regime.

Transmission of Catholic social thought and its ideas for addressing the social question also occurred through priests like Peter Dietz, one of the more interesting and, at times, problematic and perhaps tragic characters in the American social thought movement. [49] Born of German immigrant parents in New York City in 1878, Dietz broke off his studies for the priesthood at various times, and worked as a paperhanger and painter, while becoming active in the City's *Gesellen Verein.* He eventually returned to his studies, which he subsequently pursued in Germany, where he became deeply acquainted with the social thought tradition. He made it his life's work, he later wrote, "to bring *Rerum Novarum* to the people in *practice.*" He returned to the U.S. and began parish work in 1905 in Northern Ohio. He soon began lecturing in events sponsored by the Ohio *Saatsverband* of the Central Verein. Dietz eventually made contacts with the leaders of the American Federation of Labor where he made himself an important presence until the early 1920s, when he withdrew from active participation in the labor movement.

Catholic social thought was mediated to Catholic laity, including workers and unionists, in myriad ways: diocesan newspapers, books, pamphlets and study-guides, sermons and talks, through better than 100 "labor colleges" in which the Jesuits played a major sponsoring role, and through the work of labor priests.[50] Lamennais had called for priests to play such a role as early as the 1830s. In addition to Dietz, this line included John Ryan, Charles Rice (Pittsburgh), the

[47] On the significance of German Catholic immigrant influence, see the classic study by *Philip Gleason*, The Conservative Reformers: German-American Catholics and the Social Order (Notre Dame, University of Notre Dame Press 1968), esp. pp. 46–171.

[48] For a brief summary of the organization's history and activities, see, "Seventy Years of Service to Church and Country: Notable Record of Catholic Central Verein of America", in The National Catholic Welfare Conference Bulletin, Vol. 6, No. 8, January, 1925, pp. 14–15.

[49] For a biography of Dietz, see *Mary Harrita Fox*, Peter Dietz, Labor Priest (Notre Dame, University of Notre Dame Press 1953). For an interesting window on the way Dietz's work lived on, see *Michael Harrington*, "Catholics in the Labor Movement: A Case History", Labor History, vol. 1, no. 3, pp. 231–263 (1960) (detailing the history of the factional struggle within the United Electrical, Radio and Machine Workers of America over its adherence to Communist principles and the activities of the Association of Catholic Trade Unionists).

[50] On them, see *Patrick J. Sullivan*, Catholic Labor Priests in the United States: A 20th Century Story of Solidarity (Washington, D.C., Pacem in Terris Press 2014).

Jesuit John Corridan (who inspired the character, Fr. Barry, in the film, *On the Waterfront*), Francis Haas, Mort Gavin, Edward Boyle (both in Boston), George Higgins, Clement Kern (Detroit), John Donohue, John Eagan and John Hayes (Chicago), to name a very few. These men had close contacts with union members and leadership, and with politicians, and in the case of Ryan and Haas, with the author of the NLRA, Senator Robert Wagner as well as other Congressional leaders. Ryan was also a close friend of Justice Brandeis, who had played a leading role in helping to establish labor arbitration in the garment industry.[51]

Neither Congress nor Senator Wagner invented American-style collective bargaining. Its contours had been worked out in the decades before the Act's passage jointly by labor and management and in large part adopted by and integrated in the Act's terms. To the extent that Catholic social thought and teachings, along with thought and activism of the Protestant Social Gospel movement, and Jewish religious and ethical thought shaped the thinking and gave motivation to the actors, one can say that religion has influenced American labor law, and in very significant ways.

But, how much was Senator Wagner directly influenced by Catholic social thought? That question admits of no easy answer. Nevertheless, among Wagner's papers pertaining to the framing of the NLRA are two heavily annotated copies of the 1931 social encyclical, *Quadragesimo Anno* [*On the Reconstruction of the Social Order*]. Wagner also corresponded with John Ryan and extensively with Francis Haas, who served as the Director of the National Catholic School of Social Service and later, as Dean of Social Science at the Catholic University in Washington, D.C. During his years in Washington (1931–1943), Haas served in a number of New Deal agencies, including the National Labor Board (established by the National Industrial Recovery Act), the first National Labor Relations Board (the "old Board"), the Works Progress Administration, and as an original member of the Wisconsin Labor Relations Board. Haas also served extensively as a labor arbitrator and frequently appointed by the National War Labor Board, the National Mediation Board, and the U.S. Department of Labor. President Roosevelt appointed Haas as Chairman of his Fair Employment Practices Commission, charged with addressing employment discrimination, and in 1947, President Truman appointed him to his President's Committee on Civil Rights.[52]

Haas was very discreet about his relationships with politicians, and acutely sensitive to the impact anti-Catholicism might have on labor legislation. In a letter dated August 31, 1933, Haas demurred to a request that he write a piece demonstrating "the parallels between the Encyclicals and the N.R.A. (National Recovery Act)." "The thing should not be done now," Haas counseled. "No

---

[51] For a biography, see, *Francis L. Broderick*, Right Reverend New Dealer, John A. Ryan (New York, The Macmillan Company 1963).

[52] For a biography, see *Thomas E. Blantz*, A Priest in Public Service: Francis J. Haas and the New Deal (Notre Dame, University of Notre Dame Press 1982).

attempt should be made to put a Catholic imprimatur, so to speak, on what a good many people regard as political policy. Personally, I do not put this interpretation on a pamphlet such as you outline and certainly you would not do so. But there is being started a virulent campaign of criticism of the Administration which is timed to get into full swing in about a month, and the Church in my opinion should not be compromised." Haas then dismisses any notion that he has surrendered "to the idea that the Church should not speak on industrial and economic questions." That is not the point, he explains, but he continues by observing that, "The whole thing is tied up in so many complications that it would take a five page letter to explain."[53]

Without question, the NLRA, which remains the key piece of American labor legislation, bears the stamp of many influences, and certainly not all of them religiously based. Nevertheless, the strains of thought reflected in the Catholic social thought tradition help to explain and illuminate both the Act and the historically Catholic character of the American labor movement.

In a deeply perceptive and thought-provoking piece that he published now about twenty years ago, my co-panelist, colleague and friend, Reinhold Fahlbeck, reflected on what he termed the "un-American character of American labor law." Our labor law, with its emphasis on collective action and the formation of associations, he points out, stands in stark contrast to the individualistic habits and attitudes of the "archetypal American," leaving that law to appear, as he puts it, "somehow un-American." From the viewpoint of the typical American, states Fahlbeck, "[t]hose people who want and need concerted action and unions are not quite reliable. They are not like Americans at-large."[54] For the reasons I have outlined, I could not agree with him more.

Of course, the NLRA does not exhaust American social legislation, key portions of which also date from the New Deal era. What religious influence does it bear? Again, as is true everywhere, such legislation stands as something of a florilegium, a composite of ideas, needs, values and compromises. The voice of religious activists, both in the very influential Protestant Social Gospel movement, as well as those of Jewish and Catholic actors, played a key role in motivating the enactment of such legislation by giving it a moral impetus, an impetus that reflects biblical commands. Key social legislation enacted during the New Deal era, that remains in effect as part of the social fabric, include the Fair Labor Standards Act (FLSA) of 1938 and the Social Security Act (SSA) of 1935.

Briefly summarized, the FLSA provides a minimum wage for covered employees, and requires the payment of time and one-half in weeks where time

---

[53] Letter from *Francis J. Haas* to the Rev. Edward Lodge Curran, President, International Catholic Truth Association (Aug. 31, 1933), American Catholic History Research Center & University Archives, Francis J. Haas Collection, folder 28, box 26.

[54] *Reinhold Fahlbeck*, The Demise of Collective Bargaining in the U.S.A.: Reflections on the Un-American character of American Labor Law, 15 Berkeley J. Emp. & Lab. L. 307 (1994).

worked by those employees exceeds forty hours. It restricts, but does not wholly prohibit labor by children older than fourteen years. It does not put a limit on working hours for adults, nor does it require vacations or holidays.

The Social Security Act established an old-age pension system through employer and employee contributions based on a payroll tax. It also established a joint state-federal unemployment compensation system, and a lump sum benefit to survivors. The system was and remains intended as a supplemental pension system, even though for many Americans, it constitutes the sole or chief source of retirement income. Coverage under the Act has been expanded over the decades, and it formed the basis for important programs like Medicare, which provides health insurance for persons from age 65 who have paid into the program. Support for both the FLSA and the SSA came from numerous quarters, including the Catholic "Bishops' Program of Social Reconstruction," promulgated in 1919 (and in which Peter Dietz and John Ryan both played roles in implementing), which made calls for legislation of the type these statutes reflect. Both the FLSA and the SSA reflect calls made in *Rerum Novarum* and *Quadragesimo Anno.* Catholic, Protestant and Jewish social activists regarded such legislation as part of a piece.

2. *Civil Rights Legislation and Religion*

Bluntly put, without the leadership of the African-American Protestant Churches, the Civil Rights Act of 1964 would never have come to pass. The Churches formed the nodal points for organizing efforts, and their ministers constituted the core of the Civil Rights Movement's leadership, as the membership of the Southern Christian Leadership Conference and the history of their undertakings testifies. It was not for nothing that the Ku Klux Klan bombed the Sixteenth Street Baptist Church in Birmingham, Alabama on a Sunday morning in September 1963, just prior to the beginning of services – a bombing that killed four girls. African-American churches have long been the targets of such attacks.

The moving history of the Civil Rights movement well exceeds the bounds of this paper. As was true of labor legislation, however, the key role of the Churches in the passage of the landmark Civil Rights Legislation of the 1960s, which includes not only the famous Civil Rights Act, but important enactments like the Voting Rights Act, rests in providing the motives that moved a Nation to act to attempt to remedy wrongs that go pre-date its founding.[55] One of the classic examples of the appeals that pricked the conscience of the United States, and that culminated decades worth of work with the enactment of long sought for

---

[55] On these points, see *Anthony E. Cook*, Beyond Critical Legal Studies: The Reconstructive Theology of Dr. Martin Luther King, Jr., 103 Harv. L. Rev. 985 (1990) (contending that Dr. King employed the specific religious and cultural experiences of African-Americans to explain his vision of a reconstructed society).

civil rights legislation, can be found in Dr. Martin Luther King's "Letter from a Birmingham Jail." Although the letter does use the sort of rights language so familiar to Americans, it gains its special force through the use of biblical language that demanded an examination of conscience of a Nation where a majority still saw itself as the heirs of a "Judeo-Christian" tradition. For example, in answering the question, "How can you advocate breaking some laws and obeying others?" King responds that "there are two types of laws, just and unjust," and he goes on to observe that he agrees "with St. Augustine that 'an unjust law is no law at all.'" What is the difference between them? A just law," King explains

> is a man-made code that squares with the moral law or the law of God. An unjust law is a code that is out of harmony with the moral law. To put it in the terms of St. Thomas Aquinas: An unjust law is a human law that is not rooted in eternal law and natural law. Any law that uplifts human personality is just. Any law that degrades human personality is unjust. All segregation statues are unjust because segregation distorts the soul and damages the personality. It gives the segregator a false sense of superiority and the segregated a false sense of inferiority. Segregation, to use the terminology of the Jewish philosopher Martin Buber, substitutes an "I-it" relationship for an "I-thou" relationship and ends up relegating persons to the status of things. Hence segregation is not only politically, economically and sociologically unsound, it is morally wrong and sinful.[56]

"One day," he observes in closing, "the South will know that when these disinherited children of God sat down at lunch counters, they were in reality standing up for what is best in the American dream and for the most sacred values in our Judaeo-Christian heritage, thereby bringing our nation back to those great well of democracy that were dug deep by the founding fathers in their formulation of the Constitution and the Declaration of Independence."

IV. The Weakened Role of the Religion and the Future of Labor and Social Legislation in the United States

The passage of the Civil Rights Acts in the mid-1960s also marked an important turn in American's religious attachments. During this period, some substantial changes in patterns of social bonding generally began to occur. After nearly two centuries of steady growth in their memberships, which roughly paralleled the growth in population, the twelve "mainline" Protestant Churches slowly began to lose members, and today, Protestants no longer make up a majority of the U.S. adult population.[57] Since 2007, the membership in mainline Protestant Churches

[56] *Martin Luther King*, "Letter from a Birmingham Jail", in: Why We Can't Wait (Signet Classic 2000) (1963), pp. 70–71.

[57] Pew Research Center, "Ten Facts about Religion Today", (August 27, 2015) available at http://www.pewresearch.org/fact-tank/2015/08/27/10-facts-about-religion-in-america/. Also see, Pew Research Center, America's Changing Religious Landscape: Christians Decline Sharply

appears to have declined by 5 million, and the number of Catholics by about 3 million. The numbers of those referred to as "nones," persons with no religious affiliation, have increased in that same period, and now, reports the Pew Research Center, are "more numerous than either Catholics or mainline Protestants," and presently are "second in size only to evangelical Protestants among major religious groups in the U.S."[58] These trends are not isolated: membership in unions as well as other forms of associations began declining in the 1960s as well, along with increases in marriage dissolutions, etc.

One can only speculate on what these trends might mean for future labor and social legislation in the United States. Politically and culturally, Americans are the children of John Locke while the thought of John Calvin continues to exercise a diffuse but important influence on many of our attitudes. As Americans, we come by our individualism honestly and I see no likelihood of that characteristic weakening. Unlike Germany, we have no Fichte (and, without a philosophical foundation, we have had no Bismarck to bring an articulated program of social legislation into political reality either). Americans do not understand the social contract as ensuring that everyone can live from his or her work and the reciprocal notion that individuals who cannot do so have a right to support. The welfare state or social state principle, as embedded in German or Western European thought, simply has no roots with us.[59] We remain, in large part, heirs of the ideas of the "night watchmen" state. The churches that once so effectively filled the "caritas gap" through far-reaching private activities have grown weak, and among the Catholics, the ranks of women and men in religious life who devoted their lives to an astonishing range of caritative activities have all but vanished. The *kenosis,* the death to the self, described by St. Paul has little if any meaning in a culture of self-sovereignty. Little wonder that the term solidarity remains so foreign to us.

"One of the gravest problems of our day is the lack of commitment to common symbols," Mary Douglas has observed.[60] In a highly individualist nation, religion once gave Americans a set of generally understood common symbols, a body of common understandings that, among other things, generally recalled to us our duties to others. As that commonality evaporates, and as the influence of religion both in public and in private life recedes, Americans are left with the language of individual rights. Such language is ultimately egocentric and makes resolution of clashing claims of rights seem arbitrary, at least to the losing side. It also suggests that we have no duties except those to which we consent. When

as Share of Population; Unaffiliated and Other Faiths Continue to Grow (May 12, 2015), available at http://www.pewforum.org/files/2015/05/RLS-08–26-full-report.pdf.

[58] Pew Research Center, America's Changing Religious Landscape, pp. 8–10.

[59] On Fichte and the welfare state, see, e. g., *Bärbel Frischmann*, "Fichte über den Rechtsstaat als Sozialstaat," Fichte-Studien, 29 pt. II (2006), pp. 45–55.

[60] *Mary Douglas*, Natural Symbols: Explorations in Cosmology, p. 1.

it comes to values, Americans appear to find increasingly little over which consensus exits.

Perhaps this helps to explain why matters like a national health insurance scheme remain so controversial in the United States, and that even long-established New Deal programs face criticism from a variety of quarters. We are aware of the quickly expanding income gap, the collapse of the middle class, and the disappearance of a sense of community among us. As all our social relations become more fragile and evanescent, an uncomfortable awareness seems to have slowly emerged that we must find some new way to conceive of how we bound to one another. This question has become all the more urgent in light of the unprecedented demand for immigration and the refugee crisis that confront us. The social question remains as pressing as ever, both on employment and social fronts, as well as on an international scale. I fear that without some re-thinking, at least in the American context, we will have no resources intelligently to address it. As I remarked at the beginning, perhaps the basic themes of this panel exceed its apparent boundaries and address the most contemporary of concerns.

The Significance of Religion for Turkish Labour and Social Legislation

Tankut Centel

I. Introduction

The element of religion is of particular importance in today's Turkish judicial system. This is due to the fact that, along with the proclamation of the Republic, Turkey started to lay the institutional foundation for the transition to a secular judicial system. Hence, along with the establishment of the Republic, efforts to develop a secular Turkish society were initiated. Accordingly, the Republic was proclaimed on 29 October 1923 and the caliphate was abrogated one year later, on 3 March 1924.

Secularity is the main ideological characteristic of the Turkish Constitution adopted after the establishment of the Republic in 1924. First, the basic laws of Western European countries have been translated into Turkish law and legislated. In this respect, the adoption of the Swiss Civil Code and Code of Obligations as the Turkish Civil Code and Turkish Code of Obligations has been the most important example in creating the Turkish secular judicial system. Similarly, the acceptance of civil courts instead of sharia courts constitutes the main example of the new secular period[1].

[1] *Nevhis Deren-Yıldırım*, 'Ein allgemeiner Überblick über das türkische Recht', Waseda Proceedings of Comparative Law, Vol. 7, 2004, p. 60.

Thereby, all Islamic influences have been removed from the current Turkish judicial system. Therefore, the law applicable in Turkey constitutes part of the continental European judicial system. However, the element of religion continued to be the nightmare of the Turkish judicial revolution. Also, during the transition to the multi-party system, which started in the 1950s, and the advent of politicians exploiting the religious feelings of society, the element of religion became increasingly important. In this respect, it is quite significant that a conservative looking party, one that gives importance to religious elements, is governing Turkey today.

The meaning of the element of religion regarding labour and social law in the Turkish judicial system has not been researched in depth. However, freedom of religion has a particular meaning in labour law from the point of Islam. Freedom of religion usually concerns workers' lives only outside the workplace. However, the religion of Islam – which does not separate the mundane and life after death – has a comprehension that regulates everyday life as well. That is the reason why a Muslim worker can face problems at his workplace because of his/her religion[2].

Furthermore, Turkish labour law has, so far, not dealt with the workers' freedom of religion and conscience in detail. This is due to the fact that the Turkish legislation, influenced by the principle of secularity, has been purified of religious elements. Accordingly, the element of religion is not obvious in legislative regulations; yet, if we consider the underlying impact, it contributes to achieving the objectives of Islam under the influence of social reality. In this respect, regulations influenced by the element of religion in labour and social legislation are fragmented, and it is not possible to put them on common ground. Therefore, we will try to reveal the importance of the abovementioned element of religion, providing research with a potential link between different legal regulations and the principles of Islam.

II. The concept of freedom of religion

1. Scope of freedom of religion

Freedom of religion tends towards the external sphere of the person (*forum externum*) and denotes the liberty of revealing his/her religion or belief by way of teaching, practice and doing worship and performing religious ceremonies alone or within a community. Accordingly, freedom of religion, in accordance with the requirements of the belief system of a person, is an acting-out from the inner sphere to the external sphere (*forum externum*). The notion of freedom of

[2] *Ufuk Aydın*, İş Hukukunda İşçinin Kişilik Hakları, Eskişehir 2002, p. 132.

conscience, which goes along with freedom of religion in Turkish law, concerns the belief system that only resides in the inner sphere of a person[3].

2. *A short overview of the evolution of freedom of religion in Turkey*

a) The period of the Ottoman Empire

Politics regarding the converting of non-Muslim persons to Islam were not examined during the Ottoman Empire. Thus, all non-Muslims were granted the rights corresponding to their proper religion, and their personal legal matters were delegated to their own spiritual leaders. However, this conception of tolerance during the Ottoman Empire did not mean that freedom of religion was recognized. As the Ottoman Empire did not rely on secular principles, and religious elements were particularly important in its governmental structure[4], freedom of religion and the protection of churches during the Tanzimat (reform) period in 1839 started to become a subject of foreign affairs for the leaders of the Ottoman Empire[5].

b) The period of the Republic

The 1924 Constitution of the Republic period regulated freedom of religion in secular terms (Articles 70 and 75). Indeed, the provision in the 1924 Constitution defining Islam as the religion of the Turkish State – which clashes with the principle of secularism (Article 2) – was abrogated by the amendment made in 1928.

Later, the Constitution of 1961 – which considers the principle of the secular State as a key feature of the Turkish Republic – presented the most widespread freedom of religion and conscience without making any distinction between the various religions[6].

c) Freedom of religion today

Freedom of religion has been secured via Article 24 of the 1982 Constitution, essentially on an individual basis. Accordingly:

> "Everyone has the freedom of conscience, religious belief and conviction.
> Acts of worship, religious rites and ceremonies shall be conducted freely, as long as they do not violate the provisions of Article 14.
> No one shall be compelled to worship, or to participate in religious rites and ceremonies, or to reveal religious beliefs and convictions, or to be blamed or accused because of his religious beliefs and convictions.

---

[3] *Hande Seher Demir*, Türkiye'de Din ve Vicdan Özgürlüğü, Ankara 2011, p. 7.

[4] *Bihterin Vural Dinçkol*, 1982 Anayasası Çerçevesinde ve Anayasa Mahkemesi Kararlarında Laiklik, Istanbul 1982, p. 24.

[5] *Demir*, op. cit., pp. 104–105.

[6] See *Dinçkol*, op. cit., p. 38.

[...]
No one shall be allowed to exploit or abuse religion or religious feelings, or things held sacred by religion, in any manner whatsoever, for the purpose of personal or political interest or influence, or for even partially basing the fundamental, social, economic, political, and legal order of the State on religious tenets".

Article 24 of the Constitution, which stipulates freedom of religion, is a warranty provision applicable to atheists and persons of Abrahamic and non-Abrahamic religions' adherents (workers). The provision in question owes its strength to the idea of secularism. Therefore, we cannot talk about freedom of religion without talking about the principle of secularity[7].

On the other hand, should freedom of religion essentially be attempted to be used to

- disrupt the integrity of the State,
- jeopardize the existence of the Turkish State and the Republic,
- remove the basic rights and freedoms,
- make a discrimination of religion and sect,

it shall be restricted by law (Article 14/II and III and Article 24 of the Constitution)[8]. The restrictions in question are generally considered as compatible with Article 9, Paragraph 2 of the European Convention on Human Rights, which supports the principle of the possibility of limiting freedom of religion for the purpose of protecting others' rights and freedoms, public safety, public order, general health and public moral.

3. The importance of freedom of religion for Turkish law

Freedom of religion gained significance in Turkey along with the creation of the modern Turkish State. Since the granting of freedom of religion is based on secularity, it was possible for Turkish law to gain a secular character only in line with the creation of the Republic. In this sense, the principle of secularity means that the power of sovereignty of the State is legitimized in a non-religious way, the State shall not intervene in religious affairs and religious influences shall be kept apart from State affairs[9].

During the Ottoman State, Turkey was influenced by Islamic law but the reforming acts of the end of the Ottoman period brought the dichotomy of Islamic law/Western law (secular law). Following the proclamation of the Republic, the dichotomous order in question was based on secularity, and the essence of secularity constituted the core and foundation of the reform movement undertaken.

---

[7] *Demir*, ibid., p. 16; *Dinçkol*, ibid., p. 67; *Bülent Tanör/Necmi Yüzbaşıoğlu*, 1982 Anayasasına Göre Türk Anayasa Hukuku, Istanbul 2001, pp. 166 and 67.

[8] See also *Dinçkol*, ibid., p. 81; *Christian Rumpf*, Laizismus und Religionsfreiheit in der Türkei, Ebenhausen 1987, p. 30.

[9] *Rumpf*, ibid., p. 18.

In this sense, efforts were made to remove religious references from the Turkish law system during the Republic period[10]. This was due to the circumstance that during the transition from the Ottoman State to the Turkish nation state, religious elements were considered to undermine the ideal of a democratic and secular order. However, the Republican government could not escape from the influence of the social reality and religious elements started to become influential in the course of the transition to the multi-party system.

III. The influence of religious elements on employment

1. The influence of religion on the individual employment contract

The employment contract shall be kept free from religious influences both during its drafting, its application and its termination. In this respect, Article 5/I of the Labour Act provides that the employment contract shall be kept free from religious themes and includes the provision that "*discrimination on grounds of religion or sect belief or due to similar reasons must not be allowed in labour relations*". However, there are different points of view concerning the scope of the provision in question.

a) Equality during recruitment

The expression "*labour relations*" as mentioned in Article 5/II of the Labour Act is a matter of debate regarding the question of whether or not the ban on discrimination in question actually includes the period prior to the drafting of the employment contract. By assuming that the provision in question does not include the period prior to the drafting of the employment contract, the possibility to prevent the employer from discriminating between people with specific beliefs during recruitment is annihilated.

Accordingly, the restrictive interpretation of Article 5/II of the Labour Act means that the employer can discriminate between people with specific beliefs before recruitment. In this case, with respect to the Turkish mosaic composed of non-Muslim Turkish citizens or foreigners and Muslims who may, at the same time, be members of different sects, we cannot ignore that this might lead to results which would not be validated by law.

On the other hand, Article 15/II of the Constitution provides that no one can be forced to declare his/her religious conscientious convictions and thoughts and be accused on grounds of these convictions. Thus, during the recruitment of the job candidate, no question related to religion may be asked; if, however, this should happen, this kind of question must not be taken into consideration,

[10] *Demir*, op. cit., p. 22.

except in cases where the job candidate is subject to work in a religious establishment[11].

b) Equality after establishment of a labour relation

Concerning the conditions of work and the termination of the employment contract by the employer, it is out of the question that the factor of being a member of a particular religion or sect may have any influence (Article 5/II of the Labour Act). Accordingly, in the case that discriminating conditions of work are imposed on the worker due to his/her religion or affiliation with a sect, or that the employment contract is terminated, the worker may claim damages equal to up to four months' wages and appertaining rights denied to him (Article 5/VI of the Labour Act).

Further, concerning workers who enjoy legal job security, it is provided that religion cannot be considered as a valid reason to terminate the employment contract (Article 18/III of the Labour Act).

Concerning the interdiction of discrimination on grounds of religion or affiliation to a sect, Article 5/I of the Labour Act and the regulation of Article 18/III of the Labour Act work along the same lines; yet, we can see that their range of protection is different. Also, both provisions aim at the same interdiction of discrimination (discrimination on grounds of religion or affiliation to a sect). However, in case of a discrepancy (during the lawsuit), if the worker does enjoy legal job security, it is up to him to prove that he has been discriminated against; if the worker does not enjoy legal job security, he/she does not have the responsibility to prove the facts; instead, it is up to the employer to do so, which means that the obligation to produce proof is with the other party.

2. Restrictive regulations on women's employment

a) In general

When looking at the working population in Islamic countries, it can be observed that the employment rate among women is remarkably low. However, during the period before Islam (the early 7th century), Arabic women were allowed to carry out economic activities and to trade on their own. Accordingly, the first wife of Muhammad, Hatice, managed a camel caravan business and shared parts of her benefit with the men working for her. However, we can observe that this right granted to women was abolished completely. In the system installed, women were obliged to stay at home in order to deal with the housework and to ask permission from their husbands for anything they wished to do. Concerning agricultural land, that is to say the working of women in the field, it became a

---

[11] *Şükran Ertürk*, İş İlişkisinde Temel Haklar, Ankara 2002, p. 74.

common task for women to do, as such work was considered as housework and did not need to be carried out in the presence of men[12].

The employment rate among women in Turkey with its Muslim majority is remarkably low as compared to that of EU countries, where the majority is not Muslim. The respective rates in 2013 were:
- 31.8 % for the 20/64 age group,
- 29.6 % for the 15/64 age group,
- 21.5 % for the 15/24 age group[13].

In this respect, it is obvious that restrictive measures on the employment of women have resulted in lower employment rates among women.

b) The place of the housewife in labour law

aa) Permission from the husband to the married woman who wants to work

After the proclamation of the Republic, the Swiss Civil Code was translated into Turkish law in order to be legitimated as the Turkish Civil Code. In this way, efforts were made to grant Turkish women the same rights as men during the new period, rights that they had been deprived of before. Yet, the former Turkish Civil Code – which continued to be applicable until 2002 – included some dispositions which did not serve this cause. One of these dispositions is Article 159 of the former Turkish Civil Code, which provided that a married woman had to get permission from her husband if she wanted to work either permanently or independently.

This means that during the period before 2002, women had to make a choice between work (profession) and marriage (family). During this period, a woman who knew that her husband-to-be would not give her permission to work, was obliged to abstain from working. If a married woman wanted to work without getting such a permission from her husband, she had the possibility to resort to the judge (to the court) and justify that the fact of her working would be beneficial for the continuation of the marriage union. However, enforcement of this decision frequently led to divorces due to severe marital conflicts. After all, husbands who did not accept the fact that their wives worked, tended to generate trouble in their marriage and this situation could end up in divorce.

The Constitutional Court abrogated this provision after 60 years of application (in 1990)[14] and the new Civil Code that became effective in 2002 got rid of

---

[12] *İlhan Arsel*, Şeriat ve Kadın, Istanbul 1991, p. 399.

[13] http://appsso.eurostat.etc.europa.eu/nui/submitViewTableAction.do?dvsc=9.

[14] See the verdict of the Constitutional Court, dated 29 November 1990, 30/31 – Official Gazette, 2 July 1992, No. 21272. In detail: *Hüseyin Hatemi*, 'MK 159 Kuralını İptal Eden Anayasa Mahkemesi Kararına İlişkin Düşünceler', İş Hukuku Dergisi, Vol. 2, No. 4, October-December 1992, p. 566; *Cevdet Yavuz*, 'Türk Hukukunda Kadının Çalışma Hakkı İle İlgili Düzenlemeler', Argumentum, Vol. 2, p. 224.

provisions which obligated women to obtain permission from their husbands to be allowed to work.

bb) Payment of severance pay to the married woman

Women workers who decide to quit their jobs during the year after concluding the marriage obtain the right to receive severance pay (Article 1/XIV of Labour Act No. 1475). This provision relies on the idea that a working woman should not be deprived of severance pay in case her recent husband does not approve of her working. The stipulation that a person who resigns voluntarily cannot receive severance pay would otherwise adversely affect women in the above situation.

The provision granting women who get married the right to receive severance pay was adopted during the period when a married woman had to get permission from her husband if she wished to work. However, despite the fact that the Civil Code now accepts that married women no longer need such a permission, the provision in question still prevails. Moreover, the Constitutional Court considered that the provision which grants the right to receive severance pay to women who get married was compatible with the Constitution and did not abrogate it[15].

It is disputable whether the fact that this provision grants severance pay to women workers who quit their jobs after getting married constitutes a positive form of discrimination or not[16]. At any rate, there are some situations in this case that need to be discussed with a view to the possible existence of positive discrimination.

The first of these situations is governed by the fact that married women no longer need permission from their husbands to work. The second situation revolves around the circumstance that women who quit their work after getting married are free to work somewhere else the day after having received the severance pay. In this respect, the Court of Cassation does not consider it an "abuse of a right"[17] if a working woman finds a new job and continues to work after having got married and received severance pay. To conclude, women who receive severance pay can in practice continue to work in the same workplace, provided that the employer accepts this. This situation disburdens women workers who need cash when getting married as severance pay is usually paid in cash. Also, the employer is relieved because he/she will need to pay less severance pay in the future as the severance pay is calculated by considering only the services after marriage.

---

[15] See the verdict of the Constitutional Court, dated 19 June 2008, 2006–156/125 – Official Gazette, 26 November 2008, No. 27066.

[16] *Tankut Centel*, 'Kıdem Tazminatında Pozitif Ayrımcılık', Sicil, Vol. 4, No. 15, September 2009, p. 5.

[17] Court of Cassation, General Council Decision, 27 April 1988, 9–225/369 – Cevdet İlhan Günay, *Şerhli İş Kanunu*, t. 1, Ankara 1988, p. 670 No. 13; Court of Cassation, 9th Div., 25 Jan. 2001, 2000–16313/1306 – İşveren, Vol. 35, No. 11, August 2001, pp. 17–18.

In contrast, women workers who know that they will receive and save the severance pay thanks to getting married will be more willing to quit their work and to accept a life as a housewife. In addition to that, women workers, after having received their severance pay, are likely to continue to benefit from their insurances, as premiums will be paid on their behalf by the husband; this means that they will be entitled to receive pension payments in the future without having worked; or they will claim from the State the repayment of insurance premium payments made before the marriage, alleging the reason of marriage as a justification[18]. The fact that this situation encourages women to refrain from working cannot be ignored[19].

c) The socio-legal position of the married woman

aa) Civil marriage and the payment of widow's pension

Regulations restricting women's employment are targeting married women on the basis of the existence of a civil marriage. Thus, the "imam marriage" element which constitutes a social reality in terms of marriage has to be taken into consideration.

(1) The place of religious marriage in Turkish society

The reality is that civil marriage for the first time appeared in Turkey along with the adoption of the Turkish Civil Code in 1926. Accordingly, the principles of monogamy and the celebration of marriage in an official service started to lay the foundations of Turkish society under the Republic regime from this date. However, this reality does not constitute a barrier to concluding a religious marriage after the civil marriage. However, concluding a religious marriage prior to the civil marriage is subject to penal sanctions provided by the Turkish Penal Code.

Therefore, in the case of multiple marriages, a person who concludes a marriage while he/she is already married is subject to a prison sentence ranging from six months to two years according to Article 230/I of the Turkish Penal Code.

Concerning imam marriage, a prison sentence ranging from two months to six months is given to persons who have a religious marriage ceremony without being officially married. However, provided that the civil marriage is concluded thereafter, public prosecutions and adjudicated punishments will be withdrawn along with all the consequences (Article 203/V of the Turkish Penal Code). Accordingly, a person who has a religious ceremony (imam marriage) without having presented the document showing that the marriage act has been conclud-

---

[18] See III 2 c bb and cc below.

[19] *Kadriye Bakırcı*, 'İstihdamda Cinsiyetler Arası Eşitlik ve Mevzuatta Yapılması Gereken Değişiklikler', Sicil, Vol. 2, No. 8, December 2007, p. 35; *Şükran Ertürk*, Çalışma Hayatımızda Kadın Erkek Eşitliği, Ankara 2008, p. 188.

ed according to the law, is subject to a prison sentence ranging from two months to six months according to Article 230/V of the Turkish Penal Code.

Despite all these provisions, the number of people who are still living in an imam marriage cannot be underestimated. Therefore, according to the data of the Turkish Statistical Institute, while the percentage of people who both have a religious (church) wedding and a civil (official) wedding is 93.7 %, the percentage of people who only have a civil wedding is 3.3 %, and that of people who only get religiously married is 3 %. While the percentage of only religiously married people is 8.3 % in Southeastern Anatolia, this percentage falls to 0.9 % in South Marmara[20]. However, we have to keep in view that the number of people who get married by an imam tends to decrease compared to the past[21].

(2) The non-attribution of allowance to the religiously married wife

The widow of a deceased insured person is one of the persons who can benefit from the burial insurance. In this respect, as provided by legislation, 'bonds of matrimony' shall exist for the beneficiary to be considered as the widowed spouse of the deceased insured person. Accordingly, in case of the nonexistence of official bonds of matrimony between the deceased insured person and his widowed spouse, the payment of burial allowance to the surviving spouse is out of the question[22]. Thus, a merely religiously married spouse will not be able to benefit from burial allowance due to the nonexistence of a civil marriage between the insured person meanwhile deceased and herself.

The payment of burial allowance to the officially married spouse is subject to some exceptions. The first of these exceptions refers to civil marriages concluded before the application of the Turkish Civil Code in 1926. According to this, in case of death of an insured person who got married more than once before the application of the Turkish Civil Code, the burial allowance is equally shared between any surviving spouses. If one of these allowances is cut, the allowance of this person will be added onto the allowances of the other surviving spouses (Transitional Article 14 of Law No. 506; Article 70 of Law No. 5434).

The second exception provision, the "Act on unpunished registration of children born from unofficial unions", concerns the spouses. These are the mothers of children born out of wedlock but registered (recognized) at a later stage . The persons in question are considered as rightholders in terms of burial insurance and it is accepted that they benefit from burial allowance[23].

---

[20] www.tuik.gov.tr/PreHaberBultenleri.do?id=13662.

[21] See www.sdergi.hacettepe.edu.tr/makaleler/ycik.pdf.

[22] *Ali Güzel/Ali Rıza Okur/Nurşen Caniklioğlu*, Sosyal Güvenlik Hukuku, Istanbul 2014, pp. 710 and 721.

[23] Ibid., p. 710 fn. 9.

Apart from the two exceptions mentioned above, civil marriage is required for allowances to be granted and spouses married by an imam cannot be beneficiaries of burial allowances. In this respect, a recently taken decision by the Court of Cassation has accurately stipulated that the spouse in question, who was married by an imam, cannot be holder of the right to the burial allowance of her deceased spouse who was supporting her financially[24]. The legal justification of the Court of Cassation on this subject is mainly based on the fact that according to current national law, the imam marriage performed by an imam cannot constitute an obligation for third parties or for the State.

The result of this decision is accurate within the framework of the legislation in force. However, there are arguments that persons considered as not holding any rights under this law (i. e. the spouse married by an imam who was supported financially by the insured person) are nevertheless able to benefit from burial allowance, provided that there is a portion remaining as an augmented share of that allowance[25].

bb) The return of premiums to a woman that is to be married

Additional Article 1 to Social Insurance Act No. 506 has granted the right termed "*full payment*" to women workers in order for them to reacquire the total of insurance premiums paid until the date they got married during the year that they quit their work or for those who quit their work during the year of their marriage (Paras. 1 and 2).

Accordingly, half of the insurance premiums regarding disability, old-age and death that they and their employers paid will be fully refunded, upon written request, to women workers who quit their work due to marriage. This payment is called "full marriage payment" as it is made in the case that the insured person gets married.

Although the full marriage payment has a security function for women workers, it is to simplify their rupture with working life. Fact is that women workers who know that the premiums they pay until they get married will not be lost but be paid back to them, will more readily stop working and get married to a person who does not accept that the wife works.

Women workers who receive the full marriage payment reset their insurance period with effect from the date of receipt of the payment. However, women workers who are supposed to start working again after having received the full marriage payment, can reactivate their reset insurance period provided that they pay back the amount they got. Therefore, women workers who are supposed to go back to work after having received the full marriage payment can recover

[24] Court of Cassation, 10th Div., 1 March 2010, 2008–18155/2758 – Sicil, Vol. 6, No. 22, June 2011, p. 180.

[25] See *Kadir Arıcı*, 'Ölüm Sigortasından Yararlanma', Sicil, Vol. 6, No. 22, June 2011, p. 186.

the lost previous benefits provided that they pay back the premiums with an interest of 5 % from the date they received the marriage payment. The insurance period of women workers who do not pay back the premiums they have received resumes on the date they go back to work; in turn the lost insurance periods are not taken into account for the calculation of later benefits (Additional Article 1/III of Social Insurance Act No. 506).

However, as women workers who have received the full marriage payment are free to work again, the main part of Social Insurance Act No. 506 has been abrogated and has been replaced today by the Social Security and Universal Health Insurance Act No. 5510, which does not accept the full marriage payment. The fact that the full marriage payment option is not provided by law in the new legislation is considered as an accurate step to prevent this payment from encouraging women workers to quit their jobs and to be cooped up at home[26].

cc) The right of social insurance to the non-working married woman

Married women have the right to benefit from retirement and general insurance without working and within this framework, to be retired in the future and receive retirement pay by means of the provisions of "optional insurance" (Articles 50–52 of Act No. 5510).

In reality, the optional insurance of Act No. 5510 is a kind of "elective insurance" (Article 50 of Act No. 5510) for persons who want to benefit from retirement and general health insurance by way of paying a voluntary premium. Thus, persons who had "compulsory insurance" earlier and who

- do not work as compulsorily insured workers,
- did not receive allowances for their own insurances,
- are older than 18 years,
- have applied to the Social Security Institution,

can maintain their insurances provided that these conditions are met[27].

The second group of persons who meet these conditions, i. e. married women who stop working, has the right to benefit from the optional insurance. Thus, the husband will probably pay the woman's premiums and the latter will have the guarantee to receive burial allowance provided that she exclusively stays at home and takes care of her family (i. e. of the needs of the husband and children). It is obvious that this situation encourages married women to quit working life.

[26] See *also Ali Nazım Sözer*, Türk Sosyal Sigortalar Hukuku, Istanbul 2013, p. 384.

[27] See *Yusuf Alper*, Sosyal Sigortalar Hukuku, Bursa 2014, p. 116; *Güzel/Okur/Caniklioğlu*, op. cit., p. 215; *Sözer*, ibid., p. 12.

IV. The role of religion in the organization of work

1. The use of weekend holidays

After the proclamation of the "Republic" of the Turkish State on 29 October 1923, the Act on Weekend Holidays No. 394 was accepted[28]. Consequently, in all the industrial and commercial workplaces of cities with a population of more than 10,000 inhabitants, work will stop during one day per week and workers who work six days per week will have the right to rest for at least one day (Article 1 of Act No. 394).

Because of its importance for Muslims, the holiday of the week has been proclaimed to be "Friday" by Act No. 394. However, this has been changed and Friday has been replaced by "Sunday" by Article 3 of Act No. 2739 dated 27 May 1935, which took effect on 1 June 1935.

Act No. 2739, which adopted Sunday as the holiday of the week was abrogated on 17 March 1981 by the Act on Bank Holidays and General Public Holidays. However, Act No. 2429 has conserved the fact of Sunday being the holiday of the week (Article 3/A of Act No. 2429), is still applicable and the regulation concerning the fact of Sunday being the holiday of the week has not been directly repealed due to concerns that it might generate a community backlash. However, the still applicable Labour Act No. 4857 adopted on 22 May 2003[29] has definitely withdrawn the matter in question. Hence, "at least twenty-four hours of uninterrupted rest (week holiday) within a period of seven days of work" is to be given (Article 46/I of the Labour Act). In this way, the fact that a worker has worked on a Sunday will not mean that he/she has not already used the weekend holiday, provided that he/she is required to take a holiday on a day other than Sunday.

During the period of enactment of the Labour Act, some secular circles were concerned about the fact that Friday might be reaccepted as a free day. The employer class who had permanently asked for flexibility so far, stayed quiet in view of these concerns.

The new Labour Act has legally smoothed the way so that employers can chose Friday as the holiday of the week in the workplace instead of Sunday. In this case, the employers can give their workers a holiday on a particular day according to the environment (situation and conditions).

[28] Official Gazette, 21 January 1924, No. 54.
[29] Official Gazette, 10 June 2003, No. 25134.

2. *The use of the right to a holiday on religious holidays*

a) Religious holidays recognized by the law

Act No. 2429 accepted religious holidays as holidays along with bank holidays and official holidays. Therefore, the Ramadan Feast of 3.5 days and the Feast of the Sacrifice of 4.5 days are some of the religious holidays (Article 2/B of Act No. 2429).

As we can notice, the religious days recognized by the law as religious holidays concern only Muslims. The reason for this is naturally related to the fact that the majority of the Turkish population is Muslim.

However, this does not mean that non-Muslims will not celebrate their own religious holidays. Thus, workers and employers must agree on the fact that taking a holiday on the other religious holiday respectively can be considered as a right. In cases where such an agreement has not been made, it is not possible for non-Muslims to take a holiday on their own religious holidays and claim this as a right from their employer.

b) Rest during religious holidays

The worker has the right to rest on holidays. In this way, the worker enjoys the possibility to rest and to perform religious duties during a total of eight religious holidays per year.

Due to the fact that religious holidays are considered as holidays pursuant to Act No. 2429, the employer cannot force the worker to work on these days, and in the case that the worker refuses to work, the employer cannot terminate the employment contract on this ground. If this was to happen, the termination of employment effected by the employer would count as unjustified termination of the contract.

c) Remuneration during religious holidays

The employer is obliged to pay the full day of the worker without asking any work in return, irrespective of the worker's religion, during days which have been accepted as religious holidays by Act No. 2429 (Article 47/I of the Labour Act; Article 43/I of the Maritime Labour Act).

On the other side, workers can accept to work during religious holidays. In this case, workers who do not take the holiday off will be paid for each day they work instead (Article 47/I of the Labour Act). Work conducted on a religious holiday is paid double. This means that workers who accept to work on religious holidays will not receive one but two days' wage.

3. *The effect of religion on working time*

a) Practicing worship during break

Praying five times per day constitutes the basis of the religion of Islam. Furthermore, the Friday prayer performed in the group (within the religious community) around noon is of particular importance and involves a special procedure. From this perspective, the question of stopping the production during the abovementioned periods and of giving or not giving workers the possibility to worship is an issue troubling the existing legal system, but ultimately a question of organization within the workplace.

The function of organizing working time, as a general rule, rests with the employer. Accordingly, the person who has to determine the starting and finishing hours of work at the working place is the employer. That is why the employer is obliged to inform workers at their workplaces on the starting and finishing hours along with break times (Article 67/I of the Labour Act).

There is no legal obligation for the employer to take into consideration the period of prayers and especially of Friday prayer while determining break times. Therefore, Article 24 of the Constitution, while highlighting that everyone has the right to freedom of religion and conscience, assuring the right to participate in a religious ceremony and rites and not being obliged to declare his/her convictions, does not contain a provision which would aim to guarantee the right of practicing worship (Paras. 1 and 2).

In the same line, Article 68/I of the Labour Act precises that the break has to be determined at an average time of the working day and according to the needs of the workplace and the local customs. Besides, it is mentioned that the midday break should be used according to the climate, season, local customs and the nature of the workplace (Article 68/III of the Labour Act), but religious elements (prayer times) are not included in this scope.

For this reason, and as employers and workers mostly have the same religion in practice, it is preferable to ask for the employer's discretion instead of forcing the former to determine the rest periods according to prayer times; alternatively, respective provisions can be laid down on this subject in the collective labour agreement.

b) Worship at work

In the religion of Islam, it is not compulsory to worship in a group except for the Friday prayer. Thus, the question of praying at work will arise when prayer time coincides with presence expected at work. In such a case, if the employer grants authorization to the worker to worship at the workplace, he will need to assign the worker a special place for this purpose.

In January 2016, the Prime Ministry circularized that employees of public institutions and establishments who so desire will be given time off for Friday prayer, even if the time overlaps with working hours, without causing a loss in working hours[30]. In response to this, a lawsuit was filed with the Council of State, Turkey's highest administrative court, arguing that the government order goes against Turkey's secular Constitution and the new prayer practice is an exploitation of religion for political goals[31].

However, there is no provision in the legislation which obliges the employer to open a prayer room or a masjid (Islamic prayer room) at the workplace. In this case, the employer can assign a special place for worship. Even though it is not mentioned in the legislation, the parties can include provisions in the collective labour agreement in order to have a place for worship assigned at work[32]. This kind of provision in a collective labour agreement regarding religion and the conscience of freedom is legally valid and not contradictory to the Constitution and the imperative provisions of laws (Article 33/V of the Act on Unions and Collective Labour Agreement).

4. The limits of freedom of dress at work

The way of dressing and appearance is one of the worker's personal rights. In this respect, the way of dressing and appearance are considered to be individual rights of expression of the worker. Thus, be it eye-catching or conservative attire, it is considered as a notion proper to the dress sense of each worker.

However, it can be the case that the nature of the work obliges the worker to dress in a particular way or in good attire. Accordingly, work in a healthy and safe environment may require a particular dresscode and appearance. In this regard, the fact that the employer can impose a special dresscode or attire on the worker (or forbid the latter to wear certain clothes) constitutes a problem.

When we consider the freedom of dress and appearance only from the religious perspective, especially with regard to women workers in relation to the Islamic form of dressing and headscarf, or in respect to men regarding the fact of their wearing a beard or a tie, we see that this can pose a problem in practice.

In this respect, if we firstly take in hand the decisions taken by the Court of Cassation concerning workers who refuse to shave or trim their beards and wear them at work, it is difficult to say whether the Court of Cassation has settled a decision on whether wearing a beard or refusing to shave it due to employer-imposed demands does or does not constitute a reason for justified termination of

---

[30] Official Gazette, 8 January 2016, No. 29587.

[31] http://www.aljazeera.com/news/2016/01/turkey-court-challenge-friday-prayer-time-160108171547568.html; http://www.al-monitor.com/pulse/originals/2016/01/turkey-friday-prayer-criteria-for-schools.html.

[32] See V 4 below.

the employment contract. Thus, the Court of Cassation in some cases accepted the circumstance that wearing a beard and letting it grow was not a legitimate reason for a termination of contract[33]. On the other hand, the insistence of a person working as a chef to keep his beard despite cease-and-desist warnings and pay cuts is not considered compatible with health regulations and the particular nature of the work[34]. Correspondingly, it can be said that the employer can intervene with regard to the way of dressing and appearance of the worker according to the particularities of the work, within the framework of the customary and the principle of good faith[35].

Concerning the subject of Islamic form of dressing and headscarf for women workers, it is accepted that the employer requires the workers not to use clothes and accessories which demonstrate their religious beliefs or politic views. After all, this way of dressing and appearance will jeopardize the impression that the employer would like to make on the community[36]. Especially the neutrality of public servants has become a requirement of secularism. This is because public servants are understood as representing the State, and are therefore responsible for protecting the values of collective life[37].

On the other side, the bases applicable for private sector workplaces are even more frequent in the public workplaces. However, the way of dressing and appearance of workers in public workplaces is subject to the "*Regulations on Dress Code for Personnel of Public Institutions and Establishments*" of 1982[38].

In the regulations mentioned above, there is an effort to ensure that "the public officials dress with decorum and without excess keeping with the reforms of Atatürk" (Article 1 of the Regulations on Dress Code). Accordingly, women workers cannot wear sleeveless and shirts with a very low-cut neckline, blouses or dresses, jeans, stretch and legwear of similar fabric and cut; the length of their skirts shall not be shorter than knee-length and their skirts shall not be slit. Further, the clothes of male workers shall be clean, decent, ironed and simple and their shoes shall be closed, clean and polished. Workers should be bareheaded inside the building or during the accomplishing of their mission (Article 5/a and b of the Regulations on Dress Code). Concerning the provisions on the dresscode for officials working in religious affairs related to the Religious Affairs Directorate, they are applied within the framework of the basis defined and approved by the Directorate (Article 5/c of the Regulations on Dress Code).

---

[33] Court of Cassation, 9th Div., 6 February 2001, 2000–18594/1750 – Kazancı Hukuk Otomasyon 2.0, İçtihat Bilgi Bankası; *Aydın*, op. cit., p. 116.

[34] *K. Ahmet Sevimli*, İşçinin Özel Yaşamına Müdahalenin Sınırları, Istanbul 2006, p. 232 fn. 574.

[35] *Aydın*, op. cit., p. 117.

[36] *Sevimli*, op. cit., p. 234.

[37] *Amélie Barras*, Refashioning Secularisms in France and Turkey. The Case of the Headscarf Ban, London 2014, pp. 45–46.

[38] Official Gazette, 25 October 1982, No. 17849.

The rights and functions of the employer of the public sector are considerably restricted in light of the provisions mentioned above[39]. Moreover, it is legally not possible, even on the condition that agreement is made with the labour union, that the employer accepts provisions contradictory to the provisions in question in the collective labour agreement. The reason is that the regulation in question prohibits the provision of dispositions contrary to the bases mentioned in the collective labour agreement (Article 13/I of the Regulations on Dress Code).

V. Religious patterns in collective labour law

1. Freedom of association of religious officials

a) The right to unionize and to be member of a union

First of all, workers can, under their employment contract unionize or be member of an existing labour union (Article 2/IV, 6/I, 17/I of the Act on Unions and Collective Labour Agreement).

In addition, persons who carry out independent/freelance professional operations against a fee without any employment contract but according to agreements related to transportation, attorneyship, publications, commission fees and ordinary company agreements, have been granted the right to unionize (Article 2/IV of the Act on Unions and Collective Labour Agreement). Accordingly, independent drivers, carriers, writers, attorneys, commissioners and associates of ordinary companies have the right to unionize or be members of similar unions already existing provided that they do not work in accordance with an employment contract.

However, workers in religious workplaces and places of worship do not fall within the scope described. In this sense, the question arises as to what might be the union rights of workers in religious workplaces and places of worship which do not depend on an employment contract.

b) The situation of religious officials

Concerning religious officials, their affiliation is connected to the Religious Affairs Directorate, which in turn is connected to the Presidency. Religious officials of the Religious Affairs Directorate shall be subject to the Act on the Structure and the Missions of Religious Affairs Directorate No. 633 and Civil Servants Act No. 657. Accordingly, we have to say that workers in religious workplaces are in reality working under the status of "*civil servant*" in the Turkish law system.

---

[39] See also Barras, op. cit., pp. 48–49.

The unionization of religious officials who are not religious civil servants has already been prohibited in Turkey earlier on. However, Act on Labour Unions No. 274 (Article 4/I c) of 1963 and also Act on Labour Unions No. 2821 (Article 21/I 3) of 1983, provided that workers in religious workplaces and places of worship shall not be members of a labour union. During the acceptation of Act No. 274, this decision was justified, as "the religious activities have a divine character that would require to consider different kinds of discrepancies between the citizens"[40]. Besides, the interdiction in question not only concerns the religion of Islam today but also workers in religious workplaces and places of worship[41].

The interdiction of unionizing for workers in religious places and places of worship was repealed in 1988 by Article 17 of Act No. 3449[42]. However, the repeal of the act in question has not been so important. Fact is that it is important for persons in religious places and places of worship working as civil servants within the framework of the Religious Affairs Directorate to unionize within the framework of civil servants' labour unions. The unionizing of civil servants only appeared in Turkey in line with the efforts of democratization in 1995.

In the Turkey of today, where civil servants and other public workers have the freedom of association, there are no more obstacles for religious servants: they can also "unionize among civil servants" and be a member of these unions as provided by Act No. 4688. Therefore, service branch number 11, which is counted in the branches that can be created by the civil servants' union, is divided between "religious affairs and religious foundations services" (Article 5 of Act No. 4688).

2. The religious bases of the unions

a) In compliance with the characteristics of the Republic and democracy

The unions and the confederations cannot act in contradiction with the characteristics of the Republic and the democratic principles. Thus, the status, management and operation of the unions and confederations cannot be in contradiction with the principal characteristics of the Republic and democratic principles (Article 51/VI of the Constitution).

The principal characteristics of the Republic are explained in Article 2 of the Constitution. Accordingly, the Republic of Turkey is a democratic and secular State governed by the rule of law, respecting human rights, and loyal to the nationalism of Atatürk.

Concerning the democratic principles, they are relatively wide. To give a few examples, it is possible to quote basic principles like the attribution of function to managers by election, the right of management of the majority, equal treatment,

---

[40] *Öner Eyrenci*, Sendikalar Hukuku, Istanbul 1984, p. 106.
[41] See *Ergun İnce*, Toplu İş İlişkileri, Istanbul 1983, p. 73.
[42] Official Gazette, 8 June 1988, No. 19830.

the protection of the basic freedoms of the members and the application of the principle of secret vote/public count during elections[43].

b) The closing of establishments in contradiction with the established regime

aa) Contradictory activities

Article 31/I of the Act on Unions and Collective Labour Agreement provides that unions and confederations in contradiction with the characteristics of the Republic and democratic principles mentioned in the Constitution shall be closed. If the activities in question are led only by the managers of labour unions and confederations, their functions will be terminated by the court in accordance with the same provision.

On this subject, we should not lose sight of the provision of Article 24/V of the Constitution. Accordingly, "no one can use the social, economic, political and legal organization of the State, based on religious rules, in order to misuse and abuse religious feelings or matters considered as sacred by religion whatsoever the purpose, to obtain political or personal benefit or to ensure an influence". Thus, with regard to unions and confederations acting in order to exploit religious feelings of the community or use religious bases of the principal organization of the Turkish State, Article 31/I (the closing of these unions by court judgment) applies.

On the other side, the provision on the closing of unions is compatible with the consideration of these kinds of activities related to religion in terms of political activity. This is because the interdiction provided by Article 24/V of the Constitution is also applicable to political parties which will act in this way. In this regard, as political parties that act using the religious bases of the Turkish State will be closed by the Constitutional Court, no support of these parties from unions and confederations will be possible. If the unions and confederations act in violation of this principle, they will be confronted at the risk of being closed in the same way as political parties.

bb) Closing by court order

Unions and confederations which act in violation of the characteristics of the Republic and democratic principles in the Constitution in that they make use of religious bases are closed by labour court decision upon request of the public prosecutor (Article 31/I of the Act on Unions and Collective Labour Agreement). In this respect, the fact that administrative authorities do not have the function to stop particular activities and to close such unions and confederations constitutes an insurance with a view to the protection of the freedom of association.

[43] *Fevzi Şahlanan*, Sendikaların İşleyişinin Demokratik İlkelere Uygunluğu, Istanbul 1980, p. 45.

3. The approach of current unions to religious subjects

As demonstrated above[44], the creation and activity of unions and confederations based on religious principles is out of the question. However, it is not legally empeachable that the organizations in question and their directions have different approaches to religious subjects which constitute their bases at the same time.

a) On the working class

We can see three different workers' confederations at the level of the working class. One of them is the Confederation of Turkish Trade Unions (Türk-İş), a superordinate institution established in 1952 which has the most significant number of workers as members. The Türk-İş aims to protect and develop the rights and profits of workers in the understanding of the secular State, pluralistic and liberal-democratic rules and Atatürk's principles (Article 2 of the Statute of Türk-İş).

The Türk-İş is composed of working class members, generally conservatives, but is not putting forward religious elements. The main reason for this is that the Türk-İş adopted a politics which tends to stay neutral towards political powers and the phenomenon named "politics above political parties".

However, this politics has resulted in the establishing of the Confederation of Progressive Trade Unions (DISK). In this respect, DISK is a trade union whose main principle is to ensure solidarity between workers without distinguishing in terms of beliefs, religion or sect (Article 3 of the Statute of DISK).

On the other hand, Hak-İş (the Confederation of Turkish Real Trade Unions), which was created in 1976, has embraced the working class, which fights for freedom, giving utmost importance to religious elements.

Despite all these separations and divisions Türk-İş continues to be the most powerful trade union in Turkey nowadays.

b) From the employer's side

aa) The tendency of the employing professional associations

There is only one organization in terms of employing professional associations, which is the Turkish Confederation of Employer Associations (TISK). The TISK, which was established in 1962, has adopted as a basic principle the utmost encouragement of secularity and of the liberal parliamentary democratic regime[45].

---

[44] See V 2 above.

[45] http://tisk.org.tr/tr/Tisk-Temel-ilkeleri.

There is no evidence of any problem on the part of TISK as regards religious issues. The reason for this, as demonstrated below[46], is that the employer class (capital) – which gives importance to religious elements and uses this as a relationship opportunity – is active in voluntary associations of entrepreneurs.

bb) The approach of employing associations

(1) Associations of voluntary entrepreneurs

Employing associations which play an important role in working life are the Turkish Industry and Business Association (TUSIAD), the Independant Industrialist and Businessmen Association (MUSIAD), the Anatolian Lions Businessmen Association (ASKON) and the Confederation of Businessmen and Industrialists of Turkey TUSKON). One of the organizations mentioned, TUSIAD, represents important capital regarding the size of the entreprises of the members. We can say that the members of the other organizations represent rather medium and low capital.

One of these organizations, the Turkish Industry & Business Association (TUSIAD) established in 1971, aims to create and develop a collaborative organization adopted by the secular State of law in addition to other principles (Article 2 of the Statute of TUSIAD). It has been observed that, in response to this, the prominent characteristics of the members of MUSIAD composed of industrialists and businessmen are especially religious.

(2) The relations between the government and the business world

The first step of Turkish industrialization has developed in the industry and commerce chambers, membership of which is compulsory for industrialists and merchants. Regarding this step, the principal particularity of the business world is that the relations between the government and the managers of the chambers are based on representation of profit. Along with the development of the private sector, the associations of voluntary entrepreneurs started to gain influence in the 1970s. One of them, which has preserved its particularly active role and importance, TUSIAD, is not unrivalled and new (other) entrepreneurial organizations have come to compete in the business world.

However, the relations between the government and the entrepreneurs in question are undergoing a particular evolution today. In reality, since the growing influence of political Islam from the 1990s onwards, the government has developed close relations with some of these voluntary employer associations. In this respect, MUSIAD kept close relations with the only party representing

[46] See V 3 b bb (2) below.

political Islam in the 1990s. Whereas ASKON and TUSKON are two further organizations of entrepreneurs established later, their members – who form part of the political Islamic class – have been maintaining close relations with the government. Besides, President Erdoğan announced recently that he will no longer participate in TUSIAD meetings[47].

These three organizations, which focus on the element of religion in their relations with the government, are set against TUSIAD which aims at the creation of a secular law order. The use of religion as a reference in economic and political relations has led to a highly polarized business life. Accordingly, the new capitalism in Turkey has to take into consideration religious relations from now on with regard to all business relations[48].

4. Collective bargaining in relation to religion

The parties of the collective labour agreements (partners) can, usually within the framework of the autonomy of establishing general labour agreements that has been granted to them, include in the collective labour agreements provisions concerning religion or considering religious elements. However, the collective labour agreement cannot contain provisions in contradiction with the statutory legal provisions and the provisions of the Constitution (Article 33/V of the Act on Unions and Collective Labour Agreement).

Besides, the regulation on the dresscode of public workers[49] stipulates its provisions as indispensable and impossible to be amended via collective labour agreements. Accordingly, it is not legally possible to adopt provisions in contradiction with the provisions of the regulation in question, not even with the consent of the public sector employer and the trade union. The reason for this is that the regulation in question prohibits the establishment of provisions in contradiction with the provisions of the former (Article 13/I of the Regulations on Dress Code). This absolutely compulsory regulation concerning the dresscode became important due to a collective labour agreement between a military naval shipyard command and a trade union whose managers were close to a religious class. The penalty rules relevant to this collective agreement accepted that a public worker who wears a beard is not subject to penalties and increasingly not subject to a justified termination of the employment contract. However, the Court of Cassation, which debated on this, has considered the termination of the employment contract as unjustified[50] without mentioning the mandato-

---

[47] http://www.hurriyet.com.tr/ekonomi/27863705.asp.

[48] *Ayşe Buğra/Osman Savaşkan*, Türkiye'de Yeni Kapitalizm, Istanbul 2014, p. 34.

[49] See IV 4 above.

[50] Court of Cassation, 9th Div., 6 February 2001, 2000–18594/1750 – Kazancı Hukuk Otomasyon 2.0, İçtihat Bilgi Bankası.

ry provision of the regulation with regard to the dresscode of public workers (Article 13/I)[51].

Apart from that, there is no legal interdiction for the parties of the collective labour agreement to consider the period of Friday prayer or daily normal prayer periods as free times or midday break, or for them to decide that no one shall work during religious feast days, or for them to grant social help by giving extra remuneration to fasting persons who do not eat at work during the month of Ramadan, or for the employer to provide a prayer room or to designate places at work intented for such purposes in the collective labour agreement.

VI. The importance of religious communities with respect to social law

1. Religious foundations

Apart from intra-familial solidarity and professional organizations (guilds) during the Ottoman Empire, other charity organizations have also played an important role concerning the protection of the poor. These organizations are mainly based on religious rules and customs. For instance, thanks to donations and handouts like zakat and fitre (special islamic charity) we can say that the religion of Islam helps the poor through the help of the wealthy. Apart from this individual form of social solidarity, associations which were common in the Ottoman Empire have assumed the function of organization for this kind of social help. These organizations, which owe their emergence and development to the appeal of Islam to kindness and charity, have not only established the public services but also helped the poor in case of disease or in other difficult situations[52].

As there is no church tax or similar fee in Turkey, and as the financial resources of the Religious Affairs Presidency are limited[53], the old islamic tradition has been continued by keeping up the religious activities via the foundations. However, the religious foundations of the Republic period have been under the control of the State within the framework of the law[54].

The religious foundations mainly focus on the maintenance of mosques and the organization of religious schools in terms of Qur'an courses; they also encourage religious and cultural activities.

---

[51] *Sevimli*, op. cit., p. 268.

[52] *Güzel/Okur/Caniklioğlu*, op. cit., p. 30.

[53] See for the social activities of the Religious Affairs Presidency: http://www.diyanetvakfi.org.tr/5/ faaliyetler/yurtici-ve-yurtdisi-yonelik-hizmetler/hayri-ve-sosyal-hizmetler.

[54] *Rumpf*, op. cit., p. 152.

2. Community Foundations

The present Community Foundations are charity foundations constituted by the non-Muslim Turkish people before the establishment of the Republic. These foundations are various public legal entities (Article 4 of the Foundations Act) managed by the rules fixed by a direction selected by their own members (Article 6 of the Foundations Act). However, as it is not legally possible to create a foundation in order to support a particular community, it is also not possible to create a new Community Foundation. The Community Foundations which were created earlier, as sother foundations in Turkey, are monitored by the General Directorate of Foundations and the number of these foundations is still at 166[55]. However, as the creation of such a foundation is not possible and considering the efforts to change the inflexibility of previously established foundations, we cannot speak of functions of social help and solidarity on the part of the Community Foundations.

VII. Examination and assessment

1. The secular nature of the Turkish law system

We can see that the protection of freedom of religion and the place of religious elements in working life have a different meaning in Turkey compared to European countries. There are two main reasons explaining this situation.

The first is the impact of the Turkish Revolution. In reality, the Turkish Republic – which sought to draw a line under the Ottoman Empire and to adopt the European system – tried to isolate the law system from religious elements for the sake of secularity. However, the emergence of the secular system in Europe is different from developments in this context in Turkey. Therefore, the Turkish Revolution is not the result of a movement from the base up but constitutes a top-down movement of modernization – whereas the secular system in Europe developed from the bottom to the top[56]. That is the reason why the higher authorities (i.e. the law system) in relation to the secularity issue in Turkey have always felt the need to take measures against religious elements in order to prevent the risk of moving back into the past. Accordingly, Turkey is oscillating between the occidental Christian world customs and the social realities of the Islamic world customs[57].

Secondly, the different approach to secularity on the part of the Turkish law system is due to the content of the religion of Islam. This is because the religion

---

[55] http://www.vgm.gov.tr/db/dosyalar/webicerik241.pdf.

[56] *Demir*, op. cit., pp. 25–26.

[57] *Rumpf*, op. cit., p. 22.

of Islam, apart from worship, also contains religious principles that are related to mundane issues like the management of the State and other community issues. Christian religion, by contrast, is mostly disconnected from mundane issues or has merely suggestive power as regards mundane tasks.

That is the reason why in Turkey, secularity has always been considered to be opposing Islam. In fact, Turkey – which tends towards the European secular system – has kept far from the principles of the law system of the religion of Islam. The secular law system in Turkey is not against the religion of Islam and has merely been trying to separate community life and State government from the principles of the religion of Islam.

2. Purification of Turkish labour and social law from religious elements

The attempt to purify the Turkish law system from religious elements is also noticeable in labour and social law. However, while labour and social law legislation provides for the right to freedom of religion, defending the right to express one's religious views and fighting against sect discrimination and the interdiction of worship, it does not contain legal regulations which would permit the actual practice of freedom of religion. All regulations of these issues are in fact left to the collective labour agreement between the employer and the trade union.

Concerns regarding the move from secularity back into the past were intended to be dissipated firstly by way of limitations at work and the establishment of interdictions. In this respect, one typical example is the change of the holiday of the week from Friday to Sunday and the interdiction of making religious policies to labour unions. However, along with the growing integration of secularity and democratic thinking within the Turkish community, the possibility of giving up these doubts and getting rid of them is getting strong today. Accordingly, we can keep in mind that as a political party which uses religious elements as a reference, the AKP (Justice and Development Party), especially during the last 10 years, has been governing and is controlling the direction of business regulations in Turkey.

Hence, religious elements which keep women out of reach of working life are still perfidiously effective nowadays, namely under the guise of positive discrimination and the expansion of women's rights. However, the protection of women and the granting of more rights to them in our modern, globalized world discredits the continuity of women's employment in Turkish working life. In this respect, the Turkish lawmakers should see that granting excessive rights to women and isolating them from male workers in a way directly restricts the employment of women, which will result in the fact that the latter continue to be cloistered at home.

Religious Influences on Current Welfare and Labor Legislation in Israel

Rachel Barag-Hirshberg

I. Introduction

The status of religion in the Israeli judicial system arises from its complex historical and political reality. The State of Israel was established in 1948 with the termination of the British Mandate in Palestine. In the Declaration of Independence, the representatives of the Jewish community and the Zionist movement declared Israel to be a Jewish State that will

"... be based on the principles of liberty, justice, and peace, as envisaged by the prophets of Israel; will uphold the full social and political equality of all its citizens, without distinction of race, creed or sex; will guarantee full freedom of conscience, worship, education, and culture."[1]

Based on this, Israel is viewed as a Jewish and democratic state. The Israeli legal system faces many dilemmas arising from this characterization[2]. These dilemmas are also apparent in the area of labor law, as I will demonstrate in this paper.

When Israel was founded, the Zionist leadership decided to maintain a status quo on matters of religion and state. That is, it decided to continue the Ottoman system, which conferred autonomy in matters of personal status on the three main religious communities that existed in Israel at that time – Christian, Moslem, and Jewish. This status quo continues to this day, and results in state support

[1] Proclamation of Independence – The Declaration of the Establishment of the State of Israel (14/5/1948) (www.knesset.gov.il/docs/eng/megilat_eng.htm).

[2] *Daphne Barak-Erez*, The Story of Pigs and Pork Prohibitions in Israel (2015).

for autonomous religious institutions, including courts with juridical authority over family law[3].

Israel's characterization as a Jewish state encompasses in it a profound ideological rift, so far unresolved, as to the meaning of its "Jewish" nature. This is the underlying reason why Israel does not have a constitution, but rather only a group of "Basic Laws." All the state's legislative efforts and their judicial interpretations are couched under these Basic Laws.

When the separation from the British legal system occurred, it was unclear how the courts should act when faced with a legal question the answer to which could not already be found in Israeli law. It was determined that decisions to such questions of first impression should be rendered "in the light of the Jewish tradition's principles of liberty, justice, honesty, and peace"[4].

Israeli labor and welfare legislative efforts are far-reaching and extensive. They reflect Israel's commitment to the ILO and its conventions. A fundamental facet of these laws is that rights granted under them cannot be negotiated or surrendered by the parties in an employment dispute.

In Israel, labor and welfare disputes are argued in a distinct labour court system separate from other civil courts. Uniquely, these judicial efforts include lay judges, who represent both employees and employers. This court system deals with a wide range of issues including labor relations in the private sector, collective agreements, disputes between citizens and the national insurance body, procedures related to provident funds, and criminal processes resulting from breaches of employment law. In total, Israel's welfare and employment courts base their work on 93 laws, of which 35 belong to the criminal realm.

In my opinion, religion has influenced the legal field of labor and employment in Israel in three main areas. The first, which was mentioned previously, centers on the dilemma that Israel's democratic and Jewish nature poses to its legislative efforts. The second relates to an interesting phenomenon, whereby religious norms have been intentionally inserted into modern-day Israeli labor legislation. I will be demonstrating this phenomenon later in this paper by comparing religious norms to modern legislation. Finally, the third area, which I experience in my work as a judge, is the influence of religion on litigation in the Israeli labor courts, especially on cases of religious discrimination.

I will be discussing these three areas of influence in this paper, starting with the legislative.

---

[3] *Frances Raday*, Religion, Multiculturalism and Equality: The Israeli Case, 25 Israel Yearbook on Human Rights, 193–241. Hebrew version of the article: *Frances Raday*, Religion and Equality in Israeli Case Law, Berenson Book Vol. II, 341–388 (Editors. *Prof. Aharon Barak & Haim Berenson*) (2000).

[4] Section 1, Law of Justice, 1980.

II. The Dilemmas Created by Israel's Definition as a Jewish and Democratic State

In the early 1990s, Israel's legal landscape was significantly altered when two Basic Laws, both related to human rights, were passed: *Basic Law: Human Dignity and Liberty* was passed in March 1992 and *Basic Law: Freedom of Occupation* in March 1993. Prior laws could be utilized until the start of 2002, after which they were no longer considered valid if they contradicted the new laws.

Legal constitutional analysis in the Israeli system is conducted in three stages, of which the main one (and the one relevant to our discussion) is a test to validate that any infringement of a legal right meets the condition of the limitation clause, which states that there shall be no violation of the Basic Laws except by a law befitting the values of the State of Israel, enacted for a proper purpose, and to an extent no greater than is required[5].

The limitation clause does not define Israel's values. To learn these, it is necessary to consult the purpose statement of the two new Basic Laws; namely, to protect human dignity and liberty or freedom of occupation in order to establish in a Basic Law the values of the State of Israel as a Jewish and democratic state.

It's clear from the above that the State of Israel's values are the values of a "Jewish and democratic" state. As already stated, these legislative terms have led to many legal dilemmas, including in the area of labor law, as I shall now demonstrate.

In the area of labor law, one of the central cases argued in Israel's Supreme Court examined whether the 1951 Hours of Work and Rest Act, prohibiting Jewish employees from working on Saturdays – the Jewish day of rest – contradicts *Basic Law: Freedom of Occupation.* The case[6] dealt with a furniture marketing company with branches throughout Israel that had been subject to administrative fines because it employed Jewish workers on Saturdays. The company had requested that the Ministry of Labor and Social Affairs grant it a permit to employ Jewish workers on Saturdays and Jewish holidays, but the request was refused. Following this, the company sought relief in court, arguing that the 1951 Act contradicted the Basic Law and should be rendered null and void.

The Supreme Court's decision, written by its then Chief Justice, The Honorable Aharon Barak, states that the law's designation of hours of work and rest does infringe on the employers' and the employees' freedom of occupation. The infringement refers to the sphere of time. That is to say, the law does not contend with the nature of the work but only with the hours during which it is performed. The law, therefore, does infringe on the employer's desire to open the

[5] Section 8 Basic Law: Human Dignity and Liberty.

[6] Bagatz 5026/04 Design 22 – Shark Delux Furniture Ltd. & 18 others vs. The Ministry of Industry, Commerce and Employment (S. Ct. April 5, 2004).

business during weekly rest periods and on the employee's desire to work during these times[7]. However, Chief Justice Barak determined that this infringement was not sufficient to render the law invalid, since the law meets the test of the limitation clause. Namely, the law conforms to the State of Israel's Jewish and democratic values to grant human beings a day of rest every week and therefore meets standards of normative unity. Chief Justice Barak explains that human rights will always be broader than the legal ability to actuate them. These rights are the rights of a human being as part of society. This means that they are not absolute, and it is sometimes necessary to limit them in order to meet social goals[8].

Chief Justice Barak adds that the legislation dealing with weekly rest periods has two complementary aims. Its first objective is social, benefiting the employees' welfare by providing them with a consecutive weekly rest period. This social aim is reflected in the *Weekly Rest (Commerce and Offices) Convention of 1957* and in similar legal arrangements in other democratic countries such as the United Kingdom, Canada, and the United States. The decision also states that guaranteeing a single rest day – for employers and for employees – benefits the family. The legislation's second objective is of a national-religious nature; the observance of the Sabbath is viewed as a paramount national Jewish value. Thus, these two complementary aims together form a single appropriate objective[9].

I want to emphasize here that Chief Justice Barak believes that the judiciary must make every effort to actuate and harmonize Israel's values as a Jewish and democratic state.

Chief Justice Barak rejects the claim that, even if it is appropriate to legislate common rest periods, putting them on a Saturday for Jews is a form of religious coercion. He explains that requiring the rest period on a legislatively mandated day and not on a day selected by the employee or employer is coercive. However, selecting Saturday as the rest day is concordant with the Jewish understanding of the Saturday and does not constitute religious coercion[10]. In this context, quoted are the words of Chief Justice Dickson in R. v. Edwards Books and Art Ltd:

"I regard as self-evident the desirability of enabling parents to have regular days off from work in common with their child's day off from school, and with a day off enjoyed by most other family and community members ...

A family visit to an uncle or a grandmother, the attendance of a parent at a child's sports tournament, a picnic, a swim, or a hike in the park on a summer day, or a family expedition to a zoo, circus, or exhibition – these, and hundreds of other leisure activities with family and friends are amongst the simplest but most profound joys that any of us can know. The aim of protecting workers, families and communities from a diminution of opportunity to experience the fulfilment offered by these activities, and from

---

[7] Section 10.

[8] Section 11.

[9] Section 17.

[10] For further Discussion see: Shetreet, Some Reflections on Freedom of Conscience and Religion in Israel, 4 Isr. Y.H.R. 194, 214 (1974).

the alienation of the individual from his or her closest social bonds, is not one which I regard as unimportant or trivial ... I am satisfied that the Act is aimed at a pressing and substantial concern. It therefore survives the first part of the inquiry under s. 1... Religious freedom is inevitably abridged by legislation which has the effect of impeding conduct integral to the practice of a person's religion. But it is not necessarily impaired by legislation which requires conduct consistent with the religious beliefs of another person. One is not being compelled to engage in religious practices merely because a statutory obligation coincides with the dictates of a particular religion ... Legislation with a secular inspiration does not abridge the freedom from conformity to religious dogma merely because statutory provisions coincide with the tenets of a religion"[11].

Let us now examine the second area.

III. Adoption of Religious Norms in Israeli Secular Labor Legislation

There are interesting examples of religious norms reflecting Jewish culture (as manifested in its texts) being adopted into Israeli labor law. It is striking that these norms, whose origins are religious, are inserted into a legal system that is, at its base, secular. This stands in contrast to other legal systems that are inherently religious, where such insertions are expected and reflect the legal anchoring of religious norms[12].

A brief word about Jewish religious texts:

There are two primary sources of Jewish religious philosophy and life: First, the Tanach – the Jewish or Hebrew Bible – composed of the five books of Moses (the Torah), the Prophets (Nevi'im) and the Writings (Ketuvim). The second source is the Oral Law, compiled in the Talmud. According to Orthodox Jewish tradition, God gave Moses oral as well as written laws at Mount Sinai. These oral laws were passed on through the ages just as were the written ones. After the destruction of the Second Temple, Rabbi Yehuda Ha-Nasi compiled the oral laws into a written document (the Mishna) early in the third century C. E. The Mishna deals with agriculture, festivals, marriage and divorce, civil and criminal law, temple practices, and personal and religious purity. Subsequently, rabbinic authorities analyzed the document and provided extensive additional commentaries (the Gemara). The Mishna and the Gemara together are collectively known as the Talmud. The version of the Talmud most often cited today was substantially completed by the middle of the sixth century C. E.

The Oral Law is a legal commentary on the written Bible, filling in details not explicitly spelled out in it and explaining seeming contradictions or obscure passages. Thus, while there are relatively few specific references to labor rights in the

---

[11] Sections 22–23.

[12] See footnote 3 above.

Bible, Talmudic scholars noted many labor protections to meet the contingencies of an increasingly complex economy[13].

The following is a brief review of two major labor rights included in the Bible and the Talmud that have found their way into modern Israeli labor law[14].

1. Limits on Hours of Work

The first and most obvious example relates to the same topic that was discussed in part one; namely, limits on hours of work. This law is stated explicitly in the Bible: the requirement that workers be granted a day of rest[15] – quite an innovation for the Biblical Period[16]. The Sabbath – Saturday – the Jewish day of rest is one of Judaism's most important contributions to humankind, exemplifying the principle that individuals are more than merely tools to be exploited.

Indeed, Saturday and the other Jewish holidays were adopted as legislatively mandated rest days in Israel, as part of the 1951 Hours of Work and Rest Act. This was actually the first labor law that the Knesset – Israel's parliament – passed. It states:

Hours of Work and Rest Act, Chapter 3, Section 7(b):

"The weekly rest shall include –
(1) In the case of a Jew, Saturday;
(2) In the case of a person other than a Jew, Saturday or Sunday or Friday, whichever is ordinarily observed by the person as the weekly day of rest."

Section 9 of the same law prohibits employment during weekly rest periods, unless such employment has been permitted – for an individual business – by the Minister of Labor and Social Affairs, or for a whole sector of workers if it is a general permit upon a decision of a ministerial committee.

As alluded earlier in this paper[17], the principle of Freedom of Contracts cannot override this law and all sides in a labor relations setting must abide by this law and cannot forgo this weekly rest. Additionally, this law prohibits discrimination in hiring based on a candidate's refusal to work during a rest day; nor can a prospective employer demand that a candidate forgo a rest period as a condition of employment.

Another interesting regulation appears in Section 9 of the law: An employee who has not previously worked on days of weekly rest and who is requested by

---

[13] *Michael S. Perry*, Labor Rights in the Jewish Tradition, Jewish Labor Committee (1993).

[14] For a discussion of further examples that are beyond the scope of this paper, see *Michael Wigoda*, The Right to Work and Workers' Rights in Jewish Law, The Department of Jewish Law, The Ministry of Justice (2005).

[15] Exodus 20:9,10: "Six days shalt thou labor, and do all thy work: but the seventh day is a Sabbath unto the Lord thy God: in it thou shalt not do any manner of work …".

[16] See footnote 14 above.

[17] See Introduction.

the employer to work during these periods or notified that this request is imminent may, within three days of the date of the request, inform the employer that, in accordance with a prohibition imposed by commandments of the religion that the employee observes, he does not agree to work on days of weekly rest. The employer may then request that the employee present a written affidavit in support of the request within seven days. The employer may at that time make reasonable accommodations in the conditions of employment and the work schedule of the requesting employee.

However, the law exempts employers from the requirement to abide by a weekly rest if the place of employment performs work related to public security, safety, the wellbeing or health of people, hotel accommodation, power supply, and maintenance of essential supplies and services[18].

The Labor Court was asked to rule in a case[19] questioning the legality of the termination of a janitorial worker's employment in a municipal park, on grounds that the latter refused to work on Saturdays. The employing municipality argued that the work must be performed on Saturdays, and that, therefore, it was exempt from meeting the regulations just discussed. The Court stated that even if this claim was true, the termination constituted an infringement of the employee's religious rights due to the fact that the worker's employment was terminated without any effort to provide reasonable accommodations to his conditions of employment. Thus, the termination was invalidated.

The Supreme Court of Israel has currently under discussion a case[20] filed on behalf of the Israeli National League of football players demanding that the football matches not be played during the Sabbath as the players were considered workers and the National League was not exempt from meeting the regulations just discussed. An interministerial committee has been established to formulate policy regarding football matches played on the Sabbath.

Back to the Talmud! The Talmud mentions two other laws related to hours of work: the first requires that a worker be paid for hours spent walking to work – a law designed to prevent an employer from compelling a worker to leave home before the normal working day begins[21]. The second law prohibits a worker from laboring at night after working a day shift. This is an example of an ancient "Fair Labor Standards Act"[22].

---

[18] Section 11.

[19] Yigal Kashani vs. The Municiplaity of R'anana (Tel Aviv Dis. Ct. July 15, 2002).

[20] Bagatz 7635/15 The Movement for a Jewish State vs. The Minister of Culture and Sports & 19 others.

[21] *Baba Metzia* 83b: "A laborer's entry [to town] is in his own time, and his going forth [to the fields] is in his employers".

[22] See footnote 14 above.

Echoes of these Talmudic principles are found in Israeli labor laws that set the length of the working day, the duration of the working week, compensation for overtime, night shifts, and breaks during the working day and between work days. In this context, note that Section 20 of the same Hours of Work and Rest Act permits employees to pray during the working day, in accordance with their religious traditions. The time allowed for prayer will be set in consideration of the place of employment and the observance of the employee's religious tradition.

2. *Income Protection*

The second example of religious Jewish norms influencing secular labor legislation relates to income protection. A set of biblical commandments requires the prompt payment of wages: "Thou shall not oppress thy neighbor, nor rob him: the wages of a hired servant shall not abide with thee all night until the morning"[23] and "Thou shalt not oppress a hired servant that is poor and needy, whether he be of thy brethren or of thy strangers that are in thy land within thy gates [i. e. non-Israelites]. In the same day thou shalt give him his hire, neither shall the sun go down upon it ..."[24].

Perry stated that Talmudic scholars have interpreted these statements to mean that employers must pay their workers on the day that the contracted period of labor ends. The Talmud warns that employers who withhold wages are guilty of six violations: oppressing a neighbor, stealing, oppressing the poor, delaying payment of wages, failing to pay wages on the due date, and failing to pay wages before sunset. Indeed, the Talmud warns that "he who withholds an employee's wages is as though he deprived him of his life"[25]. This principle was considered so sacrosanct that the Talmudic sages reversed the burden of proof under contract law for disputes over the payment of wages[26].

In 1958, the Knesset[27] passed the Wage Protection Act which established the basic legal norm of assuring both the value of wages and the employee's right to utilize wages as desired. To achieve this aim, the law sets both the date when employers must remit wages[28] and the direct method of payment required; namely, an employee may not be compelled to purchase goods from the employer in lieu of payment[29]. Also established are documentary requirements related to wages, and limitations on debts and fines that can be garnered from wages.

---

[23] *Leviticus* 19:13.

[24] *Deuteronomy* 24:14, 15.

[25] *Baba Metzia* 111a.

[26] See footnote 14 above.

[27] Israel's parliament.

[28] Sections 9–11.

[29] Section 4.

As deterrence, the act imposes severe sanctions on employers who withhold wages – sanctions unique to the Israeli legislator, so far as I know. This sanction, known as the "in terrorem" clause, sets the compensatory payment at either 515 % of the withheld wage, or an interest rate of 20 % per month, whichever is greater[30]. When the act was passed, the Minister of Labor specifically stated that it accords with Jewish tradition[31].

IV. The Intersection of Religion and Labor Law in Labor Court Rulings

The final topic that I will address is Israeli Labor Court rulings related to religious discrimination. The use of religion as the grounds for religious discrimination suites is one of the most interesting arenas in which religion influences labor law in Israel.

Israeli anti-discrimination legislation was progressive from the State's inception[32]. Among Israel's first labor laws, the Employment of Women Act was passed in 1954, enacting, among other things, maternity leave. In 1959, when many countries were just starting to grapple with the issues of gender equality, Israeli law prohibited gender discrimination in the Government Employment Agency. In 1964, a law guaranteeing gender equality in pay was added, and in 1973, the National Labor Court determined that such equality was, in fact, to be considered public policy. That is to say, even before general legislation was passed, the Court extended this legislative intent to cover private employment contracts. These efforts were further reinforced in 1987, at which time several additional anti-discrimination laws were enacted, including gender equality in retirement age (1987), and the Equal Opportunities in Employment Act (1988), which is relevant to our discussion, and to which I shall shortly return.

I will finally mention the 1996 Gender Equality Act as well as a series of legislative orders dealing with appropriate representation, people with disabilities, sexual harassment and so on.

The number of legal actions due to religious discrimination in Israel as to date is rather small but increasing, and, in some cases, the courts have had to rule in interesting cases. As in other countries, such as Australia, many of these cases have arisen in the context of education.

---

[30] Section 17.

[31] For further elaboration on the Wage Protection Act see: *Stephan Adler*, Wage Protection Act: Law and Case Law, 7th Israel Labor Law Review, 5–46 (1995).

[32] *Guy Mundlak*, Do Anti-Discrimination Acts "Do the Work"? Israel Law, Society and Culture Review, 223–258 (2001).

Section 2(a) of the Equal Opportunities in Employment Act (as of 2000) states

"An employer shall not discriminate among employees or among persons seeking employment based on gender, sexual orientation, personal status, pregnancy, fertility treatments, in vitro fertilization (IVF), parental status, age, race, religion, nationality, country of origin, location of residence, opinions, party affiliation, or military reserve duty including the duration and frequency of such service (based on the Defense Service Act, Consolidated Version, 1986), in any of the following:
(1) Hiring;
(2) Terms of employment;
(3) Advancement in employment;
(4) Vocational training or supplementary vocational training;
(5) Termination or severance pay;
(6) Employment and retirement benefits."

As stated, the anti-discrimination legislation tries to address the full cycle of employment, from hiring to termination or retirement.

I will now discuss two cases adjudicated in the labor law courts, one dealing with a private school and the other with a public one.

The first case, which was argued at the Jerusalem Labor Court[33], dealt with a teacher in a Christian private school affiliated with a German Christian Order. The school had both Christian and Moslem female students. A teacher, who for twenty-seven years had taught classes in Arabic Language and Islam, requested that the principal grant her the right to don a Hijab during working hours. He refused, and the case went to court. The teacher argued that her right to don a Hijab emanated from her religious freedom – one of the principles of the State of Israel. It was further argued that her termination of employment as a result of covering her head was illegal based on the rights granted by the Equal Opportunities in Employment Act, because it constituted religious discrimination.

The District Court rejected the teacher's claim. It stated that the school was private, and, as such, instituted a dress code aimed at creating a climate of pluralism and mutual respect, since it served a mixed population of Christian and Moslem students. The decision further stated that the school intended to create equality, avoiding social pressure and coercion and maintaining a friendly environment. The school had thus operated for 120 years. For these reasons, the prohibition on head covering did not constitute an illegal prohibition, but rather was necessary based on the nature of the work, as stated in Section 2(c) of the Equal Opportunities in Employment Act:

"Differential treatment necessitated by the character or nature of the assignment shall not be regarded as discrimination under this section."

[33] Nadara Nimry vs. The Schmidt Girls school, Blessed Virgin Mary Ward of sisters, Arcdiocese of Cologne (Jerusalem Dis. Ct. August 23, 2010).

It is important to highlight that the Court's decision draws on the school's private status, where the norms of public education do not apply[34]. However, in public schools terminations of employment on reasonable, factual grounds are also permissible. Section 18 of the Public Education Act states that "The Council for Public Religious Education may reject, for purely religious reasons, the hiring or employment of a school principal, an inspector, or a teacher in a public religious institution."

Indeed, in the second case[35] I would like to discuss, a religious girls high school attempted to use this Section 18. In this case, a teacher in this school chose to become a single mother and her contract was therefore terminated. The school justified this termination by stating that single motherhood contradicted the values that the school wished to impart on its students. The Tel Aviv District Court stated that this termination constituted illegal discrimination, as prohibited in the Equal Opportunities in Employment Act and awarded the teacher significant monetary compensation.

As stated, unlike the first case, this was a public institution, not a private one.

The final point I wish to make could potentially be the topic of another in-depth study. It relates to utilizing religious beliefs to claim that the Labor Court has no authority to adjudicate disputes between members of the same devout religious community.

In this context, I shall mention that some communities do not recognize the authority of a civil court system on grounds of their religious world view. They believe that disputes should be settled in accordance with religious, and not civil laws. Generally, disputes in such communities are settled in intra-community institutions. The claim of lack of authority tends to arise when one side in the dispute decides to turn to a labor court, while the other side wishes to consult an intra-community adjudicator. My experience is that in such cases, the side that turns to the law court does so for two reasons: First, due to the assumption that the laws of the State of Israel will confer an advantage, and second, due the fact that these laws are more enforceable.

Labor courts have tended to reject claims of lack of authority when it comes to disputes about protective rights – rights that cannot be negotiated or surrendered by the parties in an employment dispute. However, my experience has been that such situations are rife with difficulties. Often, the side that turns to the Labor Court is subject to significant social sanctions in the community, and therefore, the decision whether the Court should tackle the issue can be complex.

---

[34] For a commentary on European headscarf cases see: *Achim Seifert*, The Constitutionality of State Neutrality Acts in Germany and Implications for the Wearing of Muslim Headscarves, 2 International Labor Rights Case Law, 101–106 (2016).

[35] Plonit vs. Almonit (Tel Aviv Dis. Ct. March 7, 2013).

I would like to close with an interesting story sited by Perry[36] about what may be the first strike recorded in history! The Talmud tells of a family that held the right to bake ceremonial bread in the Temple in Jerusalem. Temple management felt that the family held too much power and insisted that members of the family train non-family members, thus making their employment in this area possible.

The family categorically refused and decided to strike. The rabbis tried to persuade family members that their craft was holy and therefore a strike was not acceptable. When this failed, the Temple tried to employ Egyptian foreign workers to bake the bread. When the replacements were found wanting, the family demanded that its wages be doubled as a condition for them to return to work. The Talmud notes without further comment that the wages were indeed doubled.

It seems that the Talmud implicitly recognizes the right of trade unions to strike but notes that there is a strong preference to binding arbitration. The right to strike has been granted to Israeli employees, even in essential services in some cases. When ruling on a request for an injunction against a strike the National Labor Court used Jewish law to support its judgment declaring a broad right to strike. It cited the biblical phrase that "men are slaves to God and not slaves to slaves" and the Talmudic law that a worker has a right to leave his work even in the middle of the day. However, the labor courts can limit such strikes by way of injunctions. The challenge of contending with strikes in critical services is one of the challenges facing all democratic societies, and Israel among them.

[36] See footnote 14 above.

Religious Expression in the Workplace

The Case of the Federal Republic of Germany

*Achim Seifert**

* The article is the revised and updated version of a paper which I have published in the Comparative Labor Law & Policy Journal (CLLPJ). I am grateful to Professor *Matt Finkin*, general editor of the CLLPJ, for the permission to republish the paper.

I. The changing context

Questions related to religious expression in the workplace have always been a matter of discussion in German labor law. The focus, however, has changed considerably over the last few years. This change reflects the development from a relatively religiously homogeneous to a religiously diverse society in Germany, due to the constant immigration Germany has faced since the 1960s.

Indeed, religious diversity is nothing new for Germany. As a result of the protestant reformation in the 16th century and the then following confessional wars, religious tolerance was recognized within certain limits; the most important steps in this direction were the Religious Peace of Augsburg of 1555 ("cuius regio – eius religio") and the Peace of Westphalia of 1648.[1] However, these religious conflicts, torturing the population of the Holy Roman Empire for almost two centuries, were of a mere confessional character; their common ground was the Christian religion. Thus, the compromise that could be reached between the different confessions was always superimposed by a broad consensus about Christian "values". Religious tolerance therefore was typically limited to different denominations and Christian groups that existed within Christian-

[1] For an overview of the history of the confessional wars and their impact on the relationship between State and Churches see *von Campenhausen/de Wall*, Staatskirchenrecht – Eine systematische Darstellung des Religionsverfassungsrechts in Deutschland und Europa; ein Studienbuch, 4th edition, Munich 2006, pp. 9–14.

ity, whereas other religious groups, in particular the large Jewish community in Germany, could not benefit from this limited religious tolerance: Until the Napoleonic Wars in the early nineteenth century, the Jews were not only the target of repeated persecutions ("pogroms") but were also submitted to a specific and discriminatory legal regime banning them to specific districts in the towns, the "ghettos", and excluding them from a number of professional activities and from public offices. In addition, they were not allowed to practice their religious belief in the public sphere. Their situation only changed in the course of the nineteenth century when they were recognized as full citizens and entitled to exercise their belief without the former legal restrictions. However, this fragile emancipation process could not protect the Jewish community, under the Nazi regime, from falling victim to the most atrocious crimes.

The situation did considerably change with the influx of immigrants that many of the Western countries experienced during the last three or four decades. As a result of this massive migration, religious diversity has widened considerably: Today, nearly all relevant religions of the world are represented in Germany and do co-exist. In particular the Muslim community has become the most relevant and visible religious group alongside the Christian Churches, which poses a number of problems regarding integration into German society.[2]

Although this change started several decades ago, it has only been a few years that people belonging to non-Christian religious groups are exercising their religious beliefs with much more self-assertiveness than before and have been increasingly intent on claiming their religious freedom with the help of the judicial system; in particular, this applies to the numerous Muslims living in Germany. This trend forces German lawyers to revisit the existing legal framework for religious freedom. However, in addition, the entire German discussion on religious diversity is gaining much more fundamental relevance since it is embedded in the wider controversy about the need of cultural homogeneity in modern society. Immigration and its most obvious consequences, cultural and religious diversity, are regarded (especially by some German conservatives) as challenging the Christian and Occidental "dominant culture" ["Leitkultur"], which they consider to be under threat. Consequently, the religious and the cultural dimension of a diverse society are inseparably tied. It is not exaggerated to consider this debate on cultural and religious identity, for which the Muslim headscarf has become *the* symbol, as a new "Kulturkampf".

The following paper picks up on these developments. The main argument is that German law in general and German labor law in particular still have not developed a coherent concept to cope with these new challenges arising from

[2] According to the Federal Government [*Bundesregierung*], the Muslim community in Germany amounts to 3.4 million people (2006). See *Bundesregierung*, Stand der rechtlichen Gleichstellung des Islam in Deutschland, in: Bundestagsdrucksachen (BT-Drs.) 16/5033, p. 2.

religious diversity in German society. Although German law recognizes religious freedom as a constitutional right, the traditionally predominant religious communities in Germany, *i. e.* the Roman Catholic Church as well as the various Protestant Churches at State level, still have a number of legally recognized privileges whereas other religious groups, especially the different Muslim communities, so far have not acquired the same legal status. As a result, the growing religious diversity of German society has not yet been transformed into a real concept of religious pluralism founded on the idea of equal recognition of the different religious beliefs that are represented in German society. This already makes clear the necessity for an analysis of the constitutional mapping of the relationship between State and religion (II.): Religious expression in the workplace is embedded in this wider context, which therefore first must be taken into account. These constitutional foundations considerably influence the legal tools German labor law essentially provides in order to cope with conflicts arising from religious expression in the workplace (III.). However, particular emphasis will be placed on the different areas in which religious expression in the workplace raises legal conflicts (IV.). Finally, some conclusions shall be drawn (V.).

II. The constitutional mapping of the relationship between State and religion

1. Religious freedom and religious neutrality as the main pillars

Since the Weimar Republic, founded in the aftermath of World War I (1919), the German constitutional system has been grounded on the principle of separation of Church and State. In the wording of Article 137, Para. 1 of the Weimar Constitution, the provision is still in force (incorporated in the German Constitution [*Grundgesetz* – abbr. *GG*] in terms of its Article 140): "There is no State Church." In this respect, the Weimar Constitution marked a considerable change in the relationship between the State and its Churches. Indeed, Section 147 of the constitution of the 1848/49 National Assembly in Frankfurt (the so-called Constitution of St. Paul's Church) already promised the separation of Church and State. However, this first democratic constitution of Germany did not come into force due to the failure of the revolutionary movement in 1849; and after the foundation of the German Empire in 1871 by *Bismarck* the German states still maintained a strong influence on the Churches, in particular on the Protestant Churches, until the end of World War I:[3] The princes of the respective states (e. g. the king of Prussia) remained the heads of the Protestant Church in their states.

[3] See *von Campenhausen/de Wall*, op. cit., pp. 26–30.

Today's German constitutional law addresses the protection of religion and the relationship between the religious groups and the State in various provisions. Indeed, the core elements are the guarantee of religious freedom enshrined in Article 4 GG and the principle of religious neutrality of the State. However, these principles are superimposed by the so-called "Church articles" of the Weimar Constitution (Articles 137–141) that have been incorporated by Article 140 GG into the GG and that still favor the big Christian Churches in Germany.

a) Religious freedom under Article 4 GG

The wording of Article 4, Para. 1 GG is as follows: "Freedom of faith and of conscience, and freedom to profess a religious or philosophical creed, shall be inviolable". Article 4, Para. 2 GG supplements this right in guaranteeing the undisturbed practice of religion. The fundamental right of religious freedom is not, contrary to the guarantee of religious freedom in Article 135 of the Weimar Constitution, under the reservation that the legislator limits the freedom by statutory law. It is guaranteed without any reserve, which underlines the eminent value religious freedom has in German constitutional law.

aa) Scope

Religious freedom under Article 4, Para. 1 GG essentially has two dimensions. On the one hand, it protects the religious freedom of the individual. This implies the right of the individual to freely choose a religious belief and to live according to the rules of this belief. Consequently, Article 4 GG not only guarantees the *forum internum but also the forum externum*. In addition, the guarantee of individual religious freedom also implies the right not to have a religious belief and not to join a religious community or to abandon a certain religious belief.[4] This so-called negative religious freedom guarantees, according to the explicit rule of Article 136, Para. 3 of the Weimar Constitution, the right not to participate in religious festivities; moreover, negative religious freedom prohibits the installing of a Christian crucifix in classrooms of public schools[5] or common prayer in public schools (except when the participation in the prayer is not mandatory).[6]

On the other hand, religious freedom under Article 4 GG has a collective dimension. The constitutional guarantee also implies the freedom of individuals to form religious groups and to exercise their religious beliefs collectively. In addition, religious communities themselves can invoke the constitutional guar-

[4] See *BVerfG*, decision of December 17, 1975 – 1 BvR 63/68, BVerfGE 41, p. 29, at 49; decision of February 8, 1977 – 1 BvR 329/71 et al., BVerfGE 44, p. 37, at 49; decision of May 16, 1995 – 1 BvR 1087/91, BVerfGE 93, pp. 1 et seq., at p. 15.

[5] See *BVerfG*, decision of May 16, 1995 – 1 BvR 1087/91, BVerfGE 93, p. 1, at pp. 15 et seq.

[6] *BVerfG*, decision of October 16, 1979 – 1 BvR 647/70 and 7/74, BVerfGE 52, pp. 223–255.

antee of religious freedom.[7] This guarantee of collective religious freedom under Article 4 GG is complemented by the provisions of the Weimar Constitution on religious societies (in particular Article 137 of the Weimar Constitution) that have been incorporated into the GG by Article 140 GG; they will be considered in greater detail below.[8]

bb) Complementary prohibition of discrimination on grounds of religious belief

The guarantee of religious freedom under Article 4 GG is supplemented by the prohibition of discrimination on grounds of religious belief (Article 3, Para. 3 GG). Whether Article 3, Para. 3 GG only covers direct or also indirect discrimination,[9] is still subject of a debate[10] that, after two recent decisions of the Federal Constitutional Court, seems to be decided in favor of the submitting of indirect discrimination.[11] As far as access to the public service is concerned, Article 3, Para. 3 GG is complemented by Article 33, Para. 3 GG that guarantees, *inter alia*, access to all public offices independently from religious belief.[12]

b) The principle of State neutrality

The German Constitution does not explicitly guarantee the principle of State neutrality in religious matters. However, doctrine and jurisprudence deduce this important constitutional principle from a synopsis of different constitutional provisions, in particular of religious freedom (Article 4 GG), the prohibition of discrimination on grounds of religious belief (Article 3, Para. 3 GG), equal access to the public service (Article 33, Para. 2 GG) as well as of the principle that

---

[7] See *BVerfG*, decision of June 26, 2002 – 1 BvR 670/91, BVerfGE 105, p. 279, at p. 293; decision of February 5, 1991 – 2 BvR 263/86, BVerfGE 83, p. 341, at p. 354 (*Bahá'i*).

[8] See *infra* II 2.

[9] The distinction between direct and indirect discrimination has been developed by the anti-discrimination law of the EU. Direct discrimination arises when a person is treated less favorably on one of the grounds forbidden by EU law (*e. g.* gender, religious belief, handicap etc.) than another is, has been or would be treated in a comparable situation. In contrast to this, indirect discrimination targets measures of employers that are discriminatory in effect, though they do not expressly make a distinction between individuals of different gender, religious belief etc. To take the example of gender discrimination: it is considered discriminatory to apply a gender-neutral measure, criterion or practice when in fact this measure disadvantages a much higher percentage of women than men, unless that difference can be justified by objective factors unrelated to any discrimination on grounds of sex. For a more in-depth analysis of this distinction see *Catherine Barnard*, EU Employment Law, 4th edition, Oxford 2012, pp. 354–356 with further references.

[10] For further details see *Lerke Osterloh & Angelika Nußberger*, in: Sachs (ed.): *Kommentar zum Grundgesetz*, 7th edition, Munich 2014, Art. 3, note 255 with further references.

[11] See *BVerfG*, decision of November 27, 1997, 1 BvL 12/91, BVerfGE 97, pp. 35 et seq., at p. 43; decision of January 30, 2002, 1 BvL 23/96, BVerfGE 104, pp. 373 et seq., at p. 393.

[12] See also Section. 9 of the Act on the Status of Civil Servants [*Beamtenstatusgesetz*] and *BVerwG*, decision of November 24, 1988 – 2 C 10/86, BVerwGE 81, pp. 22 et seq.

civil rights do not depend on a certain religious belief (Article 136, Para. 1 of the Weimar Constitution), the right of every citizen not to be forced to participate in religious festivities (Article 136, Para. 4 of the Weimar Constitution) and the prohibition of a State Church (Article 137, Para. 1 of the Weimar Constitution).[13]

In particular, this principle prohibits the establishment of a State Church, the privileging of certain confessions or religious beliefs, and the ban of other religions. The State has the duty to equally treat the different religious groups represented in Germany and cannot identify with one of them. However, this does not mean that the Constitution requires a strict separation of State and religion. Religious neutrality has to be understood in the sense of an open attitude, equally promoting the different religious confessions. The Federal Constitutional Court had to clarify this principle on various occasions. One famous example will suffice: in 1995, the Court banned crucifixes from the class rooms of Bavarian public schools.[14]

2. *Attenuation of a strict separation of Church and State*

Religious neutrality of the State and religious freedom are undoubtedly the pillars of the constitutional relationship between State and religion under the GG. Their underlying concept is the separation of State and religious groups. However, these two constitutional principles are only one side of the constitutional medal. They are not only supplemented but also attenuated by Articles 136–141 of the Weimar Constitution; these constitutional provisions have been incorporated into the GG by Article 140 GG and are therefore applicable constitutional law of the Federal Republic of Germany. The core element of the so-called Weimar Church Compromise is the privileged status of religious societies [*Religionsgesellschaften*] (see A.). The constitutional guarantee of Sunday as the day of weekly rest and legally recognized holidays affect the relationship between State and religion (see B.).

a) The constitutional guarantee of autonomy of religious societies

Although there is no State Church in Germany (Article 137, Para. 1 of the Weimar Constitution) the German Constitution privileges religious societies, particularly the Catholic and the different Protestant Churches, in various ways. These privileges have their constitutional basis in Article 137 of the Weimar Constitution and also affect the labor law status of their workers. By consequence,

---

[13] See *BVerfG*, decision of December 14, 1965 – 1 BvR 413/60, 1 BvR 416/60, BVerfGE 19, pp. 206, at 216; decision of October 16, 1968 – 1 BvR 241/66, BVerfGE 24, pp. 236 et seq., at p. 246; BVerfGE 33, 23, 28; BVerfGE 93, 1, 17. See also *Juliane Kokott*, in: Michael Sachs (ed.), Kommentar zum Grundgesetz, 7th edition, Munich 2014, Art. 4 GG, Paras. 4–5 with further references.

[14] See *BVerfG*, decision of May 16, 1995 – 1 BvR 1097/81, BVerfGE 93, pp. 1 et seq.

the strict separation of Church and State is attenuated in favor of a mutual co-operation between both. This particular relationship has been characterized as a "limping separation of Church and State".[15]

aa) What is a religious society?

Article 137 of the Weimar Constitution does not define what constitutes a religious society. Religious groups can be accorded the legal status of an association according to the rules of the Civil Code [*Bürgerliches Gesetzbuch* – abbr. *BGB*] (Article 137, Para. 4 of the Weimar Constitution) or can obtain the recognition of the State authorities as a statutory corporation [*Körperschaft des öffentlichen Rechts*] (Article 137, Para. 5 of the Weimar Constitution). The only explicit requirement for this recognition is that their constitution and the number of their members guarantee for a durable existence.

The following are traditionally recognized as religious societies under Article 137, Para. 5 of the Weimar Constitution: dioceses, certain parishes and various institutions (e.g., *Caritas*) of the Roman Catholic Church, the Protestant Churches at State level [*Landeskirchen*], *Diakonisches Werk*, the charity of the Protestant Church in Germany, several Jewish communities at local level and their umbrella organization, the Central Council of Jews in Germany [*Zentralrat der Juden in Deutschland*], various Lutheran communities, other communities of the Evangelical Church, the Old Catholic Church and the Russian Orthodox Church.[16] In recent times, also other religious communities have been trying to acquire the status of statutory corporations. In the case of the *Jehovah*'s *Witnesses*, the State of Berlin refused to give them recognition as a religious society. The then following law suit against the State before the administrative courts did not succeed: the Federal Administrative Court [*Bundesverwaltungsgericht*],[17] in the last instance, ruled that the State's refusal to recognize the *Jehovah's Witnesses* as a religious society was lawful, since the status of a statutory corporation would require a minimum of constitutional loyalty, which was missing in the case of the *Jehovah's Witnesses*. In this context, the *BVerwG* essentially relied on the *Jehovah's Witnesses* refusal to participate in municipal, State or federal elections. The Federal Constitutional Court,[18] however, overruled this decision of the

[15] That is the famous characterization of the relationship between the State and the Churches under the Weimar Constitution expressed by *Ulrich Stutz*, Die päpstliche Diplomatie unter Leo XIII nach den Denkwürdigkeiten des Kardinals Domenico Ferrata, in: Abhandlungen der Preußischen Akademie der Wissenschaften, Volume 25, Philosophisch-historische Klasse, Berlin 1926, p. 54 (footnote 2).

[16] For an overview of the religious societies recognized as statutory corporations see *Bundesregierung*, Stand der rechtlichen Gleichstellung des Islam in Deutschland, BT-Drs. 16/5033, pp. 25–26 and pp. 75–76.

[17] *BVerwG*, decision of June 26, 1997 – 7 C 11/96, BVerwGE 105, p. 117 et seq.

[18] *BVerfG*, decision of December 19, 2000 – 2 BvR 1500/97, BVerfGE 102, pp. 370–400, at pp. 392–399.

Federal Administrative Court and decided that the *Jehovah's Witnesses* had to be recognized as a religious society by the State authorities. According to the Federal Constitutional Court, Article 137, Para. 5 of the Weimar Constitution only requires from religious societies, that they respect the fundamental constitutional principles mentioned in Article 79, Para. 3 GG such as the core elements of the fundamental rights (Articles 1–19 GG), the rule of law, the principle of democracy, and the welfare State clause (Article 20, Para. 1 GG). A further constitutional loyalty of religious societies would not be in line with the principle of autonomy of religious societies enshrined in Article 137, Para. 3 of the Weimar Constitution. However, in the case of the Church of Scientology, the Federal Labour Court has refused to recognize this group as a religious society under Article 137 of the Weimar Constitution:[19] The main argument was that Scientology was a business organization and not a religious society.

As far as the various Muslim communities in Germany are concerned, many of them also claim to be legally recognized as religious societies under Article 137, Para. 5 of the Weimar Constitution. They want to obtain the same legal privileges as the Christian Churches.[20] So far, there has only been one community formally demanding the status of a statutory corporation.[21] The major legal problem to be raised in this context is that the Muslim communities have no formal affiliation. Contrary to the affiliations to Christian Churches or other religious societies, Muslim communities do not require a formal joining in terms of the corporate law. However, Article 137, Para. 5 of the Weimar Constitution requires that the society's constitution and the number of its members guarantee for a durable existence.[22] Thus, the structure of Islamic communities itself is an obstacle for the recognition as a statutory corporation. It remains to be seen how the courts will deal with this challenge.

bb) Autonomy of religious societies

The key element of the status of religious societies is their autonomy under Article 137, Para. 3 of the Weimar Constitution. They shall have the right to regulate and to administer their own affairs within the limits determined by the law applying to everyone [innerhalb der Grenzen des für alle geltenden Gesetz-

[19] See *BAG*, decision of March 22, 1995 – AZB 21/94, NZA 1995, pp. 823–834.

[20] See, for instance, the political claims of the Islam Council for the Federal Republic of Germany, available at: www.islamrat.de.

[21] See *Bundesregierung*, Stand der rechtlichen Gleichstellung des Islam in Deutschland, BT-Drs. 16/5033, p. 25. The administrative procedure in this case is, according to my knowledge, still pending.

[22] See *Gerhard Czermak*, Religions- und Weltanschauungsrecht, Heidelberg 2008, Para. 210. See also *Michael Klöpfer*, Der Islam in Deutschland als Verfassungsfrage, in: Die öffentliche Verwaltung (DÖV) 2006, pp. 45–55, at p. 53; *von Campenhausen/de Wall*, op. cit., p. 87; *Bundesregierung*, Stand der rechtlichen Gleichstellung des Islam in Deutschland, BT-Drs. 16/5033, p. 26.

es]. All institutions belonging to a religious society benefit from this autonomy status, regardless of their legal structure.[23] Consequently, Article 137, Para. 3 of the Weimar Constitution covers all social institutions run by Churches (hospitals, schools, nurseries, kindergartens etc.) or that are organizationally associated with a Church.

This constitutional autonomy covers, in principle, all matters that are considered by the religious society as own affairs,[24] namely relating to internal constitution and structure, rules concerning the membership within the group, its activities (e.g. the maintenance of charity institutions), and also rules concerning the service within the Church, particularly the statute of the so-called Church civil servants [*Kirchenbeamten*].[25] Furthermore, the jurisdiction of the Federal Constitutional Court and the legislature deduce from this principle a specific status of religious societies within State labor law; this point shall be considered more fully at a later stage.[26]

The autonomy of the respective religious society is only limited by "laws applying to everybody". This criterion has been controversially discussed over the years.[27] The Federal Constitutional Court[28] considers that these State laws are not identical with State laws binding every citizen, regardless of religious belief. Instead, only those State laws are considered as "laws applying to everybody" which do not affect the Churches harder than they affect other "citizens".[29] Thus, a judicial control by State courts, for instance, of internal Church acts that have no immediate effect on the State sphere is not in line with the autonomy of religious societies under Article 137, Para. 3 of the Weimar Constitution.[30]

---

[23] See *BVerfG*, decision of June 4, 1985 – 2 BvR 1703, 1718/83 and 856/85, BVerfGE 70, pp. 138 et seq., at pp. 162 et seq.

[24] For further details see *von Campenhausen/de Wall*, op. cit., pp. 100–106. On the historical background of these State subsidies see *Josef Isensee*, Staatsleistungen an die Kirchen und Religionsgemeinschaften, in: Joseph Listl & Dietrich Pirson (eds.), Handbuch des Staatskirchenrechts der Bundesrepublik Deutschland, 2nd edition, Berlin 1994, volume II, § 35 A I 1.

[25] See *von Campenhausen/de Wall*, op. cit., pp. 149–196 with further references.

[26] See *infra* III 2.

[27] For an overview of this debate see *von Campenhausen/de Wall*, op. cit., pp. 107–114 and *Konrad Hesse*, Das Selbstbestimmungsrecht der Kirchen und Religionsgemeinschaften, in: Joseph Listl & Dietrich Pirson (eds.), Handbuch des Staatskirchenrechts der Bundesrepublik Deutschland, Volume I, 2nd edition, Berlin 1994, § 17 IV.

[28] *BVerfG*, decision of September 21, 1976 – 2 BvR 350/75, BVerfGE 42, pp. 312 et seq, at p. 334.

[29] See *BVerfG*, decision of February 17, 1965 – 1 BvR 732/64, BVerfGE 18, pp. 385 et seq., at p. 386; *BVerfG*, decision of September 21, 1976 – 2 BvR 350/75, BVerfGE 42, pp. 312 et seq., at pp. 334 et seq.; *BVerfG*, decision of June 4, 1985 – 2 BvR 1703, 1718/83 and 856/85, BVerfGE 70, pp. 138 et seq., at p. 167.

[30] *BVerfG*, decision of February 17, 1965 – 1 BvR 732/64, BVerfGE 18, pp. 385 et seq., at p. 386; *BVerfG*, decision of December 9, 2008 – 2 BvR 717/08, NJW 2009, pp. 238 et seq.

cc) Other privileges of religious societies

As statutory corporations, religious societies are not integrated into the administrative hierarchy of the State. They do not fulfil any State function and are not controlled by the State authorities. However, these religious societies have considerable privileges compared to religious societies that are not recognized as statutory corporations and to all other religious groups.

One core element of their legal status is the privilege that most of the states levy Church taxes and collect them from the Church members.[31] Article 137, Para. 6 of the Weimar Constitution only provides that religious societies, recognized as statutory corporations, have the right to levy taxes on the basis of the tax lists of the respective state. The Federal Constitutional Court, however, has ruled that this State support related to Church tax collection is in line with the constitutional principle of the separation of Church and State (Article 137, Para. 1 of the Weimar Constitution).[32] As a result, they are not in the same situation as common law associations that have to enforce their membership fee claims before the civil courts; Churches benefit from the severe implementing rules of the fiscal code in favor of the State.

Although Article 138, Para. 1 of the Weimar Constitution provides that existing State subsidies for religious societies are to be removed by State law, there has not been any State regulation on this issue since the coming into force of the Weimar Constitution in 1919. The religious societies still obtain State subsidies (e.g. for the maintenance of their sacral buildings) to a considerable extent.[33] Furthermore, religious societies have to be admitted to religious services and worship within the army, State-run hospitals, penitentiary centers and other public institutions where there is a need for worship (Article 141 of the Weimar Constitution). As far as public schooling is concerned, Article 7, Para. 3 GG derogates from the principle of separation of Church and State and imposes on the State the duty to establish religious instruction within public schools. The content of this religious instruction shall be determined in conformity with the principles of the corresponding religious societies. In practice, this means that the Catholic Church or the Protestant Churches decide autonomously on the teaching program and are entitled to choose the personnel for these classes.[34]

---

[31] For an overview see *Czermak*, op. cit., Paras. 235–247 with further references.

[32] *BVerfG*, decision of October 25, 1977 – 1 BvR 323/75, BVerfGE 46, pp. 266 et seq.; *BVerfG*, decision of October 23, 1978 – 1 BvR 439/75, BVerfGE 49, pp. 375–377; *BVerfG*, decision of May 25, 2001 – 1 BvR 2253/00, in: Neue Zeitschrift für Verwaltungsrecht (NVwZ) 2001, p. 909. See also Federal Financial Court [*Bundesfinanzhof* – abbr. *BFH*], decision of July 4, 1975 – VI R 173/72, BFHE 116, p. 485 et seq.

[33] For more details see *Czermak*, op. cit., Paras. 352–363.

[34] However, it should be noted that there have been various efforts at State level in recent times to establish classes for religious education for Muslims at public schools. This instruction in the Muslim religion is not organized in cooperation with the various Muslim federations in Germany. For an overview of existing religious education classes at State level see *Bundes-*

Finally, they have certain privileges in tax law[35] and receive various forms of State subsidies.[36]

b) Constitutional protection of Sunday as the day of weekly rest

Finally, also the constitutional protection of Sunday as the day of weekly rest is linked to religious freedom under the Constitution. According to Article 139 of the 1919 Constitution of Weimar, Sunday and legally recognized holidays remain protected as days of rest and of moral exaltation [*seelische Erhebung*]. The provision does not guarantee individual rights to the citizens but only contains an institutional guarantee to protect Sunday and the then (in 1919) legally recognized holidays.[37] It, moreover, does not protect the maintenance of specific religious holidays.[38] Also Article 139 of the Weimar Constitution has to be considered as part of the so-called Weimar Church Compromise. It is interesting to note that a large majority of the members of the National Assembly voted in favor of a constitutional protection of Sunday and legally recognized holidays as days of rest.[39] The reason for the great acceptance of Article 139 is, certainly, that both Christian traditionalists as well as secularists were satisfied with the wording: it combined Christian doctrine with the social democratic idea of a protection of Sunday and legally recognized holidays. The provision not only protected, on a constitutional level, traditional (Christian) holidays, but also had to be considered as a constitutional "program" to legally recognize secular holidays such as a War Memorial Day or the first of May as Labor Day; a political compromise on which holidays shall be legally recognized, however, could not be reached during the Weimar Republic (1919–1933).[40]

The main impact of this constitutional provision on labor law is the prohibition of Sunday work in line with the statutory regulation of working hours (see Section 1, Para. 2 of the Working Time Act [*Arbeitszeitgesetz* – abbr. *ArbZG*])

---

regierung, Stand der rechtlichen Gleichstellung des Islam in Deutschland, BT-Drs. 16/5033, pp. 44–52.

[35] See *Bundesregierung*, op. cit., BT-Drs. 16/5033, pp. 69–71.

[36] For a critical overview of these State subsidies see *Czermak*, op. cit., Paras. 50 and 365.

[37] *BVerfG*, decision of September 18, 1995 – 1 BvR 1456/95, Neue Juristische Wochenschrift (NJW) 1995, pp. 3378 et seq., at p. 3379.

[38] *BVerfG*, decision of September 18, 1995 – 1 BvR 1456/95, NJW 1995, pp. 3378 et seq., at p. 3379.

[39] For a more in-depth analysis of the discussion on Article 139 of the Weimar Constitution within the National Assembly see *Georg Kaiserberg*, Art. 139 – Feiertagsschutz, in: Hans Carl Nipperdey (ed.), Die Grundrechte und Grundpflichten der Reichsverfassung, Berlin 1930, second volume Art. 118–142, pp. 428–429. See also *Andreas Grube*, Der Sonntag und die kirchlichen Feiertage zwischen Gefährdung und Bewährung – Aspekte der feiertagsrechtlichen Entwicklung im 19. und 20. Jahrhundert, Frankfurt am Main 2003, pp. 134–137 and *Jan Heinemann*, Grundgesetzliche Vorgaben bei der staatlichen Anerkennung von Feiertagen, Frankfurt am Main 2004, pp. 94–96.

[40] See *Grube*, op. cit., pp. 137–145.

and the statutory limitation of the opening hours of retail shops on Sundays in Section 3, Para. 1 of the Act governing the hours of trading [*Ladenschlussgesetz*]. However, recently there has been a trend to soften these statutory restrictions and to jeopardize the guarantee of Sunday as the day of rest. The prohibition of Sunday work has been undermined by considerable exceptions in Sections 9–13 ArbZG. In addition, many federal states [*Bundesländer*] have deregulated the shop closing times on Sundays since the Federalism Reform of 2006, when the regulation of shop closing times shifted from federal to State competence.[41] The Federal Constitutional Court limited, however, this undermining of Sunday as the day of rest in a seminal decision of December 1, 2009.[42] Pursuant to this ruling, State legislature has a positive obligation [*Schutzpflicht*] to ensure that Sunday remains *the* day of rest. As a result, legislature needs to justify Sunday work.

III. Legal mechanisms to cope with conflicts arising from religious expression at the workplace

This constitutionally determined relationship between State and religion has a considerable impact on how German labor law copes with conflicts arising from religious expression in the workplace. This raises the question as to what essential tools German labor law provides to master these difficult problems. There are, in particular, four legal mechanisms that shall be discussed in the following sections. Traditionally one important tool is the horizontal effect of religious freedom under Article 4 GG (I.): Thus, workers whose religious freedom at the workplace is limited by the employer can invoke Article 4 GG against their employer. The second tool is the constitutional guarantee of autonomy of religious societies under Article 137, Para. 3 of the Weimar Constitution, which according to the Federal Constitutional Court and the doctrine provides for a specific status of religious societies within the State labor law (II.). As the third tool, collective labor law shall be analyzed (III.). And finally, anti-discrimination law, originally leading a shadowy existence, is increasingly becoming the most important legal instrument in dealing with the issue of religious expression at the workplace (IV.).

1. The horizontal effect of religious freedom

The constitutional guarantee of religious freedom under Article 4 GG – as most of the other constitutional rights enshrined in the GG – only binds the State in exercising its legislative, executive, and judicative power (Article 1, Para. 3 GG).

[41] See *Jürgen Kühling*, Ladenschluss nach der Föderalismusreform – Öffnungszeiten und Arbeitnehmerschutz, in: ArbuR 2006, pp. 384–386.

[42] BVerfG, judgment of December 1, 2009 – 1 BvR 2857/07 and 1 BvR 2858/07, BVerfGE 125, pp. 39 et seq.

Following this traditional understanding of fundamental rights, Article 4 GG protects, first and foremost, the individual vis-à-vis the power of the State. However, the Federal Constitutional Court has already recognized in its famous Lüth decision of January 15, 1958[43] that the fundamental rights also have an impact on the relationships between individuals, the so-called horizontal effect of the fundamental rights [*Drittwirkung der Grundrechte*]. This means, that the judge always has to take into consideration fundamental rights in contractual or other legal relationships in the field of private law. Contrary to some early decisions of the Federal Labour Court[44] that were inspired by its then president *Hans Carl Nipperdey*,[45] the Federal Constitutional Court has not favored a direct but only an indirect horizontal effect of the fundamental rights: Accordingly, the judge has to interpret the general clauses of the Civil Code such as the *boni mores* [*Gute Sitten*] (Section 138 BGB), the principle of good faith [*Treu und Glauben*] laid down in Section 242 BGB or the principle of equitable discretion [*billiges Ermessen*] (Section 315, Para. 1 BGB, Section 106 German Trade Act [*Gewerbeordnung* – abbr. *GewO*]) in the light of the constitutionally guaranteed fundamental rights. One important impact of this doctrine is that judges have the constitutional duty to intervene in contractual relationships in order to compensate an otherwise arising disequilibrium between the parties by controlling the terms of contract on the basis of the principle of equity and good faith. It is obvious that this constitutional duty plays an important role for the employment contract characterized *per definitionem* by the dependence of the worker.

These principles also apply to the protection of religious freedom within the employment relationship. The horizontal effect of religious freedom under Article 4 GG can have an important impact on the workers' position. According to the general rules of the BGB on the non-performance of an obligation (Section 275, Para. 3 BGB), the obligor is entitled to refuse the work performance if he is to perform the work in person and if, after balancing the obligee's interest in the work performance and the impediment to performance, the work performance cannot be reasonably required of the obligor. There is no doubt that this general rule of law of obligations also applies to performance obstacles resulting from religious duties of the obligor.[46] Another example is the employer's directing power, which has to be exercised, according to Section 106 GewO, in respect of the principle of equity. The Federal Labor Court, in its constant

---

[43] 1 BvR 400/51, BVerfGE 7, p. 198 at 203–212; see also the decision of October 19, 1993 – 1 BvR 567, 1044/89, BVerfGE 89, p. 214, at pp. 231–234.

[44] *BAG*, decision of January 15, 1955, Arbeitsrechtliche Praxis (AP) Art. 3 GG No. 4.

[45] See *Nipperdey*, Gleicher Lohn der Frau für gleiche Leistung – Ein Beitrag zur Auslegung der Grundrechte, in: Recht der Arbeit (RdA) 1950, pp. 121; *id.*, in: Enneccerus/Nipperdey, Allgemeiner Teil des Bürgerlichen Rechts, 15th edition, Tübingen 1959, 1st volume, § 15 II 4.

[46] See ErfK/*Preis*, 16th edition, Munich 2016, BGB § 611, Para. 687 with further references.

jurisprudence,[47] considers that the employer shall take into account a religious or conscience conflict of his workers when directing the work performance. However, one criterion in balancing the interests of the parties is whether the worker could foresee the conflict when concluding the employment contract: Thus, also considerations of fault might apply in this context.

2. *The labor law of religious societies*

These general principles do not fully apply to employment relationships involving religious societies under Article 137 of the Weimar Constitution. According to estimates, about 1.2 million workers are employed by Church institutions in Germany.[48]

a) Church civil servants

As already pointed out, religious societies in the legal form of a statutory corporation are entitled under Article 137, Para. 3 of the Weimar Constitution to establish their own Church civil servant law [*Kirchenbeamtenrecht*]:[49] They can employ Church civil servants [*Dienstherrenfähigkeit*]. In particular priests as well as deacons in the Protestant Church and persons employed in certain positions within the Church administrations (e. g. of the diocese or of the Protestant Church at State level) have the status of Church civil servants.[50] The Protestant Church in Germany [*Evangelische Kirche in Deutschland* – abbr. *EKD*] – the umbrella organization of the different Protestant State Churches at Federal level – has established its own Act on Civil Servants of the Church, while the different State Churches have established specific Acts on the Service as a Pastor [*Pfarrerdienstgesetze*];[51] to the other Church civil servants, the civil servant law acts of the corresponding Church at State level apply. Also in the Roman Catholic Church priests have the status of Church civil servants: Their status

[47] See *BAG*, judgment of February 24, 2011 – 2 AZR 636/09, NZA 2011, pp. 1087 et seq; *BAG*, judgment of May 22, 2003 – 2 AZR 426/02, AP § 1 KSchG 1969 Wartezeit No. 18; judgment May 24, 1989 – 2 AZR 285/88, NJW 1990, pp. 203 et seq.; decision of December 20, 1984 – 2 AZR 436/83, AP § 611 BGB Direktionsrecht No. 27. See also *Fritz-René Grabau*, Die Wahrnehmung religiöser Pflichten im Arbeitsverhältnis, in: Betriebs-Berater (BB) 1991, pp. 1257 et seq.

[48] See *Harald Schliemann*, Europa und das deutsche kirchliche Arbeitsrecht, in: NZA 2003, p. 407.

[49] See *supra* II 2 a.

[50] For an overview of the legal situation in the Roman Catholic Church and in the different Protestant Churches at State level see *Dietrich Pirson*, Das Dienstrecht der Geistlichen und Kirchenbeamten, in: Joseph Listl & Dietrich Pirson (eds.), Handbuch des Staatskirchenrechts der Bundesrepublik Deutschland, 2nd edition, Berlin 1995, volume II, § 64 I 2.

[51] E. g. the Act on the Status of Pastors of the State Church of *Hesse* and *Nassau* [*Evangelische Kirche in Hessen und Nassau*]. The Act is accessible under: http://www.kirchenrecht-ekhn.de/#section_12_offset_top.

is defined by the rules of the *codex iuris canonici* in conjunction with episcopal acts at diocese level.[52]

b) Individual labor relations

In the case that religious societies create employment contracts with their workers, they have chosen as applicable law the rules of State labor law and are, in principle, bound by them. Consequently, the statutory rules protecting workers such as the Protection Against Dismissal Act, the provisions on sick pay, the Working Time Act, or the State labor law rules on health and safety at work are applicable to their employment relationships. However, Article 137, Para. 3 of the Weimar Constitution, in the interpretation of the courts and of the dominant doctrine, guarantees to religious societies a specific status in labor law. The Federal Constitutional Court, in its seminal decision of June 4, 1985,[53] holds that religious societies, as far as they act as employers, are entitled, under Article 137, Para. 3 of the Weimar Constitution, to order the service in the Church according to their self-concept; only by making use of this competence are the Churches able to maintain their authenticity in their service. Thus, the Churches can impose specific loyalty duties on their workers corresponding to the fundamental rules of their religious dogma and ethics and can within certain limits "clericalize" the employment relationship. The Christian Churches usually characterize their self-conception of the service in the Church as a Christian service community [*Christliche Dienstgemeinschaft*]. The Catholic Church, for instance, has concretized the loyalty duties of its workers in the "Basic Regulation regarding Service in the Church in the context of Employment Relationships" [*Grundordnung des kirchlichen Dienstes im Rahmen kirchlicher Arbeitsverhältnisse*].[54] It is perfectly in line with this case law of the Federal Constitutional Court that the federal legislature has created with Section 9, Para. 2 of the 2006 General Act on Equal Treatment [*Allgemeines Gleichbehandlungsgesetz* – abbr. *AGG*][55] a statutory provision saying that the loyal duty Churches impose on their workers does not constitute discrimination on grounds of religious belief; the provision transposes the so-called "Church clause" of Article 4, Para. 2 of Directive 2000/78/

---

[52] See e.g. Regulation of the Archdiocese of Freiburg on Church civil servants [*Kirchenbeamtenordnung für die Erzdiözese Freiburg*] of December 28, 2011, OJ 2011, pp. 190 et seq.

[53] 2 BvR 1703/83, 2 BvR 1718/83, 2 BvR 856/85, BVerfGE 70, pp. 138–173.

[54] The "Basic Regulation" is based on a resolution of the German Bishops' Conference and needs to be transposed by each diocese; cf. *Ulrich Rhode*, Kirchenrecht, 1st edition, Stuttgart 2015, p. 41. It has been revised by the German Bishops' Conference in 2015. The text is available at http://www.dbk.de/ueber-uns/vdd/dokumente-vdd/. For a fuller analysis of this important document see *Reinhard Richardi*, Die Grundordnung der katholischen Kirche für den kirchlichen Dienst im Rahmen kirchlicher Arbeitsverhältnisse, in: NZA 1994, pp. 19–24.

[55] See *infra* III 4 b.

EC.[56] It is obvious that these higher loyalty duties for workers employed by the Churches and their institutions might come into conflict with the individual religious freedom of workers. Some of these conflicts will be considered in greater detail below.[57]

c) Collective labor law

As far as collective labor law is concerned, Article 137, Para. 3 of the Weimar Constitution, in the predominant interpretation of this provision, justifies far-reaching restrictions in the institutions of religious societies.

aa) Collective bargaining and the concept of a "third way" of the Christian Churches

Thus, the Federal Constitutional Court[58] and the Federal Labor Court have recognized that the peculiarities to which employment relationships with ecclesiastical institutions are submitted (their *propria*) shall be taken into account by labor law. In this vein, the Federal Labor Court has ruled that Article 137, Para. 3 of the Weimar Constitution gives religious communities the right to abrogate the rules of State labor law on collective bargaining as well as the judge-made principles on the right to strike and to replace them by an ecclesiastical system of regulation of working conditions which relies on the idea of an intensive cooperation between the Church and its employees.[59] The Federal Labor Court has therefore recently recognized that religious communities may exclude the strike as dispute resolution machinery: Pursuant to two important judgments of 2012,[60] religious communities may determine the *proprium* of employment in their institutions according to the idea of cooperation and the ideal of a "community of service".

---

[56] For a more in-depth analysis of this "Church clause" see *infra* III 4 b with further references.

[57] See *infra* IV 2.

[58] See BVerfG, judgment of 17 February 1981 – 2 BvR 384/78, BVerfGE 57, pp. 220 et seq.

[59] See *BAG* – 1 AZR 179/11, AP Art. 9 Grundgesetz "Arbeitskampf", No. 179; BAG, judgment of 20 November 2012 – 1 AZR 611/11, AP Art. 9 Grundgesetz "Arbeitskampf", No. 180; for a fuller analysis of this case law see *Reinhard Richardi*, Arbeitsrecht in der Kirche, pp. 167 et seq. This case law does not hinder a religious society from applying the rules on collective bargaining on a voluntary basis such as the Protestant Church of the Northern Elbe Region; for this specific case see *BAG*, judgment of 20 November 2012 – 1 AZR 611/11, AP Art. 9 Grundgesetz "Arbeitskampf", No. 180.

[60] *BAG*, judgment of 20 November 2012 – 1 AZR 179/11, AP Art. 9 Grundgesetz "Arbeitskampf", No. 179 ; *BAG*, judgment of 20 November 2012 – 1 AZR 611/11, AP Art. 9 Grundgesetz "Arbeitskampf", No. 180. A constitutional complaint of the Ver.di Union was dismissed by the Federal Constitutional Court: see *BVerfG*, resolution of July 15, 2015 – 2 BvR 2292/13, NZA 2015, pp. 1117 et seq.

Instead, the Catholic Church and the regional Churches within the Protestant Church in Germany [*Evangelische Kirche in Deutschland* – abbr. *EKD*][61] determine the working conditions of their workers by the so-called "third way". This means that the working conditions are not unilaterally determined by the ecclesiastical employer ("first way") nor by collective bargaining ("second way") but on behalf of a procedure provided by ecclesiastical law which places emphasis on the co-operation between the ecclesiastical employer and his workers and aims to avoid confrontation between them ("community of service"). Both the Catholic Church as well as the Protestant Churches in Germany have created commissions composed of employers' as well as workers' representatives. In the Catholic Church, each diocese has established such a commission[62] which shall determine the working conditions. The Protestant Churches have established so-called labor law commissions [*Arbeitsrechtliche Kommissionen*]. Both models rely on a mediation and arbitration procedure in case of disagreement between the groups represented within the commissions.

bb) Institutionalized forms of employee participation

By the same token, the constitutional guarantee of religious societies, in the interpretation of the Federal Constitutional Court, requires that the statutory works council system, laid down in the Works Constitution Act [*Betriebsverfassungsgesetz*], does not apply to them. As long as they have the status of a statutory corporation, they are exempted from it by Section 130 of the Works Constitution Act [*Betriebsverfassungsgesetz*] excluding all statutory corporations from the scope of the works council system. Furthermore, Section 118, Para. 2 BetrVG explicitly exempts their establishments from the scope of the works council system. Hence, in Church hospitals or in nursing homes run by a Church the workforce is not represented by works councils [*Betriebsräte*]. In addition, the worker representation system for the public sector [*Personalvertretung*] does not apply to the establishments of religious societies either (Section 112 of the Federal Act on Worker Representation in the Public Sector [*Bundespersonalvertretungsgesetz*]); at least as far as religious societies have the status of a statutory corporation it would be logical to submit the Churches to the public sector representation system.

The Catholic as well as the different Protestant Churches, however, have established their own worker representation systems [*Mitarbeitervertretungen*] by

---

[61] For an overview on the "third way" see *Reinhard Richardi*, Das kollektive kirchliche Dienst- und Arbeitsrecht, in: Joseph Listl & Dietrich Pierson (eds.), Handbuch des Staatskirchenrechts der Bundesrepublik Deutschland, Band II, 2nd edition, Berlin 1995, § 67 III. For a critical perspective on the "third way" see *Rainer Keßler*, Die Kirchen und das Arbeitsrecht, Darmstadt 1986, pp. 23 et seq.

[62] Commission for the determination of the law governing employment contracts [*Kommission zur Ordnung des Arbeitsvertragsrechts* – abbr. *KODA*].

Church law.[63] But in general, these representation systems are below the participation standards of the public sector representation system. The Churches have often been criticized for their "second class" representation regime. However, the general exemption of the Churches from the works council system in Section 118, Para. 2 BetrVG has never been seriously questioned.

The regime of the board-level co-determination [*Mitbestimmung*] also does not apply to Church institutions: Section 1, Para. 3 of the 1976 Co-determination Act as well as Section 1, Para. 2 of the Act on Co-determination by One Third [*Drittelbeteiligungsgesetz*] just repeat the wording of Section 118, Para. 2 BetrVG and therewith exempt Church institutions from the co-determination. As a result, workers in Church institutions organized in the legal form of a stock corporation [*Aktiengesellschaft*] or a limited company [*Gesellschaft mit beschränkter Haftung*] have no representatives in the supervisory boards of these corporations.

3. The contribution of collective labor law

One of the traditional instruments of labor law to protect workers is to give them a collective voice. Collective labor law is still a very important tool in protecting worker interests at the workplace. Therefore a glance shall be thrown at the contribution of German collective labor law to the protection of religious freedom at the workplace. In this context, the two main pillars of German industrial relations – both collective bargaining as well as the participation of the works councils [*Betriebsräte*] at establishment level – merit a closer look.

a) Collective bargaining

aa) Religiously inspired trade unions

As far as collective bargaining is concerned, one strategy of workers to influence their workplace in the sense of the religious doctrine they belong to has been – by far more in the past than in the present – to build or to join religiously oriented trade unions.

In principle, the constitutional guarantee of freedom of association (Article 9, Para. 3 GG) permits the formation of unions with a religious orientation: Their program, therefore, can rely on the dogma of a Church or another religious

[63] For further details on the worker representation within the institutions of the Churches see *Reinhard Richardi*, Arbeitsrecht in der Kirche: staatliches Arbeitsrecht und kirchliches Dienstrecht, 7th edition, Munich 2015. For the recent reform of these systems of worker representation in the Churches see *Gregor Thüsing*, Kirchliches Arbeitsrecht – Rechtsprechung und Diskussionsstand im Schnittpunkt von staatlichem Arbeitsrecht und kirchlichem Dienstrecht, Tübingen 2006, § 4.

group.[64] It is part of the internal autonomy of coalitions to determine their political or religious direction. Freedom of association does not oblige unions to be politically and religiously neutral. The only restriction resulting from the guarantee of freedom of association in Article 9, Para. 3 GG is that unions lose their privileged status of a coalition if religious societies or Churches have a dominating influence on the union making impossible the autonomous pursuit of workers interests:[65] This would be the case, for instance, if a Catholic bishop could take decisions with binding force for the workers of a Catholic trade union.

The only religiously inspired trade unions existing in Germany are the Christian trade unions. They have existed since the *Wilhelminian* Empire (1870–1918).[66] From their beginning on, they have been inter-confessional organizations uniting both Catholic as well as Protestant workers.[67] The current Christian Union Confederation of Germany [*Christlicher Gewerkschaftsbund Deutschlands* – abbr. *CGB*], as an umbrella organization, organizes around 280,000 workers[68] in sixteen Christian sector unions, the most important of which are the Christian Metalworkers' Union [*Christliche Gewerkschaft Metall* – abbr. *CGM*] and the Christian Union of the Chemical Industry. According to his own understanding, the *CGB*'s union activity rests on the Christian social doctrine, although it does not become clear what that means for the collective bargaining policy of its affiliated unions *in concreto*. The Christian trade union movement has only little relevance in German industrial relations: The unions affiliated to the *CGB* have only few members compared to the big unions organized within the German Confederation of Trade Unions [*Deutscher Gewerkschaftsbund* – abbr. *DGB*]. Since the legal capacity of a trade union to create collective agree-

---

[64] With view to the Christian Union Confederation of Germany [*Christlicher Gewerkschaftsbund Deutschland* – Abbr. *CGD*] see Regional Labor Court of *Düsseldorf* [*LAG Düsseldorf*], decision of December 14, 1957 – 1 BVTa 1/57, AP No. 2, Art. 9 GG.

[65] See *Manfred Löwisch* & *Volker Rieble*, Kommentar zum Tarifvertragsgesetz, 3rd edition, Munich 2012, § 2, Para. 88; *Hartmut Oetker*, in: Herbert Wiedemann (ed.), Kommentar zum Tarifvertragsgesetz, 7th edition, Munich 2007, § 2, Paras. 331–7.; *Franz Gamillscheg*, Kollektives Arbeitsrecht, Munich 1997, volume I, pp. 409 et seq.

[66] The origins of the Christian trade union movement and its development until 1933 is analyzed by *Michael Schneider*, Die christlichen Gewerkschaften: 1894–1933, Bonn 1982; for an overview see *Klaus Schönhoven*, Die deutschen Gewerkschaften, Frankfurt am Main 1987, pp. 72–76 with further references.

[67] However, it has to be mentioned that there was an important debate within the Catholic Church on whether Catholic workers were allowed to join inter-confessional trade unions. The Prussian bishops, in the so-called Fulda Pastoral of August 22, 1900, only recognized Catholic workers' associations under the guidance of Catholic priests, whereas Pope Pius X, in his Encyclical *Singulari quadam* of September 24, 1912, allowed under certain circumstances that Catholic workers would join inter-confessional unions. The Encyclical is published in: Bundesverband der Katholischen Arbeitnehmerbewegung – KAB (ed.), Texte zur katholischen Soziallehre, 8th edition, Bornheim 1992, pp. 41–59.

[68] That is the figure the *CGB* has published. See http://www.cgb.info/aktuell/imblickpunkt.php.

ments [*Tariffähigkeit*] (Section 2, Para. 1 of the Act on Collective Agreements [*Tarifvertragsgesetz*]) requires, according to the settled case law of the Federal Labor Court, a minimum of social power, their capacity to conclude collective agreements has been challenged.[69] However, there is a recent tendency of the *CGB* unions to compete in collective bargaining with the big unions of the *DGB* by concluding collective agreements whose social standards are much below the standards guaranteed by the *DGB* agreements.

Beside the unions of the *CGB*, there are two Catholic workers' and employers' associations that should be mentioned here although they have practically no relevance. The Catholic Workers' Movement [*Katholische Arbeitnehmerbewegung* – abbr. *KAB*][70] guarantees to its members legal advice and offers seminars and various insurances, but is not a collective bargaining actor. On the employers' side there is only the Confederation of Catholic Entrepreneurs [*Bund Katholischer Unternehmer – BKU*]. The *BKU* is a network of 1,200 Catholic entrepreneurs and executive staff members and is not involved in collective bargaining.[71]

bb) Religious freedom in collective agreements

Theoretically, questions related to religious freedom at the workplace might be addressed by collective bargaining. It is imaginable, for instance, that the right to wear religious symbols at the workplace (e g. the Muslim headscarf or a Sikh turban) or to take a leave of absence in order to fulfil religious duties such as the visit of worship or prayers is determined by collective agreements. As far as the practice of collective bargaining in Germany is concerned, however, these questions seem to have no relevance at all. The important collective agreements, e.g. the public service agreements,[72] do not address these conflicts. Even the collective provisions that concretize the workers' right to claim the salary in case of an inconsiderable absence based on a reason in his person (Section 616 BGB) do not deal with the religiously justified absence of workers from the workplace (e.g. to attend a worship).[73]

There are several reasons for this omission. One important reason is certainly that workers with non-Christian beliefs are underrepresented within the unions

---

[69] See *BAG*, resolution of March 28, 2006 – 1 ABR 58/04, AP § 2 TVG Tariffähigkeit, No. 4, in which the Court conceded the legal capacity to conclude collective agreements to the Christian Metalworkers' Union *CGM* challenged by the competing metalworkers' union *Industriegewerkschaft (IG) Metall*. The Federal Labor Court, however, recognized in this decision the *CGM*'s capacity to conclude collective agreements.

[70] Further details on the *KAB* are available on the website at: http://www.kab.de.

[71] Further details on the *BKU* are accessible on the website at: http://www.bku.de/index.php.

[72] Sec. 52 Federal Agreement for Employees [*Bundesangestelltentarifvertrag* – abbr. *BAT*] and Section 29 Collective Agreement for the Public Service [*TVöD*].

[73] The relevance of Section 616 BGB for religiously motivated absences at the workplace will be analyzed *infra* IV. 4.

of the German Confederation of Unions (*DGB*). Their collective voice is normally not strong enough to force the unions to put questions of religious expression in the workplace on their collective bargaining agenda. A second reason for this lack might be that collective bargaining at sector level still is prevalent in German industrial relations[74] whereas many of the questions of religious freedom are raised in the workplace and therefore have to be resolved at that level: the need for a decentralized settling of these conflicts becomes obvious when making complex working time schemes compatible with the exercise of religious duties of workers (e.g. the duty to say a prayer also during working hours, to observe *Ramadan* or celebrate a religious holiday that is not legally recognized). Sector level collective bargaining is often not the right level to face the problems that are connected with religious expression at the workplace.

b) The role of the works councils

Much more interesting than collective bargaining might be the worker representation at establishment level exercised by works councils according to the 1972 BetrVG. Works councils shall be established in workplaces with at least five workers; they represent the whole workforce at establishment level, unionized or not, and have significant participation rights vis-à-vis the employer.[75]

There are several provisions of the Works Constitution Act that are particularly interesting in the context of religious expression at the workplace. One of them is Section 75, Para. 1 BetrVG extending the principle of equal treatment to the works constitution: according to that provision, works councils and employers have to ensure that all persons working in the establishment are treated according to the principles of law and equity. Section 75, Para. 1 BetrVG considers the prohibition of discrimination as a core element of law and equity, *inter alia* discrimination that grounds on religion and belief. The content of this prohibition is considered to be identical with Directive 2000/78/EC and Sections 1 and 7 AGG. Hence, works councils and employers have to avoid not only direct but also indirect discrimination on grounds of religion.

As far as the missions of the works council are concerned, Section 80, Para. 1, No. 7 BetrVG does address religious expression at the workplace in an indirect but nonetheless important way. The rule obliges the works council to promote the integration of workers with a foreign nationality in the company and to deepen the mutual understanding between them and the German workers. The provision in its current version has only been established by the Works Consti-

[74] See *Achim Seifert*, Employment protection and employment promotion as goals of collective bargaining in the Federal Republic of Germany, in: IJLLIR 1999 (15), pp. 343–363, at pp. 344–347.

[75] For a detailed analysis of the German works council system see *Manfred Weiss* & *Marlene Schmidt*, Labour Law in the Federal Republic of Germany, 2008, Paras. 551–621.

tution Reform Act of 2001 and addresses, in particular, the integration of foreign workers with other cultural or religious backgrounds such as the numerous Turkish workers, who are Muslims in their majority. One important element of their integration certainly is that they are represented within the works councils.[76] However, this is not self-evident in practice. Section 80, Para. 1, No. 7 BetrVG is supplemented by the employer's duty to include in his report to the general assembly of the workers also some observations on the integration of workers with foreign nationalities into the company (Section 43, Para. 2, Sent 3 BetrVG) and by the workers' right to also talk about integration matters at the general assembly (Section 45, Sent. 1 BetrVG). Furthermore, works councils and employers can conclude so-called voluntary works agreements [*Betriebsvereinbarungen*] on measures regarding the integration of workers with foreign nationalities (Section 88, No. 4 BetrVG).

Works councils can accomplish this integrationist mission by exercising their participation rights. A few examples will suffice: The works council has a co-decision right as far as the workers' behaviour in the establishment and the work rules are concerned (Section 87, Para. 1, No. 1 BetrVG), which also implies co-decision on the establishment of dress codes by the employer:[77] works councils therefore have to ask themselves, for instance, whether a certain dress code can be an obstacle to or may promote the integration of Muslim workers wearing a headscarf. Furthermore, the works council has a co-decision right regarding the working time schedule (Section 87, Para. 1, No. 2 BetrVG) and thereby can take into consideration the interests of Muslim workers with regard to their duty to pray when determining the pauses. Further, in exercising their co-decision right regarding the administration of social institutions of the employer (Section 87, Para. 1, No. 8 BetrVG) such as company restaurants the works council can make sure that the different religious groups represented within the company can have menus that comply with their religious nutrition duties. Finally, works councils can fight the recruitment of persons who might disturb the peace in the shop by violating the principles of law and equity, in particular by xenophobic attempts (Section 99, Para. 2, No. 6 BetrVG) and they are entitled to request protection from the employer for the same reasons with a view to dismissal of these workers (Section 104 BetrVG).

---

[76] See *Michael Blank*, Gleichbehandlung und Integration ausländischer Arbeitnehmer im Betrieb, in: Arbeit und Recht 1993, pp. 286–292, at p. 292. The Works Constitution Act, however, does not promote the representation of immigrant workers or of workers belonging to (religious) minorities within the works councils. Sec. 15, Para. 1 *BetrVG* only requires that the different departments of the company and the different professional activities performed in the companies shall be represented within the works council. And Section 15, Para. 2 *BetrVG* reserves works council seats to the minority gender at least in the same proportion in which it is represented within the whole workforce.

[77] *BAG*, decision of January 17, 2012 – 1 ABR 45/10, NZA 2012, pp. 687 et seq. with further references.

There is no empirical evidence regarding the extent to which works councils (and employers) make use of these provisions to protect religious freedom in the workplace. Thus, statements on the effectiveness and the usefulness of the works councils' activity in this regard have no empirical basis.

4. The growing relevance of anti-discrimination law

For a very long period of time, the constitutional principle of equal treatment (Article 3 GG) has only had a shadowy existence. There has not been a considerable case law of the courts on the constitutional prohibition of discrimination on grounds of religious belief under Article 3, Para. 3 GG although the Federal Labor Court has recognized that a dismissal violating the principle of equal treatment under Article 3, Para. 3 GG is contrary to public policy and is therefore void (Section 134 BGB).[78] Also the aforementioned equal access to all public offices independent from religious belief (Article 33, Para. 3 GG) has not left its traces in the case law.

The reasons for this insignificance of the constitutional principle of equal treatment for the protection of religious expression in the workplace are twofold. As far as the scope of Article 3 GG is concerned, the Federal Constitutional Court has always considered that the provision exclusively covers direct, but not indirect, discrimination; only recently – and apparently under the influence of EU anti-discrimination law that had to be transposed into German law – did the Federal Constitutional Court seem to abandon this restrictive interpretation of Article 3 GG.[79] Another reason for the missing relevance of the constitutional principle of equal treatment in labor law might be that, contrary to EU anti-discrimination law (e.g., Article 10 of Directive 2000/78/EC), the courts have not accepted a shift of the burden of proof in anti-discrimination cases.[80]

[78] *BAG*, decision of September 28, 1972, 2 AZR 469/71, Entscheidungssammlung zum Arbeitsrecht [Abbr. EzA] Nr. 25 zu § 1 KSchG.

[79] See *BVerfG*, decision of November 27, 1997, 1 BvL 12/91, BVerfGE 97, pp. 35 et seq., at p. 43, and decision of January 30, 2002, 1 BvL 23/96, BVerfGE 104, pp. 373 et seq., at p. 393. For further details see *Osterloh & Nußberger*, in: Sachs (ed.): Kommentar zum Grundgesetz, 7th edition, Munich 2014, Art. 3, Para. 255 et seq. with further references.

[80] According to Article 10, Para. 1 of Directive 2000/78/EC, Member States shall take such measures as are necessary, in accordance with their national judicial systems, to ensure that, when persons who consider themselves wronged because the principle of equal treatment has not been applied to them may establish, before a court or other competent authority, facts from which it may be presumed that there has been direct or indirect discrimination. It shall then be for the respondent to prove that there has been no breach of the principle of equal treatment. It is certainly no exaggeration to say that the shift of burden of proof in such cases has become a general principle of the anti-discrimination law of the EU.

a) General principles of anti-discrimination legislation

This shadowy existence of anti-discrimination law in Germany only ended recently as a result of the rapid development of European anti-discrimination law and its transposition into German law in the General Act on Equal Treatment [*Allgemeines Gleichbehandlungsgesetz* – abbr. *AGG*] of August 2006.[81]

As far as discrimination on grounds of religious belief is concerned, Directive 2000/78/EC of November 27, 2000 establishing a General Framework for Equal Treatment in Employment and Occupation,[82] for the first time in EU law laid down a legal framework for combating discrimination in the workplace. It is not exaggerated to say that the Directive overshadowed by far the relevance of Article 3 GG. The Directive has been transposed by the Federal Republic of Germany – after a heated political debate and with a delay of several years[83] – through the adoption of the AGG. Only a few words on the core elements of this new anti-discrimination legislation will be necessary in the present context.

Sections 1 and 7, in conjunction with Section 3, Paras. 1–2 AGG prohibit direct as well as indirect discrimination on grounds of religious belief. Furthermore, Section 3, Para. 4 AGG considers harassments related to the religious belief of a worker as discrimination. The same applies to instructions to discriminate against persons on any of the grounds prohibited by the AGG (Section 3, Para. 5 AGG). The prohibition of discrimination on grounds of religious belief covers – as the prohibition of discrimination on other grounds enumerated in Section 1 AGG – *inter alia* the conditions for access to employment, employment and working conditions, and pay (Section 2, Para. 1 AGG). Although Section 2, Para. 4 AGG explicitly provides that the Protection Against Dismissal Act [*Kündigungsschutzgesetz*] should only apply for dismissals, the Federal Labor Court has recently ruled that the provisions of the AGG shall be taken into consideration when interpreting the notion of social justification in Section 1, Para. 2 of the Protection Against Dismissal Act. By this, the Court avoids an obvious conflict with Article 3, Para. 1 (c) of Directive 2000/78/EC according to which also "conditions of dismissals" fall under the scope of the prohibition of discrimination based on religion.[84]

Direct discrimination on grounds of religion or belief is forbidden in general. Section 8, Para. 1 AGG, however, considers unequal treatment not to be a discrimination where, by reason of the nature of the particular occupational activities concerned or of the context in which they are carried out, such a characteristic constitutes a genuine and determining occupational requirement, provided

[81] OJ of the FRG 2006 Part I p. 1897 [*Bundesgesetzblatt Teil I*].

[82] OJ of the EC L 303/16 of December 2, 2000.

[83] For this reason, the European Court of Justice (ECJ) has condemned the Federal Republic of Germany. See *ECJ*, decision of February 23, 2006, C-43/05 (OJ C 131/23).

[84] *BAG* decision of November 6, 2008 – 2 AZR 701/07, NZA 2009, p. 361; see also *BAG* judgment of December 19, 2013 – 6 AZR 190/12, NZA 2014, p. 372.

that the objective is legitimate and the requirement is proportionate. In a modern society, however, there will be only very few cases in which the religion of the worker is a legitimate occupational requirement under Section 8, Para. 1 AGG.[85]

In addition, employers are not only obliged to abstain from discrimination in the sense of the AGG. They also have a prevention duty (Section 12, Para. 1 AGG): They have to guard against discrimination of their workers by taking the necessary measures. The employer fulfills this prevention duty by instructing his personnel on how to comply with the anti-discrimination legislation (Section 12, Para. 2 AGG).

The AGG provides several sanctions for discrimination on grounds of religious belief. Leaving aside the right of the victim to complain (Section 13 AGG), the victim of a harassment is entitled to refuse to perform his/her work without losing his/her remuneration (Section 14 AGG). Furthermore, the victim may claim from the employer who has discriminated against him/her compensation for material damage (Section 15, Para. 1 AGG) as well as for immaterial damage suffered (Section 15, Para. 2 AGG); if the discrimination concerns recruitment, the compensation for immaterial damage suffered is limited to a three months' salary if the victim has not been the best qualified candidate and would not have been recruited without the discrimination.

So far, there is no case law of the *ECJ* and of German labor courts on discrimination on grounds of religions or belief. However, there are currently two cases pending at the ECJ which raise questions related to the wearing of the Islamic headscarf at the workplace: The case of *Samira Achbita* goes back to a request for a preliminary ruling from the Belgian *Cour de cassation* [*Hof van cassatie*] and raises the question whether a company policy of strict religious and ideological neutrality, excluding the wearing of a headscarf at work, constitutes a direct discrimination on grounds of religion under Directive 2000/78/EC.[86] According to the opinion of Advocate General *Juliane Kokott*, such company rules may be considered as operational requirements under Article 4, Para. 1 of Directive 2000/78/EC.[87] In the case *Asma Bougnaoui*,[88] the French *Cour de cassation* asked the Court whether the wish of a customer of an information technology consulting company to no longer have the services of that company provided by an employee wearing an Islamic headscarf may be a genuine and determining requirement in the sense of Article 4, Para. 1 of 1 Directive 2000/78/EC. It is presumable that the decisions of the *ECJ* in these two preliminary proceedings will

---

[85] See *Gregor Thüsing*, Allgemeines Gleichbehandlungsgesetz § 8, Para. 33, in: Münchener Kommentar zum Bürgerlichen Gesetzbuch, 7th edition, Munich 2015, volume I/2.

[86] Case C-157/15.

[87] Opinion of Advocate General *Juliane Kokott* delivered on May 31, 2016.

[88] Request for a preliminary ruling from the French Cour de cassation lodged on 24 April 2015, Case C-188/15.

have an important impact on the headscarf problematic in the Member States. We will come back to this point when discussing some areas of conflict.[89]

b) Anti-discrimination law and employment relationships with Church institutions

As far as occupational activities within Churches or other religious groups are concerned, the German legislature has tried to cement the privileges of religious societies under Article 137, Para. 3 of the Weimar Constitution.

According to Section 9, Para. 1 AGG, unequal treatment of a religious society on grounds of religion shall, notwithstanding the exception of Section 8 AGG, not be considered as discrimination a certain religious belief constitutes a justified occupational requirement considering the self-conception of the religious society or the nature of the professional activity. And Section 9, Para. 2 AGG states that the prohibition of discrimination on grounds of religion does not affect the right of religious societies and their institutions to claim loyalty from their workers in the sense of their religious doctrine; thus, Section 9, Para. 2 AGG codifies the settled case law of the Federal Constitutional Court and of the Federal Labor Court rooting in the autonomy of religious societies under Article 137, Para. 3 of the Weimar Constitution and leaving it up to the religious societies to determine autonomously the content of the loyalty duty of their workers, according to their religious dogmata.[90]

Section 9 AGG goes back to the so-called "Church-clause" of Article 4, Para. 2 of Directive 2000/78/EC entitling the Member States to maintain existing rules

> "pursuant to which a difference of treatment, based on a person's religion or belief shall not constitute discrimination where, by reason of the nature of these activities or of the context in which they are carried out, a person's religion or belief constitute a genuine, legitimate and justified occupational requirement, having regard to the organisation's ethos".

Furthermore, Article 4, Para. 2 underlines that, provided its provisions are otherwise complied with, the Directive shall not prejudice the right of Churches and other public or private organizations, the ethos of which is based on religion or belief, acting in conformity with the national Constitution and laws, to require individuals working for them to act in good faith and with loyalty to the organization's ethos. The "Church-clause" has been integrated into the Directive on the initiative of the Republic of Ireland advocating the interests of the Churches within the legislation process.[91] Article 4, Para. 2 aims at concretizing the – legally not binding – EU Council Declaration on the status of Churches and

[89] See *infra* IV.

[90] See *supra* III 2.

[91] See *Peter Hanau* & *Gregor Thüsing*, Europarecht und kirchliches Arbeitsrecht: Bestandsaufnahme und Perspektiven, Baden-Baden 2001, p. 31.

non-confessional organizations of June 18, 1997[92] which has become a binding rule with the Treaty of Lisbon (Article 17 TFEU).

So far, the extent to which Article 4, Para. 2 of Directive 2000/78/EC privileges Churches still remains unclear. The *ECJ* has not had the opportunity yet to clarify the meaning of the "Church-clause". However, there is a request of the Federal Labor Court for a preliminary ruling pending at the ECJ, raising the question whether an ecclesiastical employer is entitled under Article 4, Para. 2 of Directive 2000/78/EC to request from his workers a certain religion as essential operational requirement.[93] It is not excluded that the *ECJ* will interpret the rule in a restrictive sense emphasizing the nature of the work performed by a worker and will gradate the loyalty duty of workers in relation to their closeness to the *propria* of the Church: Thus, a teacher in a Catholic school would be submitted to a much more intense loyalty duty than a charwoman in a Catholic hospital.

IV. Relevant areas of conflict

The foregoing rather abstract observations require some illustration on the basis of the existing case law of the labor courts. This permits us to develop the relevant areas of conflict between the operational interests of employers and their workers' religious expression in the workplace.

It is interesting to note that, contrary to other countries, proselytism on the part of employers is not a relevant phenomenon in Germany: To my knowledge there is only one case of proselytism decided on by the administrative courts where the employer tried to proselytize his apprentices.[94] The focus is clearly on the workers' religious freedom in the workplace. The conflicts concern, in particular, the employer's right to question candidates in the hiring process (I.), the limits of the loyalty duty of workers employed by religious societies (II.), the presence of religious symbols at the workplace (III.), and the limits religious freedom imposes on the workers' duty to work (IV.). These different areas of conflict merit a closer look.

[92] OJ EC No. C 340/133. In this declaration, the Council declared that "the EU respects and does not prejudice the status under national law of Churches and religious associations or communities in the Member States"; furthermore, the Council stated that the EU equally respects the status of philosophical and non-confessional organisations.

[93] BAG, decision of March 17, 2016 – 8 AZR 501/14 (A) (not yet published).

[94] See *BVerwG*, decision of November 9, 1962 – VII C 84.59, NJW 1963, p. 1170; see also the appeal decision of the *Oberverwaltungsgericht (OVG) Rheinland-Pfalz* of October 16, 1956 – 2 A 15/56, in: Betriebs-Berater (BB) 1956, p. 1107.

1. Religious freedom in the hiring process

As far as the hiring process is concerned, religious expression or rather the freedom not to express a religious belief, can be at stake when the employer intends to obtain information on the religious orientation of the candidates.

Since the religious belief is normally not relevant for the performance of the work, the employer does not have the right to ask the candidate in an interview which religious belief he or she belongs to.[95] This corresponds to Article 136, Para. 3 of the Weimar Constitution, according to which no one can be obligated to reveal his or her affiliation to a religious group. This constitutional provision does not only protect the individual vis-a-vis State authorities, but also in relation to other individuals. Hence, it has been consented that this question would violate the candidate's privacy and is therefore to be considered as unlawful in principle.[96] The candidate has the right not to answer or to give a wrong answer to the question ("right to lie"). The employer is not entitled to void the employment contract for wilful deceit according to Section 123, Para. 1 BGB or for error (Section 119, Para. 2 BGB) after discovering that the worker has given a wrong answer to the question. In addition, also Sections 1 and 7 AGG exclude questions from the employer on the religious orientation of candidates since this is a forbidden discrimination on grounds of religion or belief unless the religious belief is a genuine and determining occupational requirement, provided that the objective is legitimate and the requirement is proportionate (Section 8, Para. 1 AGG);[97] the anti-discrimination rules also explicitly apply to conditions for access to employment (Section 2, Para. 1, No. 1 AGG).

However, there is one important exception from this principle. The Federal Constitutional Court considers constitutional, in constant jurisdiction,[98] the Church tax law rules [*Kirchensteuergesetz*], demanding from the employer to ask his workers about their affiliation to a religious society, in order to pay the

---

[95] See *Achim Seifert*, in: Simitis (ed.), Bundesdatenschutzgesetz, 8th edition (2014), § 32, Para. 39 with further references.

[96] ErfK/*Preis*, 16th edition, Munich 2016, § 611 BGB, Para 274.

[97] See also *Grabau*, BB 1991, pp. 1257–1262, at p. 1260, arguing with the constitutional principle of equal treatment (Article 3 *GG*).

[98] *BVerfG*, decision of February 17, 1977 – 1 BvR 33/76, BVerfGE 44, pp. 103–105; *BVerfG*, decision of October 25, 1977 – 1 BvR 323/75, BVerfGE 46, pp. 266 et seq.; *BVerfG*, decision of October 23, 1978 – 1 BvR 439/75, BVerfGE 49, pp. 375–377; *BVerfG*, decision of May 25, 2001 – 1 BvR 2253/00, in: Neue Zeitschrift für Verwaltungsrecht (NVwZ) 2001, p. 909. See also Federal Financial Court [*Bundesfinanzhof* – abbr. *BFH*], decision of July 4, 1975 – VI R 173/72, BFHE 116, pp. 485 et seq. For a critical review of these decisions see *Johannes Wasmuth & Gernot Schiller*, Verfassungsrechtliche Problematik der Inpflichtnahme von Arbeitnehmern und Arbeitgebern beim Kirchlohnsteuereinzug, in: NVwZ 2001, pp. 852–859; *Roman F. Adam*, Religionsfreiheit im Arbeitsrecht, in: Neue Zeitschrift für Arbeitsrecht (NZA) 2003, pp. 1375–1380, at pp. 1379–1380. For the constitutionality of the Church tax Acts see *Hans Ulrich Anke & Diana Zacharias*, Das Kirchenlohnsteuereinzugsverfahren aus der Sicht des Verfassungsrechts, in: DÖV 2003, pp. 140–147.

workers' Church tax in case that they are affiliated to a religious society in the legal form of a statutory corporation under Article 137, Para. 5 of the Weimar Constitution. Thus, the right not to reveal an affiliation to a religious group does not exist for a large number of workers, in particular those who belong to the Roman Catholic or to one of the Protestant Churches. Whether this jurisdiction is in line with the prohibition of discrimination on grounds of religious belief under the Directive 2000/78/EC remains to be seen.

2. The loyalty duty of workers in religious societies

It has been shown above[99] that the autonomy of religious societies under Article 137, Para. 3 of the Weimar Constitution implies their right to define the content of the loyalty duty their workers are submitted to. This principle has recently been codified in Section 9, Para. 2 AGG. The loyalty duty can even affect their conduct of life beyond the working hours. It has often occupied the labor courts. Just a few significant examples will suffice.

One famous case is known as the *Rommelfanger* case. In its ecision of June 4, 1985, the Federal Constitutional Court had to decide upon the dismissal of a doctor employed by a Catholic hospital who had signed a public statement with other doctors favoring a liberalization of the abortion legislation (Section 218 Criminal Code). The doctor was immediately dismissed by the Church institution, its argument being that the statement was not compatible with the Catholic Church's doctrine on abortion. The Federal Constitutional Court held that it was up to the Churches to determine their services according to their dogmata and can claim from their workers the respect of the fundamental rules of this dogma. Thus, behavior such as that of the dismissed doctor can justify, in principle, a dismissal for disloyalty. Other examples are the dismissal of a female teacher employed by a Catholic Church institution who had sexual relations with the schoolmaster, a monk,[100] and the dismissal of a governess in a Protestant kindergarten who, at the same time, was active for the Universal Church.[101] The Federal Constitutional Court considered the dismissals in both cases as justified by the autonomy of religious societies under Article 137, Para. 3 of the Weimar Constitution: the behavior of the dismissed workers violated, in both cases, their loyalty duty vis-à-vis the Church and thereby damaged the credibility of the Church in the public.

Dismissals of workers from Catholic institutions for having officially left the Church for which they were working are problematic. According to canon law, Church secession is a major misconduct. The "Basic Regulation regarding

[99] See *supra* III 2.

[100] See *BVerfG*, decision of January 31, 2001 – 1 BvR 619/92, in: NZA 2001, pp. 717 et seq.

[101] See *BVerfG*, decision of March 7, 2002 – 1 BvR 1962/01, in: NZA 2002, pp. 609 et seq. *Idem* the decision of the Federal Labor Court in the same case: see *BAG*, decision of February 21, 2001 – 2 AZR 139/00, in: AP § 611 BGB Kirchendienst, No. 29.

Service in the Church in the context of Employment Relationships" [*Grundordnung des kirchlichen Dienstes im Rahmen kirchlicher Arbeitsverhältnisse*], in its Article 5, Para. 2 No. 2 a) underpins this. Originally, the Federal Labor Court did not consider Church secession of workers as such as a sufficient reason for dismissal:[102] The Court required a gradation according to the proximity of the work performance to the mission of the Church ["Verkündigungsnähe"]. The Federal Constitutional Court in its important decision of June 4, 1984,[103] however, overruled the Federal Labor Court and held that the autonomy of religious societies under Article 137, Para. 3 of the Weimar Constitution guaranteed the right of Churches to regulate employment in their institutions according to their own religious dogmata and ethics. Violations of these loyalty duties by the worker, such as the resigning from the Church may justify a dismissal. Nonetheless, there are some labor courts that still follow the old jurisdiction of the Federal Labor Court and gradate the loyalty duty according to the worker's proximity to the mission of the Church.[104] Whether this case law may be maintained under Directive 2000/78/EC and the AGG is more than questionable: The so-called "Church-clause" of Article 4, Para. 2[105] only considers those differences of treatment within Church institutions not to be discriminatory where, "by reason of the *nature* of these activities or of the *context* in which it is carried out, a person's religion or belief constitute a genuine, legitimate and justified occupational requirement, having regard to the organisation's ethos". The emphasis Article 4, Para. 2 is placing on the nature of the work performed by the worker and the context in which it is carried out is rather an argument for a gradation of the loyalty duty of Church workers according to the function they are performing. Taking this as a basis, the loyalty duty of a housekeeper obviously cannot be as far-reaching as that of a teacher in a confessional school. But also the European Court of Human Rights requires a balancing.[106] In *Schüth v Germany* the Court has recognized that, on the one hand, Article 9 combined with Article 11 ECHR guarantees the right of Churches to base their employment contracts on the concept of a "community of service" but that on the other hand the Church shall also consider the fundamental rights of the employee such as the right to respect of the private sphere under Article 10 ECHR.[107]

---

[102] See *BAG*, decision of March 4, 1980, AP Art. 140 GG, No. 4; decision of March 23, 1984, AP Art. 140 GG No. 16 and decision of December 12, 1984, AP Art. 140 No. 21.

[103] 2 BvR 1703, 1718/83 and 856/85, BVerfGE 70, pp. 138 et seq., at pp. 162 et seq.

[104] See e. g. *LAG Rheinland-Pfalz*, decision of September 30, 2004 – 6 Sa 346/04 (juris-doc.) and *LAG Brandenburg*, decision of November 13, 2003 – 2 Sa 410/03 (juris-doc.).

[105] See supra III. 4. b).

[106] Application No. 1620/03, Paras. 53 et seq.; judgment of September 23, 2010, application No. 425/03 (*Obst v Germany*), Paras. 39 et seq.

[107] Judgment of September 23, 2010, application No. 1620/03 (*Schüth v Allemagne*), Para. 74; see also ECtHR (Grand Chamber), judgment of July 9, 2013 – application No. 2330/09 (*Sindicatul Pastorul Cel Bun v Roumanie*), Paras. 159 et seq.

It seems however that the Federal Labor Court is returning to its original concept of a gradation of the employee's loyalty duty. In a judgment of April 25, 2013,[108] the Court recognized that leaving the Catholic Church was not as such a reason for dismissal and that the constitutional autonomy of religious communities under Article 137, Para. 3 of the Weimar Constitution and the rights of the employee needed to be balanced. In the case at hand, the interests of the Church prevailed since the work of the dismissed employee, a social worker of the *Caritas*, was closely linked to the mission of the Church. Even though the Court left open the question whether the leaving of the Church of an employee whose work is rather remote from the mission of the Church (*e.g.* a janitor of a Catholic hospital or a gardener of a Catholic nursing home) constituted a reason for dismissal, it seems clear from the judgment that the Court will differentiate in the future according to the proximity of the work to the mission of the Church.

These recent developments have influenced the German Catholic Church. As a matter of fact, the German Bishops' Conference revised its "Basic Regulation regarding Service in the Church in the context of Employment Relationships" in 2015 in the sense that it now recommends a consideration of all circumstances of the case before a dismissal may be pronounced by Church institutions if the employee has left the Church.[109]

3. *Religious symbols at the workplace*

By far more discussed in recent times is the question of the point at which workers can express their religious belief through religious symbols at the workplace. It is obvious that religious symbols at the workplace can affect the employer's interests as well as interests of colleagues not sharing the same religious belief as the worker who shows symbols of his or her religion during working time. The range of possible cases is wide: It can be a matter of a crucifix or religious posters hanging in the office of an employee or the wearing of religious garb such as the red garb of the *Baghwan* sect (*Mala*)[110] or a *Sikh* turban during working hours. The religious symbol *par excellence*, however, that has come up to the German courts is undoubtedly the Muslim headscarf. It is no exaggeration to say that the ongoing public debate on religious freedom in the workplace is focusing on the headscarf problematic. Therefore it is justified to concentrate on the headscarf cases in the following. As far as the admissibility of the wearing of a Muslim headscarf during working hours is concerned, differentiation must be made between the public and the private sector.

[108] 2 AZR 579/12, NZA 2012, pp. 1131 et seq.

[109] Cf. Article 5, Para. 3 Basic Regulation in the version of 27 April 2015.

[110] *LAG Düsseldorf*, decision of March 22, 1984 – 14 Sa 1905/83, in: Der Betrieb (DB) 1985, p. 391.

a) The public sector

As far as the public sector is concerned, the headscarf has been especially problematic in public schools. The Federal Constitutional Court had to deal with this issue on various occasions, most recently in 2015. Its general policy has undergone considerable development since the first decision the Court rendered in 2003.

aa) The decision of the Federal Constitutional Court in the Ludin case

The first "headscarf decision" of the Federal Constitutional Court concerned a case that became particularly famous and caused a heated public debate in Germany: the *Ludin* case.

After finishing her traineeship [*Referendariat*] at a State secondary school, a young female teacher demanded from the State of *Baden-Württemberg* to be employed as a teacher. The State refused to recruit the woman, the argument being that she intended to wear a headscarf during working time as an expression of her religious belief. The school administration argued that the headscarf was not in line with the constitutional principle of religious neutrality of the State. Therefore Ms. *Ludin* did not have the necessary eligibility required by Article 33, Para. 2 GG for access to the public office.[111] Following this, Ms. *Ludin* brought the State of *Baden-Württemberg* before the Administrative Court and claimed her eligibility. Her lawsuit was dismissed on all points. The Administrative Court mainly held that the constitutional principle of religious neutrality of the State justified the State's denial to hire Ms. *Ludin* as a teacher. The wearing of a headscarf as a symbol of her religious belief during working hours could, according to the administrative judges, have a determining religious influence on the pupils.[112]

The Federal Constitutional Court, in an important and highly discussed ruling of September 24, 2003[113] held that the State school administration was not authorized to forbid the plaintiff to wear the headscarf as a symbol of her religious belief during school lessons. The Court recognized that the refusal of the school administration to employ Ms. *Ludin* restricted her religious freedom under Article 4 GG. However, it did recognize that the headscarf could come into conflict with other constitutional rights. The State's duty to provide a public school system (Article 7, Para. 1 GG) that respects the constitutional principle of religious neutrality of the State was at stake in this case: The Court interprets this principle in the sense of open neutrality that tries to resolve arising conflicts in the spirit of tolerance within the public schools. Another conflicting consti-

---

[111] Following Article 33, Para. 2 *GG*, every German enjoys equal access to public offices according to his eligibility, ability and qualification.

[112] See Federal Administrative Court [*Bundesverwaltungsgericht* – abbr. *BVerwG*] of November 23, 2000 – 3 C 40/99, NJW 2000, p. 3344.

[113] 2 BvR 1436/02, BVerfGE 108, pp. 282 et seq.

tutional right is the parents' right under Article 6, Para. 2 GG to educate their children, also implying the right to educate their children in religious matters. Finally, the negative religious freedom of pupils (Article 4 GG) who do not belong to the Islam community was also at stake: As they are submitted to public schooling, they cannot avoid the demonstration of the teacher's religious belief during school lessons by being absent from them. The Federal Constitutional Court admits that there is no empirical evidence for the assumption that a teacher's wearing of a headscarf while teaching might have a determining influence on the pupils' religious orientation. Nevertheless, it is, according to the Court, not in the competence of the school authorities to resolve these conflicts. As a result of the constitutional principle of the parliamentary reservation with regard to material matters relevant to fundamental rights [*Parlamentsvorbehalt*], the Court held that only the democratic legislature of the individual federasl states was competent to provide a solution to these matters. The Federal Constitutional Court therefore considered the school administration's refusal to recruit Ms. *Ludin* as a violation of her constitutional rights.

However, the Court made clear that the federal states were free to establish parliamentary acts settling these complex conflicts arising from the presence of religious symbols in public schools. But in doing so, the state legislature shall take into account the fundamental rights of the teacher, the pupils, their parents, and the constitutional principle of religious neutrality of the State. The Federal Constitutional Court gave much discretionary power to the state parliaments in exercising their authority in this context: The state parliaments may choose between an inclusive model integrating religious diversity into the public school system and a more laic model emphasizing more on the dissociation between religion and public schools. Thus, the Federal Constitutional Court passed the ball back to the political arena.

bb) Adoption of Neutrality Acts in the states

Shortly after this seminal decision of the Federal Constitutional Court, several federal states captured the ball and swiftly established what has come to be known as "Neutrality Acts", which explicitly outlaw the wearing of religious garb or of religious symbols and thereby Muslim headscarves for teachers during school lessons [e.g., *Baden-Württemberg*][114] or even in the whole public sector [e.g., *Hesse*][115]. Other States have not adopted Neutrality Acts. From a constitutional point of view, several Neutrality Acts are questionable as far as they explicitly allow reference to "Christian and occidental values" or to the "Christian occidental

[114] Cf. the new Section 38, Para. 2 of the Act on public schools of April 1st, 2004 (OJ of the State of *Baden-Württemberg* 2004, p. 178).

[115] See Section 68, Para. 2 of the Hessian Civil Servants Act [*Hessisches Beamtengesetz*] of October 21, 2004 (OJ of the State of *Hesse*, Part I, p. 306).

tradition" in public schools. They clearly express the state legislatures' view that the different non-Christian religions represented in Germany are not on the same level as the Christian Churches. Although different models exist in the various federal states, one overarching tendency can be identified. With the exception of the Neutrality Act of the State of *Hesse*, which bans religious symbols from the whole public sector, the majority of the rules are trying to limit the restrictions of religious freedom of workers and civil servants to the cases in which State neutrality really might be affected such as is the case with teaching in public schools.

The Federal Administrative Court considered the Neutrality Act of *Baden-Württemberg* as being in line with the constitutional principle of religious neutrality of the State.[116] And the Constitutional Court of Bavaria [*Bayerischer Verfassungsgerichtshof*][117] held that the Bavarian neutrality provision in Article 59, Para. 2 of the Bavarian Act on Education and Instruction did not violate the constitutional rights of Muslim teachers: According to this provision religious symbols or religious garb worn by teachers during school lessons are not admissible in cases where they can be considered by pupils or by their parents as being contrary to the constitutional order including the values of the Christian-occidental culture. As far as the access to the compulsory school traineeship [*Referendariat*] is concerned, the Federal Administrative Court softened the effect of these Neutrality Acts: In a ruling of June 26, 2008,[118] the Court held that a general exclusion of applicants refusing to abstain from wearing religious symbols during school lessons was illegal since this would equal a general prohibition to work as a school teacher; it has to be taken into account that also private schools normally only recruit teachers who have passed the traineeship within the public school service.

cc) The Federal Constitutional Court's new orientation

In its judgment of January 27, 2015, the Federal Constitutional Court has revised its former position.[119] The decision concerned the Neutrality Act of the State of North Rhine-Westphalia (NRW). This Act forbids teachers in public schools to express views of a political, religious, ideological or similar nature which are likely to endanger, or interfere with, the neutrality of the *Land* with regard to pupils and parents, or to endanger or disturb the political, religious and ideological

[116] *BVerwG*, decision of June 24, 2004 – 2 C 45.03, BVerwGE 121, pp. 140 et seq. The decision has been highly criticized: see *Czermak*, op. cit., Para. 314.

[117] Decision of January 15, 2007 – Vf. 11-VII-05.

[118] 2 C 22/07, NJW 2008, pp. 3654 et seq.

[119] Case 1 BvR 471/10 and 1 BvR 1181/10, BVerfGE 138, pp. 296 et seq. For a critical analysis of this decision see *Achim Seifert*, The Constitutionality of State Neutrality Acts in Germany and Implication for the Wearing of Muslim Headscarves, in: International Labor Rights Case Law 2 (2016) 101–106. The new position of the Federal Constitutional Court has been confirmed by a decision of October 18, 2016 – 1 BvR 354/11 in which the 2nd chamber of the Court's first Senate invalidated a statutory rule of a state act on nurseries forbidding that nursery workers wear religious symbols during the working hours.

peace at school. The decision marks a shift from a position that left it up to the legislature how to ensure State neutrality in religious matters in public schools to a more inclusive attitude which also tries to ensure the protection of religious freedom in public schools. As a result, a general ban of religious symbols from public schools is only exceptionally allowed when the headscarf entails a specific danger to the pupils' and the parents' rights. The only example the Court gives is that the wearing of the headscarf by a teacher would provoke conflicts with pupils and parents so that school life and the fulfillment of education would or might be affected. One main problem resulting from the decision is that the Court does not give further indications of when exactly a specific danger to the pupils' and parents' rights is provoked. Furthermore, the decision may provoke the adverse effect of what the judges had intended: The requirement of a specific danger for school peace may even provoke or aggravate conflicts in public schools because parents and pupils could feel encouraged to sharpen conflicts expressly to create a specific danger, thus enabling school authorities to prohibit the wearing of headscarves in school.

Another result of the decision is that the Court declared as unconstitutional a provision in the NRW Education Act privileging the presentation of Christian and occidental educational and cultural values and traditions in public schools.[120] The Court made clear that the prohibition of discrimination on grounds of religious belief under Article 3, Para. 3 and Article 33, Para. 3 GG did not authorize any privileging of the Christian religion in public schools. Thus, those states which have enacted similar rules[121] need to revise their Neutrality Acts.

dd) Perspectives

Furthermore, it remains to be seen whether the ECJ will accept headscarf bans as compatible with the prohibition of discrimination on grounds of religion under Directive 2000/78/EC. As has been shown above,[122] there are currently two headscarf cases pending at the ECJ. Even though the requests for a preliminary ruling in these cases have come from France and Belgium, the decisions in these cases may also have important impacts on German law and may force the Federal Constitutional Court to adapt its case law to the ECJ's line.

Additionally, it is highly questionable whether the reference made in several of these Neutrality Acts to the "Christian occidental tradition" complies with Directive 2000/78/EC. As the Directive also applies to public sector employment relationships (Article 3, Para. 1), all questions regarding the expression of religious belief at the workplace raised in the Member States now have to be reconsidered in the light of its provisions. It is obvious that a ban of the Muslim headscarf from

---

120 Sec. 57, Para. 4 (iii) of the NRW Education Act.

121 See *supra* IV 3 a bb with further references.

122 See *supra* III 4 a.

public schools or even from the public sector, with Christian symbols in schools being tolerated all the same, puts Muslim workers at a particular disadvantage compared to their Christian colleagues. The Neutrality Acts thereby constitute an indirect discrimination on grounds of religion. They are only admissible when the apparently neutral criterion or provision putting, for example, Muslim workers at a particular disadvantage compared to workers of other religious beliefs is objectively justified by a legitimate aim, and if the means of achieving that aim are appropriate and necessary (Section 8, Para. 1 AGG). Indeed, the safeguarding of State neutrality might be such a legitimate aim justifying the exclusion of religious symbols in the public service. However, the question has to be raised whether these State acts are really necessary to achieve State neutrality.

b) The private sector

In the private sector, however, the interests at stake are of a different nature on the employers' side than in the public sector. Here, instead of the constitutional neutrality duty of the State, the constitutional guarantee of free enterprise has to be taken into consideration.

The leading case for the private sector is the "headscarf" decision of the Federal Labor Court of October 10, 2002.[123] A saleswoman employed in a big department store in a small town, upon returning from her parental leave, informed the employer that she had changed her religious belief and that from now on she intended to wear a Muslim headscarf during working hours as an expression of her religious belief. As the employer feared that his customers, who in their majority held "rural and conservative views", would not tolerate the headscarf, he dismissed the saleswoman. The resulting lawsuit forced the Federal Labor Court to balance the worker's constitutionally guaranteed religious freedom of enterprise. The judges argued that the employer was obliged to discover by trial whether the worker's wearing of a headscarf would eventually cause the kind of problems with colleagues or with customers' preferences that the employer had anticipated. As a result, the employer had the contractual duty to figure out the actual limits of the customers' tolerance of religious diversity in his workplace; mere allegations of contradicting customers' preferences were not taken into account by the Court. If customers indeed did not tolerate the saleswoman's headscarf, the employer would have to try to solve the problem in another way than by dismissing the worker. The Court, consequently, aimed at protecting a maximum of religious freedom in the workplace and considered the dismissal as void.

[123] Decision of October 10, 2002 – 2 AZR 472/01, NJW 2003, pp. 1685–1688. For a more in-depth analysis of this important "headscarf decision" of the Federal Labour Court cf. *Achim Seifert*, Federal Labor Court strengthens religious freedom at the workplace, in: 4 German Law Journal No. 6 (1 June 2003), accessible at http://www.germanlawjournal.de/article.php?id=280. Cf. also *Achim Seifert*, in: Gladstone (ed.), International Labour Law Reports (ILLR) 23 (2004), pp. 111 et seq.

Since the "headscarf decision" of the Federal Labor Court in 2002, the legal environment has changed considerably. Now the problem of religious symbols at the workplace has to be reconsidered under the provisions of the AGG, transposing Directive 2000/78/EC into German law. Employers can only prohibit the presence of religious symbols such as the Muslim headscarf at the workplace if their directions do not directly or indirectly constitute a form of discrimination against workers on grounds of their religious belief. The provisions of the AGG even strengthen the worker's position: In most cases, the general prohibition of the headscarf during working hours (e. g., by neutrally formulated company dress codes) will be an indirect discrimination on grounds of religious belief. Furthermore, workers are now benefitting from a shift of the burden of proof, if they consider themselves to be victims of discrimination and can establish facts from which it may be presumed that they have been discriminated against (Article 10, Para. 1 of Directive 2000/78/EC, Section 22 AGG). It is obvious that this new legal framework also strengthens the position of workers as far as other religious symbols at the workplace are concerned.

For airlines, the headscarf problem may have the opposite effect. Flight attendants flying to Iran or to other Islamic countries may be obliged to wear a headscarf when outside the plane in one of these host countries. Thus, the German airline Lufthansa, for instance, has established a work rule providing that female flight attendants shall wear a headscarf when stopping over in Teheran.[124]

4. Conflicts between religious freedom and the duty to work

Another area of conflict discussed in German labor law is that of how to reconcile the religious freedom of workers with work schedules in companies. The exercise of certain religious duties can conflict with the work schedule determined by the employer.

a) Day of rest and religious holidays

The working calendar in Western countries typically privileges Christian workers. The weekly working schedule in which Sunday is *the* day of rest (Article 139 of the Weimar Constitution),[125] obviously disadvantages Muslims who consider Friday as a day of rest, or Jews who celebrate the Sabbath on Saturday. The same applies to the legally recognized religious holidays. The different Holidays Acts [*Feiertagsgesetze*] of the various federal states almost entirely recognize Christian holidays only.

[124] See Die Welt, available at: http://www.welt.de/wirtschaft/article153996175/Air-France-Stewardessen-sollen-Kopftuch-tragen.html.

[125] For further details see *supra* II 2 b.

aa) Day of rest

The observance of a day of rest required by religious rules can be very important for persons who aim to respect the rules of their religion. The Federal Administrative Court, for instance, ruled in the early 1970s that parents might be entitled to claim an exemption of their children from the compulsory school attendance on Saturdays if they belong to a religious group respecting the biblical command to sanctify the Sabbath.[126]

As far as the employment relationship is concerned, of course, there is no general contractual duty of the employer to respect the religious beliefs of his workers and to determine individually the day of rest according to the religious belief of each worker. Such far-reaching religious tolerance would cause extremely complex problems for companies in their efforts to reconcile the different interests within their workforce when determining the work schedule. Notwithstanding this, the employer as the obligee has the general duty resulting from Section 241, Para. 2 BGB to be considerate of the rights and interests of the worker as an obligor: This means that he has to take into account the fundamental rights of the workers such as his or her religious freedom. The Regional Labor Court of *Schleswig-Holstein*, in a ruling of June 22, 2005, recognized this principle[127] and held that a worker belonging to the Seventh-day Adventist Church could be entitled to refuse work on Saturday for religious reasons, unless the employer could invoke operational requirements in his favor; thus, it has been established that the labor courts shall decide on a case-by-case basis. In deciding that way, the Regional Labor Court of *Schleswig-Holstein* just applied the principles of the Federal Labor Court's "headscarf decision" of October 10, 2002.[128]

Regarding the job placement service of the Federal Employment Agency [*Bundesagentur für Arbeit*], the Federal Social Security Court [*Bundessozialgericht* – abbr. *BSG*] has ruled that the Agency is not allowed to penalize an unemployed worker (belonging to the Seventh-day Adventist Church) who refused a workplace on grounds that the work would not allow him or her to respect Saturday as a day of rest.[129]

bb) Religious holidays

Concerning religious holidays that are not legally recognized, there is no uniform solution provided by the law.

Most state acts on holidays [*Feiertagsgesetze*] concretize the principle enshrined in Section 275, Para. 3 BGB, according to which the worker can refuse

[126] *BVerwG*, decision of April 17, 1973 – VII C 38.70, BVerwGE 42, pp. 128 et seq. *Czermak*, op. cit., Para. 262 et seq.

[127] *LAG Schleswig-Holstein* – 4 Sa 120/05 (not published).

[128] See *supra* IV 3 b with further references.

[129] *BSG*, decision of December 10, 1980 – 7 Rar 93/79, NJW 1981, p. 1526.

to perform the work if the performance cannot be reasonably required by the employer, and oblige employers to give their workers belonging to a Church or to a religious society the opportunity to attend the service during a Church holiday that is legally recognized. However, the majority of these State regulations only privilege workers who belong to a recognized religious society under Article 137, Para. 5 of the Weimar Constitution, *i. e.* the Roman Catholic Church or the Protestant Church.[130] Only the Holiday Act of North Rhine-Westphalia[131] and that of Bavaria extend this right to the attending of worship during working hours to certain Jewish holidays (*Yom Kippur* and *Rosh Hashanah*). It is highly questionable whether this limitation to the worship of recognized religious societies is in line with the prohibition of discrimination on grounds of religion and belief under Directive 2000/78/EC: After all, workers who do not belong to a religious society under Article 137, Para. 5 of the Weimar Constitution are, in respect of the services on religious holidays that are not legally recognized, put at a particular disadvantage compared to their Catholic or Protestant colleagues.

It is interesting to note that Section 7, No. 7 of the Regulation on Special Leave for Federal Civil Servants and Judges of the Federal Government [*Verordnung über den Sonderurlaub für Bundesbeamtinnen, Bundesbeamte, Richter und Richterinnen des Bundes* – abbr. *SUrlV*] even goes further and entitles federal civil servants to a remunerated special leave of three working days (and in special cases even up to five days per year) in order to participate, as a member of a Church or another religious society having the status of a statutory corporation, in the meetings of committees of the latter, unless there are conflicting operational requirements; the same applies to the participation in Congresses of the Catholic or Protestant Church [*Kirchentag*]. The issue has not been raised up to now, but in my view these provisions for civil servants need to be read in the light of the rules of the anti-discrimination law[132] and have therefore to be extended to members of other religious communities.

As to the worker's remuneration for the period of his or her absence, it is not clear whether workers who exercise their religious freedom by attending worship on a religious holiday can claim a salary from the employer for that time. According to Section 2, Para. 1 of the Continuation of Remuneration Act [*Entgeltfortzahlungsgesetz* – abbr. *EFZG*], the worker can only claim the salary for holidays that are legally recognized. Hence, there is no continuation of remuneration in

[130] E. g. Section 4, Para. 1 of the Holiday Act of the State of *Hesse*.

[131] Sec. 9 Holiday Act of North Rhine Westphalia.

[132] The Federal Administrative Court, however, applies the provision strictly *à la lettre* and does not concede the right to a special leave to civil servants who are members of a religious community that is not recognized as a statutory corporation. See *BVerwG*, decision of November 13, 1984 – 2 C 74/81, NVwZ 1987, pp. 699 et seq.

cases where religious holidays are not legally recognized.[133] As far as Section 616 BGB is concerned, the situation is even more vague. Although it has been recognized that religious duties can be a reason in the worker's person hindering their work performance under this statutory provision,[134] one Court decision posits that Section 2 EFZG contains an exhaustive regulation of the salary payment in the case of (religious) holidays.[135] The affected workers, therefore, have to take a leave without remuneration, to take vacations according to the Federal Act on Vacations [*Bundesurlaubsgesetz*] in order to fulfil their religious duties.

The future will show whether this legal situation is in line with the provision of the AGG and with Directive 2000/78/EC. So far, the debate on a non-discriminatory determination of the workers' day of rest and of religious holidays is only beginning in Germany.

b) Working time interruption for prayer

Another conflict between the working time schedule and the religious freedom of workers can arise from Muslim workers' demands to interrupt their work for prayer during working time. In 2002, the Labor Court of Appeal of Hamm had to decide on such a case, but only in a procedure that concerned a demand for an interlocutory injunction:[136] The plaintiff requested from his employer to be granted a working time interruption of three minutes between 6 and 8 a.m. for his morning prayer, but the employer refused. Nonetheless, the plaintiff said his prayer without the authorization of his superior and received several warning notices by the employer. In the subsequent lawsuit he demanded that the employer revoke the warning notices. The Labor Court of Appeal of Hamm dismissed the lawsuit arguing that the plaintiff could not claim from the employer the demanded working time interruptions for his morning prayer. The Court conceded that the prayer was covered by the constitutional right of religious freedom (Article 4 GG) and that, in principle, the employer had the duty to take this right into consideration. However, the plaintiff could not demonstrate that the protection of his religious freedom prevailed over operational requirements protected by the employer's right of free enterprise (Article 12, Para. 1 and Article 14 GG).

Until now, the ruling of the Labor Court of Appeal of *Hamm* is the only labor court decision that has dealt with this problem. Although this situation might occur in many companies, employers have not yet addressed it in their works agreements with their works councils or company agreements with a trade union.

---

[133] *Martin Henssler*, in: Franz Jürgen Säcker & Roland Rixecker (eds.), Münchener Kommentar zum Bürgerlichen Gesetzbuch, 6th edition, Munich 2012, § 616, Para. 46.

[134] *Henssler*, op. Cit., § 616, Para. 45 with further references.

[135] In this sense *LAG Düsseldorf*, decision of February 14, 1963 – 7 Sa 581/62, in: Der Betrieb (DB) 1963, p. 522.

[136] Decision of January 18, 2002 – 5 Sa 1782/01, NJW 2002, p. 1970 et seq.

However, it can be expected that the question will continue to occupy the labor courts in the future.

c) Work performance and the observance of Ramadan

A specific problem for Muslim workers can be the observance of the fasting month of *Ramadan*. The strict observance of these religious rules might conflict with the duty to work and might make necessary work interruptions for Muslim workers or their temporary transfer to other workplaces. So far, the labor courts have not had to decide on the employer's duty to be considerate of these religious interests of workers. There is no doubt that the employer has the duty, resulting from Section 241, Para. 2 BGB in conjunction with Article 4 GG, to take into consideration these religious duties of Muslim workers as far as they do not conflict with operational requirements. In practice, these problems seem to be settled in companies in an uncomplicated way by granting these workers leave or by using the flexibility of working time schemes that exist in many companies.

d) Other cases

Beyond these types of cases, there are also other cases in which the courts have had to resolve conflicts between religious freedom and the duty to work. The judgment of the Federal Labor Court of February 24, 2011,[137] for instance, concerned a Muslim employee of a service station who was asked to work in the store of the service station, which also included the dealing with alcoholic beverages. The Court held that the employer should take into account the employees' fundamental right to religious freedom when giving instructions related to the work. In the event that the employer is not able to move the employee to another workplace, a dismissal may be socially justified. The Regional Labor Court of Hamm decided recently that an employee in a call center, who generally finished his phone calls with customers with the phrase "Jesus loves you", was in breach with his duty to work since he could not furnish conclusive evidence to the Court that the use of this phrase was commanded by a religious rule which he had to respect.[138]

[137] *BAG* – 2 AZR 636/09, NZA 2011, pp. 1087 et seq.

[138] See *LAG Hamm*, judgment of April 20, 2011 – 4 Sa 2230/10, Neue Zeitschrift für Arbeitsrecht – Rechtsprechungsreport (NZA-RR) 2011, pp. 240 et seq.

V. Conclusions

As has been pointed out, religious expression in the workplace is an increasingly relevant issue in German labor law. At the beginning, it was basically an issue that concerned the balancing of worker protection by state labor law and the constitutional autonomy of religious societies under Article 137, Para. 3 of the Weimar Constitution, privileging in particular the Christian Churches; as a result, a specific "Church labor law" [*Kirchenarbeitsrecht*] has been established recognizing a far-reaching loyalty duty of workers employed in Church institutions. However, the increasing relevance of non-Christian religions in German society, in particular the growing presence of Islam which, going back to heavy immigration during the post-war decades, has shifted the attention to how labor law has to cope with the challenges arising from this social process. In this respect, religious diversity and immigration are strongly linked issues in the German debate.

So far, German law has not developed a coherent concept of how to cope with the various conflicts that arise nowadays from religious expression in the workplace and to equally recognize the different religious communities existing in Germany. The overall picture is rather contradictory. There is still preferential treatment of the traditionally predominant Christian Churches. One important example is the specific labor law of the Churches that has "clericalized" the employment relationships of workers in Church institutions to a certain extent: The core element is their right to determine the character of the service in the Churches according to their dogmata and to define accordingly the loyalty duty of their workers (Section 9 AGG). In spite of the religiously neutral character of this provision, non-Christian communities such as those of Islamic nature will have difficulties obtaining this status because of their believers missing the particular affiliation required by that article. Another example is the way various federal states are presently dealing with the headscarf problem in the public sector: Although religious neutrality has been recognized as a fundamental constitutional principle, the so-called Neutrality Acts of some of the federal states emphasize the Christian and occidental tradition as being admitted to the public sphere.

On the other hand, serious attempts have been made by the labor courts to also protect the religious freedom of workers belonging to non-Christian religious communities. The Federal Labor Court's headscarf decision of 2002 is one definitive example in this context. Perhaps this process towards religious pluralism that is based on an equal recognition of the existing religions will be hastened by one "dark horse" that should not be underestimated in this context: The impact of European anti-discrimination law on German labor law. It remains to be seen to what extent the future jurisdiction of the *ECJ* regarding the prohibition of discrimination on grounds of religious belief under Directive 2000/78/EC will have an impact on religious expression at the workplace in German law.

List of Authors

Prof. Dr. *Jörg Althammer*, Professor of Economic Ethics and Social Policy, Katholische Universität Eichstätt-Ingolstadt

Hon. Judge *Rachel Barag-Hirshberg*, The Regional Labour Court of Jerusalem

Dr. *Gwenola Bargain,* Associate Professor of Private Law, Université François Rabelais de Tours

Prof. Dr. *Tankut Centel,* Professor of Labour Law and Social Security Law, Koç University Law School Istanbul

Prof. em. Dr. *Reinhold Fahlbeck*, Department of Law, Lund University

Prof. Dr. *Thomas C. Kohler*, Concurrent Professor of Law and Philosophy, Boston College Law School

Prof. Dr. *Achim Seifert,* Professor of Private Law, German and European Labor Law and Comparative Law, Friedrich Schiller Universität Jena

Rechtsvergleichung und Rechtsvereinheitlichung

Edited by the
Gesellschaft für Rechtsvergleichung e.V.,

represented by
general secretary Martin Schmidt-Kessel

Comparative Law and Unification of Law is a new series which deals with changes in comparative law. Comparative law has become a function of the unification of law as well to a larger extent than it used to be, in particular the unification of law in a European setting.

ISSN: 1861-5449
Suggested citation: RuR

All published volumes at *www.mohr.de/rur*

Mohr Siebeck
www.mohr.de